Impact of Sexual Abuse on Mental Health of Children

By the Same Author

—Children in Agony
—Mental Depression: A Silent Killer

About the Authors

Sibnath Deb is a senior faculty in Applied Psychology, Calcutta University, Kolkata. Earlier, he worked in a professional research company as Senior Research Manager and also in an international NGO as Research Officer. He is the Council Member of the International Society for Prevention of Child Abuse and Neglect (ISPCAN), USA; Founder Vice-President of the Indian National Society for Prevention of Child Abuse and Neglect; Founder Secretary of MIDSW—an NGO involved in child protection; and Member of the Board of Editors, Journal of Interpersonal Violence, USA. He was Steering Committee Member of the UN Secretary General Study on 'Violence Against Children'. He was also involved in ITPI Project of Country Project Leader which was, launched in 12 countries under the sponsorship of OAK Foundation, Switzerland. Dr. Deb has to his credit many books including Children in Agony (recipient of 'Best Book Award 2007'); Contemporary Social Problems in India; Styles of Parenting Adolescents: The Indian Scenario; Narcotic Drugs and Psychotropic Substances; Impact of Sexual Abuse and Child Abuse and Neglect: South Asian Scenario. Also, Dr. Deb has published more than 70 research papers and dealt with more than 40 large scale studies for different agencies like the WHO, IDRC, DFID, CRS, CARE, UNICEF, The John Hopkins University and so on. He can be reached at sibnath23@rediffmail.com / sibnath23@gmail.com

Aparna Mukherjee, M.Sc. and Ph.D. in Applied Psychology, has worked on two research projects—one on the impact of early marriage on girl children and the other on perception of health service providers about care and support services for the HIV/AIDS patients. She has five years research experience in the field of early marriage, child sexual abuse and HIV/AIDS. Her areas of research interest include child trafficking, behaviour of high risk group people and prevention of early marriage.

Impact of Sexual Abuse on Mental Health of Children

Dr. Sibnath Deb
Dr. Aparna Mukherjee

CONCEPT PUBLISHING COMPANY, NEW DELHI-110 059

Cataloging in Publication Data—DK
Courtesy: D.K. Agencies (P) Ltd. <docinfo@dkagencies.com>

Deb, Sibnath, 1962-
Impact of sexual abuse on mental health of children / Sibnath Deb, Aparna Mukherjee.
p. cm.
Study conducted among the selected young girls from Kolkata, West Bengal, India.
Includes bibliographical references (p.)
Includes index.
ISBN 13: 9788180695759
ISBN 10: 8180695751

1. Teenage girls—Abuse of—India—Kolkata. 2. Child sexual abuse—India—Kolkata. 3. Teenage girls—Mental health—India—Kolkata. I. Mukherjee, Aparna, joint author. II. Title.

DDC 362.760 954 14 22

ISBN-13: 978-81-8069-575-9
ISBN-10: 81-8069-575-1

First Published 2009

Published and Printed by
Ashok Kumar Mittal
Concept Publishing Company
A/15-16, Commercial Block, Mohan Garden
New Delhi-110 059 (INDIA)

Phones : 25351460, 25351794
Fax : 091-11-25357103
Email : publishing@conceptpub.com

Foreword

The sexual abuse and exploitation of children is a world-wide problem. Statistics on the number of children subjected to prostitution, trafficking, and sexual abuse are a major concern for all countries and international organizations such as the World Health Organization, UNICEF, and the International Society for the Prevention of Child Abuse and Neglect (ISPCAN). In some western countries, there are statistics that, while known to be underestimated, reveal staggering numbers of children affected by sexual abuse. In India, there are few studies that have documented the number of children affected and more research is needed in order to bring national attention to the problem.

This ground-breaking book takes a close-up look at a group of young girls in India who were victims of sexual abuse and clearly describes the consequences of their abuse. The book is based on a well-designed research study in which abused girls were compared to non-abused girls in the same area of India to document the long-term devastating effects of a history of sexual abuse. The study was carefully designed and implemented in order to be able to generalize the results and provide a strong empirical basis for the conclusions. The author Aparna Mukherjee, Ph.D. and the mentor, Sibnath Deb, Ph.D. are to be complemented for the thoughtfulness and integrity of this study of young Indian girls.

The book will be useful to a wide variety of readers. It will be (1) an excellent example of a well-designed study for college students to read, (2) a book to inform legislators and policy-makers, and (3) an addition to the international literature on child sexual abuse. The credibility of the information provided in this book has the potential to lead to changes in the protection of children in India, both boys and girls, from future sexual abuse and exploitation. I extend my sincere appreciation and admiration to Dr. Mukherjee and Dr. Deb for this important contribution to the prevention of child sexual abuse in India.

Barbara L. Bonner, PhD
Professor of Pediatrics
Past-President, ISPCAN
University of Oklahoma Health Sciences Center
Oklahoma City, OK, USA

Preface and Acknowledgements

Child abuse and neglect, especially child sexual abuse, has a long lasting effect on personality, adjustment and future career of the children. This is not merely the problem of developing countries but a global phenomenon. In Indian society, child sexual abuse has been regarded as normal phenomenon except for the instance of forceful sexual encounter. Even in cases of forceful sexual encounter, the victim and their family members do not report it to the Police because of perceived harassment and/or subsequent social boycott. However, in the recent past, some perpetrators were brought to justice and media has become more serious about the issue, predominantly, for the purpose of newspaper publicity. One such bright example of yesteryear is the case of Dhananjay Chatterjee, who raped and murdered a school-going girl, and was hanged to death by the Court of Law, after prolonged legal battle of 20 years.

Seldom is anything accomplished without the assistance or encouragement of others, especially when one wishes to work on uncharted territory like the issue above. This study was no exception. In India, a number of NGOs are working for the welfare of the children in different capacities, but in isolation. Their rich experience is not disseminated much. Hence, it does not benefit the larger society. Through this systematic study, we made an effort to understand the mental disposition of sexually abused girl children for sharing the outcome with others so that it helps the NGOs working with this population to take up evidence-based intervention programme. It is relevant to mention here that our association with different activities of the International Society For Prevention of Child Abuse and Neglect has led us to think over this issue for investigation and for writing this document for publication. Therefore, we are grateful to ISPCAN authorities and all the Council Members for their role worldwide in addressing the issue of child abuse and neglect. We would also like to extend our gratitude to ISPCAN authorities for arranging fund for organizing multi-disciplinary training programmes on child abuse and neglect for the professionals in India. We strongly feel that the ISPCAN effort to prevent child abuse and neglect will have lasting impact in India.

The greatest inspiration for this project, were the countless young girls who are living in the different shelters across the length and breadth of the country, in a world, vastly different from our own. We have much respect and appreciation for the way they have embraced life, optimistically, even after suffering from such trauma. Each and every one of the girls we interviewed gave their precious time, co-operated fully and assisted in collecting the data associated with this study.

We cordially thank Mrs. Indrani Sinha, Projects Director and Dr. Reetichanchal Biswas of Sanlaap—an NGO, Mrs. Lakhsmi Chatterjee, Vice-President and Ms. Kasturi Mukherjee, Vice-President of All Bengal Women's Union, Mrs. Aloka Mitra, Founder of Child Care Home and the Directorate of Social Welfare, Government of West Bengal for allowing us to carry out the research in the one and only governmental shelter for girls, viz., Sundarbhai Mulchand Home in Liluah. We are also grateful to all the Faculty Members in the Department of Applied Psychology, Calcutta University for their valuable suggestions from time to time in carrying out the study.

Special appreciation is expressed for counsellors in the above organizations, namely, Ms. Swagata Deb, Ms. Ramneek Kaur, Mrs. Anusuya Ganguly of Sneha, the shelter of Sanlaap, situated in a tranquil atmosphere in greater Kolkata, Mrs. Susmita Chatterjee, Dr. Mrs. Urmi Chatterjee of the home of All Bengal Women's Union, Mrs. Anindita Mukherjee and Mrs. Sanchita Mitra of the Sundarbhai Mulchand Home in Liluah, Howrah.

We are also grateful to Dr. Barbara Bonner, Professor of Paediatrics and CMRI/Jean Gumerson Endowed Chair, Child Study Centre, Oklahoma University Health Sciences Centre,

OK, USA and Prof. U.N. Dash, Centre of Advanced Study in Psychology, Utkal University for reviewing the document and giving their valuable feedback.

We are indebted to the Librarian of the Department of Applied Psychology, University of Calcutta and other staff members for their assistance. Gratitude is extended to authors of all the books, articles and research papers that have added academic value to our work. We are deeply indebted to our parents for their support, encouragement and unconditional love. It would be a serious lapse on the part of the authors, if thank is not given to Ruhi Sinha and Anindita Choudhury for editing the document.

We have sought to do this research up to the best of our potential. We do hope to get valuable suggestions from the experienced persons working with abused children, which will direct us to carry on further work for benevolent social causes. Judicious caution was taken to present the data systematically and interpret the same logically and meaningfully without any prejudice. However, if there exists any mistake and/or typing error, the same is regretted.

Sibnath Deb
M.Sc., Ph.D., LL.B.

Aparna Mukherjee
M.Sc., Ph.D.
Department of Applied Psychology,
Calcutta University
92, A.P.C. Road, Kolkata-700 009, India
E-mail: sibnath23@rediffmail.com

Contents

1

Introduction

Child Sexual Abuse: An Overview

Child sexual abuse is a very old phenomenon. The sexual exploitation of children—males and females—has occurred throughout history, yet it was not until the 16th century that legislation was enacted in England that began the process of protecting children from sexual abuse: boys were protected from forced sodomy, and girls under the age of ten years from forcible rape. By the time of the settlement of the United States, sexual prohibitions were becoming more stringent (Oates, 1990). Illick (1974 as cited in Oates, 1990) reported that in Connecticut, in 1672, a father was found guilty of incestuous acts with his daughter and executed. The case also exemplified an attitude still encountered today: victim blaming. In the Connecticut case, this resulted in the child being sentenced to a whipping for her part in the crime.

In the 1700s some educators began warning parents to supervise their children at all times, and to ensure they were never nude in front of other adults, in order to protect them from sexual abuse. This constituted one of the first indications that society at large recognized the potential for children to be sexually abused (Conte and Shore, 1982). By the late 1900s welfare groups were familiar with child sexual abuse, and that its most common form was intrafamilial assault (Wurtele and Miller-Perrin, 1992). However, by the 1920s sexual abuse had become characterized as extrafamilial assault, committed by 'strangers', with the victim perceived as being a 'temptress' rather than an innocent child (Gordon, 1990, as cited in Wurtele and Miller-Perrin, 1992).

Societies continued to turn a 'blind eye' to child sexual abuse until after the 're-discovery' of child maltreatment in the early 1960s by Kempe and his colleagues in the United States (Kempe et al., 1962). Kempe's construction of the 'battered child syndrome' has been expanded extensively over the past three decades to encompass sexual abuse, emotional abuse and neglect. The continuing growth of concern about child sexual abuse is frequently attributed to child advocates and the feminist movement (Reppucci and Haugaard, 1993). This greater awareness grew particularly out of the latter's work as advocates for adult victims/survivors of rape and other sexual assault.

Why child sexual abuse wasn't widely identified prior to the 1960s? As Oates (1990) states, while society could cope with 'stranger danger' and the threat of the stereotypical child molester assaulting children, it was much more threatening to acknowledge that sexual abuse was commonly occurring within the family, committed by family members upon whom children were dependent and should have been able to trust. The acknowledgement of sexual abuse was therefore a threat to the structure of the family. It has been contended that some researchers, for example Kinsey and associates (1953, as cited in Goddard and Carew, 1993) 'minimized' or played down the sexual abuse of children because they felt society had not reached a point where it was able to acknowledge intrafamilial sexual abuse.

In any discussion of child sexual abuse it should be recognized that there might be interest groups that believe that there are benefits for children in having sexual relationships with adults (Tower, 1989; Korbin, 1990). Enmore (1986, as cited by Goddard and Carew, 1993) asserted that arguments used by such groups to gain rights for those who engage in, or wish to engage in sexual relationships with children are similar to those used to assist the gay rights movement. That is, they claim that their activities are normal, human and valuable experiences. The proponents of 'child love' assert that children are not always traumatized by a sexual relationship, which may enable them to 'satisfy instinctual drives [or] to test in reality an infantile fantasy ... [where the child's] emotional balance is...in favour of contentment' (Bender and Blau, 1937, as cited in DeYoung, 1982:46).

One of the more convincing arguments against this view has been presented by Finkelhor (1984) who asserted that modern society is based upon the idea of free will and the ability to consent: true consent is only possible if one has knowledge and authority, and Finkelhor contended that children lack both.

Occupying a position of less personal power and control in comparison with adults (Korbin, 1990), children have no authority in a legal or psychological sense. Moreover, they lack 'knowledge of the meanings of sexuality, information to enable them to anticipate the direction of the sexual relationship, or any idea of how others will react to their sexual involvement' (Tower, 1989:103).

For a number of decades there has been debate on the prevalence of child sexual abuse. The research has suffered from lack of common methodology, unclear definitions, use of questionable techniques for retrospective studies, such as *memory recovery*, bias, unjustified presumptions and other factors. Goldman (2000) notes that 'the absolute number of children being sexually abused each year has been almost impossible to ascertain' and that 'there does not seem to be agreement on the rate of children being sexually abused'. A meta-analytic study by Rind, Tromovitch, and Bauserman (1998) found that reported prevalence of abuse for males ranged from 3.0% to 37.0%, and for females from 8.0% to 71.0% with mean rates of 17.0% and 28.0% respectively. A study by Fromuth and Burkhart (1987) found that depending upon the definition of CSA use, prevalence among men varied from 4.0% to 24.0%.

Another common question often asked is: 'Why does child sexual abuse, rape, women battery, sexual harassment happen?' Violence has always been a part of human behaviour. It was once important for physical survival in a dangerous environment. But, in modern-day society, at a time when our survival actually depends on one another, violence still continues to increase. According to well-known Wits University academic, Llyod Vogelman (1990), by 1981 it was estimated that there had been 4 million murders in the twentieth century, and figures for rape and sexual abuse exceed this number many times over.

Child sexual abuse is regarded as particularly reprehensible in many modern societies; however, the ambiguity of the definition and the intensity of fear and reprehension prompted some critics to argue that in some respects this is a result of mass hysteria and not rational view towards specific problems. The attitudes towards various sexual activities also vary between countries. For example, in many countries going to sauna or public bath together by children and adults is acceptable. In Japan, strange activities such as groping schoolgirls in trains are tolerated to some degree. Child prostitution is often tolerated in poor societies as a way to support the family.

Definition of Child Sexual Abuse

Sexual abuse refers to sexual exposure or contact by a person older than a child for the purpose of sexual stimulation or exploitation regardless of the use of force or any accompanying physical injury. However, in definitions of the term given in scientific literature there are considerable variations in terms of criteria and specificity. In common use the term 'sexual abuse' is sometimes mistakenly used interchangeably with sexual offence, which means sexual activities that are prosecuted by law. Often it also refers to activities that are morally condemned in society.

However, this is a very ambiguous definition, because moral norms, socially accepted behaviour and laws vary greatly both nationally and internationally and because the definition is too wide to be useful. Many researchers note that this leads to incompatible study findings and wrong generalizations, when different phenomena are often lumped together as if they had similar causes and results. Okami (1990) criticizes much of current research on adult-child sexual behaviour and notes that 'much of the current victimology-based research employs polemical devices and research methods that blur the line between social science and social criticism'.

Having said that, it is undisputable that some of the phenomena covered by this definition are real, harmful to the children and relatively prevalent, thus warranting attention to the problem. The following are some definitions of child sexual abuse by leading academicians and researchers:

...the involvement of dependant, developmentally immature children and adolescents in sexual activities that they do not fully comprehend and to which they are unable to give their informed consent or that violates the social taboos of family roles (Schecter and Roberge, 1976).

...any sexual activity or experience imposed on a child those results in emotional, physical or sexual trauma (Sandra Butler, 1985).

Child sexual abuse is the adult (or older child) exploitation of the normal childhood development process, through the use of sexual activity. Examples of the types of sexual activity might include touching, kissing, fondling, manipulations of the genitals with the fingers, and actual sexual intercourse (Stovall, 1981).

According to Oates (1996), sexual abuse of children means involvement of dependent, developmentally immature children and adolescents in sexual activities, which they do not fully comprehend and to which they are unable to give informed consent. Sexual abuse includes touching, fondling and penetration.

Types of Child Sexual Abuse

Child sexual abuse seems much more common today, and can partly be explained by looking at the vulnerable, dependent role which children and adolescents find themselves in. Children and adolescents in modern society are frequently exposed to a wide range of sexual exploitations by adults, both within and outside their families.

Categories of Child Sexual Abuse are:

- Incest—sexual activity between family members,
- Pedophilia—the preference of an adult for young children as sex objects,
- Exhibitionism—the exposure of genitals by an adult male,
- Molestation—behaviours such as touching, fondling, kissing and masturbation,
- Sexual intercourse—including oral-genital, anal-genital, penile-genital contact,
- Rape—sexual or attempted intercourse without consent of victim,
- Sexual sadism—the infliction of bodily injury as a means of obtaining sexual excitement,
- Child pornography—the production and distribution of material involving minors in sex acts,
- Child prostitution—the involvement of children in sex acts for profit.

These categories sometimes overlap and show various activities to which children may be subjected to. The most common acts of child sexual abuse take the form of:

- Handling the genitals, or forcing the child to handle the older offender's genitals,
- Acts of exhibitionism by the offender,
- Manipulating the child into sexually scintillating poses and clothes, sometimes for the purposes of photography,
- Making suggestive comments about the child's sexually developing body.

The sexual and/or physical abuse of children often take place over time and the child may suffer both forms of abuse. The differences between the two are:

Sexual

- Trauma primarily psychological,
- Motivation of perpetrator is sexual/psychological gratification,
- Society less overtly tolerant,
- Pre-adolescents primarily vulnerable.

Physical

- Trauma primarily physical,
- Motivation of perpetrator is physical harm,
- Society more tolerant,
- Younger children most vulnerable.

Child sexual abuse differs from rape although rape is a category of child sexual abuse. Children are more often victimized by family members or friends than are rape victims.

Child victimization more often consists of repeated incidents, and less physical force and violence is used than in rape. Importantly, child sexual abuse does not necessarily involve sexual intercourse.

Sexual abuse of children is just one form of child abuse. And sexual abuse of children may be in the form of incest (in the home) or in the form of sexual assault or in the form of commercial sexual exploitation of children.

Christine Lawson describes various ways in which women can sexually abuse children (1993):

Subtle abuse is defined as behaviours that may not intentionally be sexual in nature but serve to meet the woman's emotional and/or sexual needs at the expense of the child's emotional and/or developmental needs (Lawson, 1993).

Seductive abuse is defined as sexual stimulation that is inappropriate for the child's age and/or is motivated by the woman's needs.... Seductive abuse implies conscious awareness and intention of arousing or stimulating a child sexually (Lawson, 1993).

Perverse abuse occurs when the child sexual development is distorted by the behaviours of the abusers.

Overt sexual abuse is defined as overt sexual contact between a woman and a child. Overt sexual abuse involves some form of coercion and/or threats to discourage disclosure (Lawson, 1993).

Sadistic sexual abuse includes (female) sexual behaviour that is intended to hurt the child and may be part of a general pattern of severe physical and emotional abuse. No studies have looked at the actual incidence and/or prevalence of sexual abuse by women, thus it has to be seen in relation to what is already known of the prevalence of child sexual abuse.

Serious sexual abuse in childhood (up to the age of 16 or 17) involving unwanted or coerced sexual contact occurs in at least 15.0% of females in the populations surveyed and in at least 5.0% of males. Because of various methodological factors, these are likely to be the most conservative or minimum estimates (Bagley and King, 1990 p. 70). The percentage of sexual contact by older female to be about 20.0% (range 14.0-27.0%) for male children and about 5.0% (range 0.0%-10.0%) for female children. (Finkelhor and Russell, 1984 p. 179).

Magnitude of the Problem (Available Official Statistics)

Child sexual abuse is a global problem across many societies. However, in the following section reported data of industrial and non-industrial countries have been provided separately.

Reported Data in Industrial Countries

Though estimates vary concerning the number of sexually abused children, the United Nation's Children's Fund (UNICEF) believes their numbers to exceed 100 million world-wide, not all of whom are located in "poor" or "developing" countries (Source: UNICEF, 1997). Indeed, the first *World Congress Against the Commercial Sexual Exploitation of Children* (Muntarbhorn, 1996) confirmed that large numbers of prostituted children are to be found in rich countries, including in the U.S. for which the 'End Child Prostitution, Child Pornography, and the Trafficking of Children for Sexual Exploitation' (ECPAT) estimated their numbers to be between

100,000 and 300,000 (ECPAT, 1996: 70). Other estimates suggest the numbers of sexually exploited children to be even higher (Goldman and Wheeler, 1986; Spangenberg, 2001). Certainly, experts in child sexual abuse believe the numbers of such children in the U.S. to be substantial (Greene et al., 1999; Kral et al., 1997). America's problem with child sexual abuse is widely believed to be concentrated in cities and towns that border Mexico (Azaola, 2001; Harris, 1998) and Canada (Dionne, 2001; Hecht, 1997). However, the problem also is believed to be extensive in America's coastal states where large numbers of children from Asia, Africa, Latin America and Eastern Europe enter the country illegally (DoL, 1996). Organized crime groups also appear to be involved in child pornography and child prostitution in the U.S., but especially crime organizations with ties to Russia, the Ukraine, and other countries of the Former Soviet Union (Budapest Group, 1999; Hughes, 2000b; Richard, 1999). Crime groups with ties to China, the Philippines, and Thailand also are known to be involved in trafficking children for sexual purposes into U.S. (Botti, 2000; ECPAT, 1996; Richard, 1999).

There are few national statistics on child sexual abuse in Canada. A 1994 report, *Child Welfare in Canada: The Role of Provincial and Territorial Authorities in Cases of Child Abuse*, describes the provincial laws, definitions and child welfare systems that deal with child sexual abuse. A 1996 report, *Child and Family Services Annual Report 1992-93 to 1994-95*, presents statistical data on child welfare services in Canada. The available data cannot be directly or easily compared among the provinces because the information is collected according to different definitions and parameters in each province. For example, in some provinces, data on suspected cases are combined with those on confirmed cases. In other jurisdictions, sexual abuse is not distinguished from physical abuse.

Nonetheless, the following information provides some insight into the incidence of child sexual abuse.

- It is estimated that there were nearly 12,000 investigations of child sexual abuse in Ontario in 1993.

Sexual abuse was substantiated in 29.0% of these cases and suspected in another 27.0%.

- In British Columbia, more than 500 complaints of sexual abuse were received in March 1992.
- The most extensive study of child sexual abuse in Canada was conducted by the Committee on Sexual Offences against Children and Youths. Its report indicates that, among adult Canadians, 53.0% of women and 31.0% of men were sexually abused when they were children.

Finkelhor (1984) in another study estimated the proportion of children in the United States that were exposed to some form of sexual abuse was between 9.0% and 52.0% for females and between 3.0% and 9.0% for males (depending on the definition of sexual abuse and methodology used). It is also clear that the majority of perpetrators of sexual abuse are men and that the victims are predominantly female (Finkelhor, 1979).

In the latest Australian national statistics of the prevalence of child sexual abuse, 19.0% of 28,711 substantiated cases were labeled as sexual abuse (Angus and Woodward, 1995); 74.0% of cases involved female victims. Aboriginal and Torres Strait Islander families were significantly over-represented in the national sample. However, within the Aboriginal and Torres Strait Islander sample, a significantly lower proportion of cases were classified as sexual abuse (11.0%) in comparison with the national sample. Based on substantiated cases reported by the various state child protection services, the rate of sexual abuse for the nation was 1.1 per 1000 children aged 0-16 years. Despite the comparatively low number of sexual abuse cases in the Aboriginal and Torres Strait Islander population the rate of sexual abuse for Aboriginal and Torres Strait Islander families were 2.0 per 1000 children aged 0-16 years, an indication of the over-representation of Aboriginal and Torres Strait Islander families in the national child abuse statistics.

There has been a significant increase in the recognition of child sexual assault (Leventhal, 1990), which has been reflected by a substantial increase in the number of reports made to child protection services across Australia and overseas, particularly in the last five years. However, until 1995, the substantiation rate of cases had not increased proportionately. Thus more cases were being reported, but higher numbers of cases were not being substantiated. In 1995, only 44.0% of all finalized child maltreatment cases were substantiated (Angus and Woodward, 1995). The increase in child maltreatment reports is attributed to the introduction of mandatory reporting of child sexual abuse across most states and territories, and the much greater public awareness of the problem (Clark, 1995).

Studies of male college students in 1996 have found prevalence rates from 4.8% to 28.0%. At the lower extreme of 4.8% is a study by Fritz, Stoll and Wagner (1981) in which 412 students responded to a self-report questionnaire that required them to label their experiences as 'abusive'—a method guaranteed to cause under-reporting (see discussion in section above). Risin and Koss (1987) obtained a rate of 7.3% in a national sample of 2,972 male college students. They used eight self-report behavioural descriptions about sexual behaviours before age 14. As pure behavioural descriptions, none of the items included the word 'abuse'. Finkelhor (1979) used a similar list of behavioural self-report items in a study of 266 college students and found an 8.3% prevalence rate; he included non-contact experiences and used specific age criteria (if under 14 there had to be a 5 year age difference with the perpetrator, if 14-15, a 10 year difference).

Higher prevalence rates of 20.0% and 24.0% came from Fromuth and Burkhart's (1987) study of students in two separate schools. They compared the effect of different definitions of sexual abuse on prevalence rates. However, their questionnaire utilized a gate question. The highest rates of 20.0% and 24.0% came from the most inclusive definition: the same as Finkelhor's 1979 study (including non-contact and age differential criteria), but with the addition that sexual contact between peers involving force or threat was categorized as abuse.

Research on college students also has been conducted by David Lisak and his colleagues (Lisak and Luster, 1994; Lisak, Hopper, and Song, 1996). The college samples in these studies were not typical, but consisted of men who commuted to an urban university, were an average of 25 years old, and from socio-economic background more typical of the surrounding community than many college student populations used in this research. This work yielded prevalence rates of:

- Approximately, 17.0% for child sexual abuse of males involving physical contact.
- Over 25.0% when non-contact forms of abuse were included.

A prevalence rate similar to the Lisak et al., studies was found in another study of college males. Collings (1995) used an anonymous questionnaire and defined sexual abuse as 'unwanted' sexual experiences taking place before the age of 18. The term 'unwanted' is likely to bias rates downward, as noted above, but the inclusion of subjects aged 16 and 17 is likely to increase the found prevalence rate. Not surprisingly, Collings found that 29.0% of the 284 male respondents had been sexually abused, with 20.0% reporting non-contact abuse and 6.0% reporting abuse experiences involving physical contact.

Studies with community samples have ranged in their prevalence rates from 2.8% to 16.0%. Again, methodology has been crucial. Kercher and McShane (1984) mailed a single self-report question including the word 'abuse' to a random sample of Texas drivers. They found a prevalence rate of 3.0%. Given the wording of their single question, this rate is not surprising.

Two random-sample telephone interview studies by Murphy (1987, 1989, cited in Urquiza and Keating, 1990) also demonstrate the profound effects of single questions including the word 'abuse' rather than instruments with multiple behavioural descriptions. In one of the studies (1987) the former method was employed, and it produced a rate of 2.8% with a sample of 357; in the other study (1989) the latter method yielded a prevalence rate of 11.0% with a sample of 777.

Bagley et al., (1994) conducted a community study of men aged 18 to 27 years in the Canadian city of Calgary. They first contacted subjects by phone then administered anonymous questionnaires in their homes via programmes on portable computers. Their questionnaire asked about 'unwanted' experiences before the age of 17. Bagley and his colleagues found a prevalence rate of 15.5%, and that 6.9% of their subjects had experienced multiple episodes of sexual abuse. Interestingly, this rate for multiple episodes was identical to that found for women in a previous study that employed the same methodology, despite the fact that the prevalence rate for any unwanted sexual experiences in that study was 32.0%, or double that found for males (Bagley, 1991).

The highest community-sample prevalence rate of 16.0% was found in a random telephone survey of 2,626 men, known as the 'L.A. Times Survey' (Finkelhor, 1990). In contrast to studies with women, published studies using face-to-face interviews with men have yielded very low prevalence rates, perhaps due to subjects' adherence to stereotypes about males not being victims (Urquiza and Keating, 1990). Finkelhor's (1984) face-to-face interview with Boston-area fathers yielded a rate of 6.0%. Siegel and colleagues (1987), using gate-question interviews with 1,480 Los Angeles-area men, found a prevalence rate of 3.8%. Baker and Duncan (1985) used a single question that described various sexual acts and found the highest face-to-face prevalence rate of 8.0% in their random sample of 970 men in Great Britain.

Studies with clinical samples have obtained prevalence rates from 3.0% to 23.0%. The lowest rate was reported from a study that used psychological records of 954 male and female patients of a large regional medical center (Belkin et al., 1994). In a chart review of emergency room records of a Buffalo, New York hospital, Ellerstein and Canavan (1980) found an 11.0% prevalence rate. DeJong and colleagues (DeJong et al., 1982) reviewed several clinical studies and found rates from 11.0% to 17.0%, and in their own hospital population found a rate of just fewer than 14.0% (1982). Metcalfe and his associates (1990) found a prevalence of 23.0% in their survey of 100 male psychiatric inpatients.

However, it is important to mention here that assessment for sexual abuse histories in hospitals has traditionally been *extremely poor*, and remains so in many settings. Thus these rates, based on reviews of records, are likely to be vast underestimates. For example, Briere and Zaidi (1989) reviewed intake reports on women presenting to an urban psychiatric emergency room. They randomly reviewed 50 charts before and 50 after the intake staff were instructed to question clients about previous sexual victimization. The first 50 charts had recorded rates of 6.0%, and the second set, 70.0%.

A report published in a 1992 issue of Lears Magazine looked at a study of 118 American fathers by sociologists David Finkelhor and Linda Meyer Williams:

- 26.0% of fathers who sexually abused their daughters said that they were preoccupied with their daughters' physical characteristics—feel of skin and smell of body. Many of these men regarded their daughters as sex objects from birth.
- 33.0% of fathers in the study became sexually interested in their daughters at puberty and said they were 'transfixed by her body's change.'
- 20.0% of respondents said they used their daughters' bodies as 'a receptacle' for self-gratification. These 20.0% abused sporadically, worried about the harm they were causing and felt great guilt. To alleviate their guilt some of these men convinced themselves that their daughters were aroused by the abuse.
- A little over 10.0% of respondents saw themselves as failures and looked to their daughters for 'close, exclusive, emotionally dependent relationships including sexual gratification.'
- 10.0% abused their daughters out of anger at their wives for various reasons—neglecting the husband, leaving husband, prioritizing daughter over husband. Sometimes the daughters were abused because they resembled their mothers. Sometimes fathers wanted to desecrate their daughters or possess them out of angry sense of entitlement.

- 33.0% of the respondents in the study reported being under the influence of alcohol when they committed the abuse, 10.0% on drugs, and 9.0% on both alcohol and drugs to reduce their inhibitions to abuse.
- The average age of the daughters of the men participating in the study was 6-7 years.

Reported Data in Non-Industrial Countries

According to a study released in 1997 by the Sakshi Violence Intervention Centre, based on a survey done with 350 school girls in New Delhi, India:

- 63.0% of the girls had experienced child sexual abuse at the hands of family members.
- 25.0% of the girls had been raped, forced to masturbate the perpetrator, or forced to perform oral sex.
- One-third of the girls said the perpetrator had been a father, grandfather or male friend of the family.

In a 1999 report by the Tata Institute of Social Sciences, a study done in 1994 and 1995 with 150 minor-age girls in Bombay, India showed:

- 58 of the girls surveyed had been sexually abused before age 10.
- Of this number, 50 had been abused by a family member or friend of the family.

Another study was done in 1997 by RAHI, a Delhi-based organization. This study focused on 1,000 English-speaking middle and upper class women living in Delhi, Bombay, Madras, Calcutta and Goa. Majority were graduate and under-graduate students. Findings from this study showed:

- 76.0% of respondents had been sexually abused as children; 31.0% of these by someone they knew and 40.0% by a family member. So 71.0% had been abused either by relatives or someone they knew and trusted.

- While 48.0% had been abused by a single abuser, 52.0% had been abused by two or more abusers—meaning the majority of women had multiple perpetrators.
- Abuse for 11.0% of the survivors occurred once in their lives while 42.0% were subjected to the abuse many times at different times of their lives either by the same abuser or different abusers at different times.
- 50.0% of the abuse took place when the survivors were under 12 years of age, 35.0% had been abused between 12-16 years of age. The significance of this is that victims were almost always in the care or company of some family member, caretaker or known person.
- 68.0% of those who had been abused were living in nuclear families, 16.0% in nuclear families that included grandparents, and 15.0% in extended families that comprised other relatives.
- 60.0% said their mothers were housewives and 40.0% said their mothers were employed outside the home.
- 54.0% of the survivors had told someone about the abuse compared to 36.0% who did not.
- Most of those who disclosed did so voluntarily. In a few cases, the abuse was discovered by an older person. 30.0% told a friend, 26.0% told their mothers, 12.0% told a sister, 9.0% told both parents. Only 2.0% had been to a therapist or counsellor.
- The main reasons given for not telling anyone about the abuse were: wanting to forget it happened (23.0%), fear of what people would think of them (14.0%), self-blame for the abuse (11.0%), and not having anyone to trust (11.0%). Only 3% did not tell because the abuser had threatened them. Only 1.0% did not tell because they were bribed by the abuser.
- The overwhelming responses to disclosure of abuse by the victims were: anger at the perpetrator, disbelief in the victim, and denial. The actions that followed most often did not involve confrontation of perpetrator.
- According to the study the most often cited long-lasting effects of the sexual abuse were: lack of self-confidence,

inability to express feelings, inability to trust people, feeling angry at the world most of the time. Other effects included: avoiding sex or compulsively seeking it out, experiencing chronic aches and pains, use of drugs and alcohol.

A 1996 study done in Bangalore by Samvada with high school students showed:

- 47.0% of respondents had been sexually abused; 62.0% of whom had been raped once and 38.0% of whom had suffered repeated violations.
- Where vaginal and/or oral penetration was involved, 32.0% of the girls had been under age. Where abuse did not involve penetration, 13.0% had been under age 10.
- 64.0% of those whose abuse involved penetration made total disclosure, 20.0% made partial disclosure.
- Self-blame went up as the "seriousness" of the abuse increased; 37.0% of those who were molested blamed themselves compared to 50.0% of those whose abuse involved penetration.
- Where families placed great emphasis on virginity and equated it with purity, virtue and family honour (*izzat*), the victims felt greater sense of shame, self-contempt, anger, and felt compelled to keep quiet about the abuse.
- Many of the respondents who feared the person abusing them, continued to feel it at the present time. Those who felt anger wished they could retaliate. Those whose desire for revenge (or justice) did not materialize began feeling helpless.
- Asked what they expected as a result of the abuse, 31.0% called for prevention; 17.0% said society needed to talk about sex; 13.0% said women should fight back compared to 3.0% who said girl children should learn martial arts; 8.0% said victim assistance should be available; 14.0% said abusers should be punished; 1.0% said abusers should be helped.

Symptoms of Child Sexual Abuse

Parents, grandparents, and guardians should be aware of the signs that could indicate that the child has been sexually abused. It should be noted that some of these behaviours may have other explanations, but it is important to assist the child no matter what the cause of these symptoms or behaviours.

- Changes in behaviour, extreme mood swings, isolation or withdrawal, uncharacteristic anger, fearfulness, and excessive crying.
- Disclosure by child (very rare).
- Physical evidence (very rare).
- Excessive masturbation.
- Age inappropriate knowledge of sex.
- Constantly talks about sex.
- Acting out inappropriate sexual activity or showing an unusual interest in sexual matters even with other children.
- Venereal disease.
- Constant vaginal discharge.
- Bleeding in vagina or anus.
- A sudden acting out of feelings or aggressive or rebellious behaviour.
- Regression to infantile behaviour; clinging.
- School or behavioural problems.
- Changes in toilet-training habits.
- Bed-wetting & soiling, nightmares, fear of going to bed, or other sleep disturbances.
- A fear of certain places like bathroom, people, or activities.
- Bruises, rashes, cuts, limping, multiple or poorly explained injuries.
- Pain, itching, bleeding, fluid, or rawness in the private areas.
- Nightmares.
- Sleeps too much or too little.
- Difficulty walking or sitting.

- Depression, crying over insignificant matters.
- Excessive crying.
- Exhibiting violent behaviour.
- Wearing many layers of clothing.

Causes of Child Sexual Abuse

Why would someone abuse a child? What kind of person abuses a child? Not all abuse is deliberate or intended. Several factors in a person's life may combine to move them towards abusing a child:

- General stress,
- The stress of having children in the family, when one didn't have children before,
- Dealing with a child who has a disability or difficult behaviours,
- The stress of caring for someone besides oneself,
- A personal history of being abused (childhood trauma),
- Alcohol or drug use,
- Marital conflict,
- Unemployment.

No one has been able to predict which of these factors will cause someone to abuse a child. A significant factor is that abuse tends to be inter-generational—those who were abused as children are more likely to repeat the act when they become parents or caretakers.

In addition, many forms of abuse arise from ignorance, isolation, or neglect. Sometimes a cultural tradition leads to abuse, for example, such beliefs as:

- Children are property.
- Parents (especially males) have the right to control their children in any way they wish.
- Children need to be toughened up to face the hardships of life.
- Girls need to be genitally mutilated to assure virginity and later marriage.

In a report prepared in 2002 by R.J. Estes and N.A. Weiner on Commercial Sexual Exploitation of Children in U.S., Canada and Mexico, the factors contributing to sexual abuse are elucidated as follows:

Chart I: Factors Contributing to the Sexual Abuse of Children and Youth

Domain	*Contributing Factors*
Macro/ Contextual (External)	• Socio-economic. • Societal attitudes toward children and youth. • Social anomie among children and youth, i.e., a lack of connectedness on the part of youth with the larger society and their place within it. • Poverty. • Child victims of crime and violence. • Societal responses to crimes committed against children, including sexual crimes. • The presence of pre-existing adult prostitution zones. • The presence of groups advocating child-adult sexual relationships. • Sexual behaviour of unattached and transient males including the military, seasonal workers, truckers, motor cycle gangs, conventioneers. • Community knowledge and attitudes concerning HIV/AIDS and other sexually transmitted diseases.
Micro/ Situational (External)	• Socio-Behavioural, Family dysfunction, Parental drug dependency, History of physical and/or sexual assault, Personal drug dependency, School/other social performance failures, Gang membership. • Active recruitment into prostitution by others, Peers, Parents or other family members (including siblings), Local pimps, National and or international crime organizations.
Individual (Internal)	• Psychogenic, Poor self-esteem, Chronic depression, External locus of control. • Seriously restricted future orientation.

Consequences of Child Sexual Abuse

Children and adolescents who have been sexually abused can suffer a range of psychological and behavioural problems, from mild to severe, in both the short and long term. These problems typically include depression, anxiety, guilt, fear, sexual dysfunction, withdrawal, and acting out. Depending on the severity of the incident, victims of sexual abuse may also develop fear and anxiety regarding the opposite sex or sexual issues and may display inappropriate sexual behaviour. However, the strongest indication that a child has been sexually abused is inappropriate sexual knowledge, sexual interest, and sexual acting out by that child.

The initial or short-term effects of abuse usually occur within two years of the termination of the abuse. These effects vary depending upon the circumstances of the abuse and the child's developmental stage but may include regressive behaviours (such as a return to thumb-sucking or bed-wetting), sleep disturbances, eating problems, behaviour and/or performance problems at school, and non-participation in school and social activities.

But the negative effects of child sexual abuse can affect the victim for many years and into adulthood. Adults who were sexually abused as children commonly experience depression. Additionally, high levels of anxiety in these adults can result in self-destructive behaviours, such as alcoholism or drug abuse, anxiety attacks, situation-specific anxiety disorders, and insomnia. Many victims also encounter problems in their adult relationships and in their adult sexual functioning.

Revictimization is also a common phenomenon among people abused as children. Research has shown that child sexual abuse victims are more likely to be the victims of rape or to be involved in physically abusive relationships as adults.

In short, the ill effects of child sexual abuse are wide ranging. There is no one set of symptoms or outcomes that victims experience. Some children even report little or no psychological distress from the abuse, but these children may be either afraid to express their true emotions or may be denying their feelings as a coping mechanism. Other children may have what is called "sleeper effects." They may experience no harm in the short run, but suffer serious problems later in life.

One of the greatest burdens on children who have been sexually abused is the guilt they carry, often for the rest of their lives. The long-term effects of guilt, the trauma of feeling betrayed and all the secrecy involved is terrible for abused children even when they have reached adult and parenthood themselves.

The most frightening of all the consequences of sexual abuse is self-destructive behaviour. The victim may feel that s/he is no longer worth anything for anybody and for him/herself. One of the most tragic consequences of sexual abuse is the increased possibility of the victim one day becoming an abuser. Some children have fewer scars than others but not a single one remains unchanged by the experience. The amount of trauma which a child will experience according to an academic researcher,

Groth (1978) is determined by four factors:

- The nature of the victim's relationship with the abuser,
- The duration of the relationship,
- The type of activities endured,
- The degree of violence or aggression involved.

The reactions of parents and family as well as the reaction of professionals and the type of treatment administered is also factors that can contribute to the trauma.

Possible Short-Term Effects

- Preoccupation with sexual matters,
- Premature development of adolescent interests,
- Promiscuity,
- Despair regarding inability to control sexual urges,
- Molestation of younger children,
- Venereal disease,
- Increased or public masturbation,
- Sudden rush into sexual activity,

- Prostitution,
- Pregnancy.

Interpersonal Relationships

- Frightened by contact with adults,
- Running away from home,
- Confusion about relationships with other people,
- Hostile interactions with older women,
- Homicidal interaction with older women,
- Homicidal ideas and fantasies,
- Increased affection-seeking from adults.

Educational Problems

- Truancy,
- Sudden disruptive behaviour,
- Depressed withdrawal from usual activities,
- Collapse of self-esteem,
- Learning difficulties.

Other Psychological Symptoms

- Personal guilt or shame,
- Tendency to withdraw from activities of normal childhood,
- Obesity,
- Physical symptoms,
- Behavioural problems and delinquency,
- Suicidal ideas,
- Depression,
- Sleep problems including nightmares,
- Impulsive self-damaging behaviour,
- Anorexia,
- (Acute) anxiety.

Possible Long-Term Effects

Problems in Sexual Adjustment

- Promiscuity,
- Avoidance of sexual activity,
- Incestuous relationships,
- Many unwanted pregnancies,
- Sexual molestation of children,
- Unsatisfactory sexual relationships,
- Homosexuality.

Interpersonal Problems

- Conflict with/fear of husband or sex partner,
- Conflicts with parents or in-laws,
- Social isolation,
- Difficulty in establishing close relationships with other people.

Other Psychological Symptoms

- Low self-esteem and long-lasting sense of helplessness,
- Behaviour which causes injury to him/herself,
- Obesity,
- Personality disorders,
- Chronic depression,
- Schizophrenia,
- Murder or interpersonal violence,
- Eating and body image disorders.

Reporting of Child Sexual Abuse Cases

Every published empirical study on the disclosure of child sexual abuse indicates that a high percentages of those child sexual abuse victims who report their abuse to authorities delay disclosure of their abuse, and that a significant number of children do not disclose the abuse at all. The delay between the initial occurrence and the subsequent disclosure of the abuse varies, depending on a number of factors such as the age of the victim at the time of the events, the relationship between the perpetrator and the abused, the gender of the abused, the severity of the abuse, developmental and cognitive variables related to the abused, and the likely consequences of the disclosure. Consequently, child sexual abuse is significantly underreported. When victims do report that they were abused, they often do so years after the abuse occurred. Adult retrospective studies of childhood sexual abuse underline the delay in disclosure. In a study of 228 adult female victims of childhood incest who were predominantly abused by males, Roesler and Weissmann-Wind (1994) found that the average age of first abuse was 6 years, and the abuse lasted on average 7.6 years. Only one-third of the subjects in this sample disclosed the abuse before the age of 18, and the average age of disclosure was 25.9. Arata (1998) found that only 41.0% of the 204 female participants in her study, whose average age at the time of victimization was 8.5, disclosed the abuse at the time it occurred. Lawson and Chaffin (1992) found that only 43.0% of their child subjects disclosed their abuse when they were initially interviewed. Lamb and Edgar-Smith (1994) conducted a study with 45 adult female and 12 adult male victims of childhood sexual abuse, and they found that although the average age at the time of victimization was 10, 64.0% of the victims disclosed their abuse in adulthood. In a study of childhood rape of girls, Smith et al., (2000) found that approximately half of the women waited more than eight years to disclose the abuse. The process of disclosing childhood sexual abuse varies, though it is often described within two axes: as purposeful or accidental; and as spontaneous or prompted. DeVoe and Coulborn-Faller (1999) found that child subjects in their study required assistance with disclosure. Sorenson and Snow (1991) noted that accidental disclosure was more common in preschool children, whereas purposeful disclosure was more common in adolescents. They also found four stages of disclosure in their retrospective study of 630 subjects who were aged three to 17 at the time of abuse: denial, disclosure (tentative and active), recantation and reaffirmation. These researchers also found that 72.0% of their subjects originally denied the abuse; 78.0% of the subjects who tentatively revealed their abuse progressed to active disclosure; 22.0% recanted their reports, and of those who recanted 93.0% later reaffirmed the original report. Lawson and Chaffin (1992) found that a significant factor in the disclosure process was the belief of the caretaker in the veracity of the disclosure. Bradley and Wood's (1996) research also supported the notion that the role of the caretaker is essential. Although recantations of disclosure were rare in their sample, they found that 50.0% of children who recanted did so under pressure from a caretaker. Summit's (1983) model of child sexual abuse, the Child Sexual Abuse Accommodation Syndrome, explains the hindrance to disclosure. This syndrome consists of five components: secrecy (the abuse occurs when the victim and perpetrator are alone, and the perpetrator encourages the victim to maintain secrecy); helplessness (children are obedient to adults and will usually obey the perpetrator who encourages secrecy); entrapment and accommodation (once the child is helplessly entrenched in the abusive situation, he or she assumes responsibility for the abuse and begins to dissociate from it); delayed disclosure (because the victims who report child sexual abuse often wait long periods of time to disclose, their disclosures are subsequently questioned); and retraction (as in the recantation stage described by Sorenson and Snow, the victims may retract their disclosures of abuse after facing disbelief and lack of support after their disclosure).

(i) Victim's Relationship to the Perpetrator

If the perpetrator is a relative or acquaintance, victims of child sexual abuse are less likely to report the offense, or they are likely to disclose the abuse after a delay (Arata, 1998; Smith et al., 2000; Wyatt and Newcomb, 1990).

In Arata's study, 73.0% of the victims did not disclose the abuse when the perpetrator was a relative or step-parent, and 70.0% did not disclose when the perpetrator was an acquaintance. Goodman-Brown et al. (2003) found that those children, who felt responsible for the abuse, often because the abuse occurred within the family, took longer to report the abuse. Wyatt and Newcomb found that the women who did not disclose their abuse to anyone were likely to have been closely related to the perpetrator and abused in close proximity to their home.

(ii) Severity of Sexual Abuse

Research results vary in regard to disclosure of abuse in relation to the severity of that abuse. Arata (1998) found that child victims who experienced more severe levels of sexual abuse were less likely to disclose this type of abuse. This is consistent with the findings of Gries, Goh, and Cavanaugh (1996), who reported that fondling was reported by 80.0% of their subjects who disclosed. In contrast, however, Hanson et al. (1999) found that of their 341 adult females who were victims of childhood rape, the more severe assaults were likely to be reported. DiPietro et al. (1998) also found that contact sexual offenses were those most commonly reported in their sample of 76 children.

(iii) Developmental and Cognitive Variables

Lamb and Edgar-Smith (1994) speculate that 'more astute' children may not disclose because they may 'anticipate unsupportive reactions.' They also maintain that such children may wait until adulthood to disclose when they can choose appropriate people to tell. White et al. (1986), as cited in Campis et al. (1993), found that older victims of child sexual abuse were less likely to disclose than their younger counterparts and noted that the knowledge of social consequences was a significant hindrance to disclosure. Keary and Fitzpatrick (1994) concluded that children over the age of five, who had previously disclosed sexual abuse, were more likely to disclose this information during formal assessment, but the converse was true for children under five. Similarly, DiPietro (2003) found that "developmental maturation clearly facilitates" disclosure (p. 140).

(iv) Fear of Negative Consequences

Sorenson and Snow (1991) found that fear of further harm had an impact on a child's motivation to disclose abuse and that the child victims often only felt safe enough to disclose after the departure of the perpetrator. Berliner and Conte (1995) also noted that the fear about perceived reactions of others prevents some children from disclosing sexual abuse. Roesler and Weissmann-Wind (1994) found that 33.3% of their subjects did not disclose their abuse during childhood because they feared for their safety. They also found that 32.9% of their subjects did not report their abuse during childhood because they felt guilt or shame as a result of the abuse.

(v) Gender Differences

DeVoe and Coulborn-Faller; Gries, Goh, and Cavanaugh; and Lamb and Edgar-Smith all found that girls are more likely to report abuse than boys. Reinhart found that sexual abuse of males was more likely to be disclosed by a third party. There are no methodologically sound empirical studies that indicate that males disclose at a higher rate than females. Gender does not appear to be as important, however, as victim perpetrator relationship in disclosure of abuse (Paine and Hanson, 2002).

Theories of Child Sexual Abuse by Males

Why men sexually abuse children has been one of the foremost questions guiding research on sexually deviant behaviour in the twentieth century. As with most forms of deviant behaviour, there are various explanations as to the etiology and maintenance of sexual offending. Within the specialist literature, biological, psychological and sociological theories have been designed to explain the onset of deviant sexual fantasies and behaviour. However, owing to the heterogeneity of the perpetrators of such abuse and the complex nature of this behaviour, no one theory adequately explains: (a) the motivating factors that lead an adult male to have sexual relations with a child and (b) the sustaining factors that contribute to the continuance of such relations (Bickley and Beech, 2001). Nonetheless, understanding the etiology and maintenance of sexual offending is important in order to implement policies that are appropriate for all types of sexual offenders. Chart II at the end of this section summarizes the theories on deviant sexual behaviour.

Biological Theory

Biological theorists are concerned with organic explanations of human behaviour. Therefore, when it comes to sexual behaviour, these theorists postulate that physiological factors, such as hormone levels and chromosomal makeup, have an effect on the behaviour (Berlin, 1983; Marshall and Barbaree, 1990). Androgens, which are male sex hormones, promote sexual arousal, orgasm, and ejaculation, as well as regulate sexuality, aggression, cognition, emotion and personality (Rösler and Witztum, 2000; Marques et al., 2002). As a result, biological theories about deviant sexual behaviour usually pertain to rape because it is considered an act of violence, and researchers have long hypothesized that there is a correlation between aggression and high testosterone levels (Money, 1970; Rada et al., 1976). The theories that address pedophilia most often look at abnormal hormonal and androgenic levels in the brain. Biological theories of deviant sexual behaviour are particularly concerned with the role of androgens and androgen-releasing hormones, which are known to be related to physical changes in the male. The secretion of androgens is controlled by the hypothalamus and the pituitary, and hormones are carried from the anterior lobe of the pituitary to the testes. The testes are an important contributor to the body's output of testosterone, which, once released, circulates in the blood. When not bound to proteins, the testosterone is metabolically active; if bound, androgens can only become active when in contact with receptors for testosterone. It is at this time that physical changes, such as increases in body hair, muscle mass and penis enlargement, are caused through androgenic effects (Hucker and Bain, 1990).

When males reach puberty, there is a major increase in testosterone levels in the testes. Because sex drive increases dramatically at this time, there is generally believed to be a correlation between testosterone levels and sex drive, with testosterone being the primary biological factor responsible for normal and abnormal sexual behaviour. Levels of plasma testosterone increase with erotic activity, which has been measured in males before, during and after they view erotic films (Pirke et al., 1974). Although a review of biological studies shows conflicting results about the correlation between rising hormonal levels and sexual activity, Bancroft (1978) stated that the results imply that hormone levels are affected by erotic stimulus. From a chromosomal perspective, Berlin (1983) discusses the possibility of a biological condition, such as Klinefelter's Syndrome, predisposing a male towards sexually abusive behaviour. Klinefelter's Syndrome is a condition wherein males appear to be essentially normal boys until puberty. At puberty, 80.0% of males with this syndrome display both the physical characteristics and hormonal profiles of women. Berlin proposes that males with Klinefelter's Syndrome may experience problems with regard to both their sexual orientation and the nature of their erotic desires. A review of the literature suggests that the prevalence of sexual deviation among individuals who are diagnosed with Klinefelter's Syndrome may be higher than it is among individuals who have not been diagnosed with Klinefelter's Syndrome. Although Berlin cautions against making causal inferences between sexual deviation and Klinefelter's Syndrome, he attempts to support his theory by citing evidence presented by Baker and Stroller (1968). Over 100 articles regarding Klinefelter's Syndrome were reviewed, and Berlin's conclusion was in concordance with Baker and Stroller's findings.

Psychodynamic Theory

Psychoanalytic explanations of deviant sexual behaviour were initially attributed to Freud, who proposed four states of childhood development: oral, anal, phallic and genital. He viewed sexual deviance as an expression of the unresolved problems experienced during the stages of development. These unresolved problems brought about fixations or hindrances during stages of development, with consequent distortion of a sexual object or a sexual aim (Schwartz, 1995). For example, psychoanalytic theory proposes that boys experience what is termed "the oedipal conflict" during the phallic stage of development. The oedipal conflict is characterized by competition between father and son for the mother's affection. At the same time, boys discover the differences between themselves and girls and conclude girls are actually boys whose jealous fathers have cut off their penises (Schwartz, 1995). Schwartz (1995) states that castration anxiety leads to the oedipal conflict, which is when boys no longer compete with their fathers for their mother's affections. However, if a boy fails to resolve the oedipal conflict, he may develop a permanent aversion to females as an adult if their appearance brings back this fear of castration. Psychodynamic theory also asserts that the human psyche is composed of three primary elements: the id, the ego and the superego. In order to understand how all three elements interact, Freud proposed that all human behaviour is motivated by wishes that often exist at a preconscious level (Holmes and Holmes, 2002). The id is the unconscious domain from which all the instinctual human drives originate (i.e., hunger, sex, aggression, etc.). The id is ruled by the pleasure principle that demands instant gratification of these urges. The second part of Freud's model, the ego, is the conscious part of the human psyche that serves as the mediator between the id and the external environment. This element is primarily conscious and is ruled by the reality principle that accepts that there is a time and a place for everything (Holmes and Holmes, 2002). It is this aspect of the psyche that interacts with the external environment in order to ensure survival. The final element, the superego, is more commonly referred to as the conscience. This aspect of the psyche has both conscious and unconscious aspects and, as Holmes and Holmes state, 'most lessons about the consequences of behaviour stem from experience and not perceptions of how the self would look relative to its environment' (Holmes and Holmes, 2002, p. 30). Thus, the superego is bolstered by past experiences that clearly define the behaviours that warrant punishment and reward. These notions are then internalized in such a manner as to allow for the development of a system of morals.

In sum, Freudian theory portrays the human psyche as being in a constant struggle to fulfil the primal desires of the id and the moral authority of the superego. This theory assumes that sexual aggressors are lacking in a strong superego and have become overwhelmed by their primal id. While psychologists generally once accepted this explanation, it has fallen out of favour due to its lack of empirical evidence in favour of more testable theories, such as cognitive behavioural and integrated theories.

Behavioural Theory

Behavioural theorists explain deviant sexual behaviour as a learned condition. Laws and Marshall (1990) presented a theoretical model of sexually deviant behaviour that describes how sexually deviant interests may be learned through the same mechanisms by which conventional sexuality is learned. The model is divided into two parts: the acquisition processes and the maintenance processes. There are six basic conditioning principles (Pavlovian conditioning, Operant Conditioning, Extinction, Punishment, Differential Consequences and the Chaining of Behaviour); two social learning influences (General Social Learning Influences and Self-Labelling Influences); and three maintenance processes (Specific Autoerotic Influences, Specific Social Learning Influences and Intermittent Reinforcement). The model adopts the position that maladaptive behaviour can result from quantitative and qualitative combinations of processes that are intrinsically orderly, strictly determined and normal in origin. Thus, deviant sexual preferences and cognitions are acquired by the same mechanisms by which other individuals learn more conventionally accepted modes of sexual expression.

Attachment Theory

According to attachment theory, humans have a propensity to establish strong emotional bonds with others, and when individuals have some loss or emotional distress, they act out as a result of their loneliness and isolation. As Marshall and Barbaree (1976) point out, the period surrounding pubescence and early adolescence is critical in the development of both sexuality and social competence. With adequate parenting up to this point in development, boys should have by now acquired appropriate inhibitory controls over sexual and aggressive behaviour and, thus, the transition to adult functioning, with both social constraints against aggression and the skills necessary to develop effective relationships with age appropriate partners, should not be compromised. Parents also fulfil the role of instilling a sense of self-confidence in the developing boy as well as a strong emotional attachment to others. Research indicates that there is a relationship between poor quality attachments and sexual offence. Marshall (1989) found that men who sexually abuse children often have not developed the social skills and self-confidence necessary for them to form effective intimate relations with peers. This failure causes frustration in these men that may cause them to continue to seek intimacy with under aged partners. Seidman et al. (1994) conducted two studies aimed at examining intimacy problems and the experience of loneliness among sex offenders. According to these studies, sex offenders have deficiencies in social skills (i.e., problems in accurately perceiving social cues, problems in deciding on appropriate behaviour and deficiencies in the skills essential to enact effective behaviour) that seriously restrict the possibility of attaining intimacy. The evidence suggests that deficiencies in intimacy are a distinctive and important feature of sex offenders. The rapists and non-familial child molesters in the sample appeared to be the most deficient in intimacy. Loneliness was also a significantly distinguishable variable in differentiating the sex offenders from controls and wife batterers. Mulloy and Marshall (1999) outlined Bartholomew's four-category model of attachment and made the following observations. A secure attachment style is characterized by the individual having a positive concept of both him and others. He is confident about his ability to make friends and interacts well with others. An individual with a preoccupied attachment style has a negative self-concept but a positive concept of others. He does not feel confident about his ability to deal with problems without the help of others. The fearful attachment style, wherein the individual has a negative concept of himself and others, finds that the individual is likely to blame himself for problems in his life and finds it frightening to go to others for help and to trust people around him. Those engaging in a dismissing attachment style have a positive self-concept and a strong sense of self-confidence. However, this individual has a negative concept of others and does not seek out others for help or support. This individual is likely to say that he does not care what others think of him and rarely has a strong emotional involvement in relationships. Marshall and Marshall (2002) cited Ward et al.'s (1995) proposition that sexual offenders who have a preoccupied insecure attachment style will characteristically 'court' the child and treat him or her as a lover.

Cognitive-Behavioural Theory

When individuals commit deviant sexual acts, they often try to diminish their feelings of guilt and shame through 'neutralizations.' These neutralizations generally take the forms of excuses and justifications, with the offenders rationalizing their behaviour (Scott and Lyman, 1968; Scully, 1990; Sykes and Matza, 1957). These neutralizations are cognitive distortions (CDs), or distorted thinking patterns that allow the offenders to remove from themselves any responsibility, shame or guilt for their actions (Abel et al., 1994). These rationalizations protect the offenders from self-blame and allow them to validate their behaviour through cognitive defenses. Cognitive-behaviourists explore how offenders' thoughts affect their behaviour. CDs are not unique to sex offenders, the uniqueness lies only in the content of distortion (Marshall et al., 1999:60).

All individuals have distorted thoughts, and in most situations CDs are relatively harmless (e.g., a motorist rationalizes that speeding on the highway is acceptable since there is little traffic). However, sex offenders' CDs are likely to lead to victimization (e.g., she didn't fight with me so she must have wanted sex). Though sex offenders do not form a homogeneous group of individuals, they show strikingly similar CDs about their victims, their offenses and their responsibility for the offenses. It is unclear as to whether CDs are conscious distortions or whether offenders genuinely believe these altered perceptions of reality. Some researchers suggest that CDs are self-serving, and thus, the offender consciously distorts thoughts initially (Abel et al., 1994). However, it is also suggested that the offenders eventually believe the distortions as they become more entrenched in their behaviour (Marshal et al., 1999). Regardless, CDs are considered crucial to the maintenance of offending behaviour for both rapists and child molesters because they serve the needs of the offenders to continue their behaviour without feeling guilt for their actions. There are many ways in which distortions manifest themselves in sex offenders. Sykes and Matza (1957) list five primary neutralization techniques, including the denial of responsibility, the denial of injury, the denial of the victim, the condemnation of the accusers, and the appeal to higher loyalties. Cognitive behavioural theorists have explained these techniques in terms of CDs, the most common of which are minimization and/or denial of the offense and justification of the offense. Additionally, sex offenders often lack victim empathy and show an inability to recognize the level of planning that went into their offenses (including grooming of the victims). Some researchers also label sexual entitlement as a specific CD, resulting from the narcissistic attitudes of offenders who seek only to fulfil their own desires (Hanson et al., 1998, p. 197). However, broadly or specifically the CDs are defined, these distorted thoughts are conducive towards the maintenance of deviant sexual practices. Most sex offenders minimize or deny their offenses. Several researchers have categorized types of minimization and denial (Haywood et al., 1994; Marshall et al.,

1999), and these include: complete or partial denial of the offense, minimization of the offense, minimization of their own responsibility, denial or minimization of harm to the victim, denial or minimization of planning, denial or minimization of deviant fantasies and denial of their personal problems that led to the deviant behaviour. Some sex offenders deny all or part of their offenses. They may completely deny that they committed the offense – claiming, for instance, that the victim made up the story or they cannot remember what happened – or they may not admit to aggravating factors of the offense. Partial denial, as described by Marshall et al. (1999), includes refutation of a problem (e.g., I am not a sex offender) or the refusal to accept that an act was sexual abuse (e.g., the victim consented). Though some researchers claim that denial is not an accurate predictor variable for recidivism (Hanson and Bussiere, 1998), there is a substantial body of literature that claims the opposite (Marques, Day et al., 1994; Simkins et al., 1989). Few therapists allow deniers to participate in treatment until they at least admit that they committed the offense (Marques et al., 1994). In addition to minimizing or denying their offenses, sex offenders make excuses as to why they committed the deviant acts. By justifying their actions, offenders acknowledge their guilt in the acts, but they do not take responsibility for them. Commonly, they blame the victims for their offenses or justify their offenses through the victims' actions. Justification is common in the vast majority of sex offenders since it assists in allaying remorse and guilt for the acts committed. Scully and Marolla (1990), who interviewed 114 incarcerated rapists, explain five ways in which rapists commonly justify their behaviour. They claim that the victim is a seductress, and she provoked the rape; women mean yes when they say no, or the victim did not resist enough to really mean no; most women relax and enjoy it, and they are actually fulfilling the woman's desires; nice girls do not get raped, and prostitutes, hitchhikers and promiscuous women get what they deserve; and the rape was only a minor wrongdoing, so the perpetrator is not really an "offender". Though these researchers focused on the excuses and justifications of rapists, many of their findings are also evident in child sexual abusers, who also justify their actions by neutralizing their guilt. Child molesters justify their actions in many ways. Common justifications include claims that they are helping the child to learn about sex, that sexual education is good for the child, that the child enjoys it, that there is no harm being done to the child, that the child initiated the sexual contact and that the child acts older than he or she is. Like offenders with adult victims, child molesters often assert that the child did not resist and must have therefore wanted the sexual interaction. They fail to recognize any other explanations as to why the child might not have resisted, such as fear, uncertainty about what was happening or the idea that the perpetrator is someone they knew and trusted. Ward and Keenan (1999) claim that the cognitive distortions of child sexual offenders emerge from five underlying implicit theories that they have about themselves, their victims and their environment. These implicit theories consider the following factors:

- *Children as sexual objects.* Children, like adults, are motivated by a desire for pleasure and are capable of enjoying and desiring sex.
- *Entitlement.* The desires and beliefs of the abuser are paramount and those of the victim are either ignored or viewed as only of secondary importance.
- *Dangerous world.* The abuser views other adults as being abusive and/or unreliable and perceives that they will reject him in promotion of their own needs.
- *Uncontrollability.* The abuser perceives his environment as uncontrollable wherein people are not able to exert any major influence over their personal behaviour and/or the world around them.
- *Nature of harm.* The abuser considers the degree of harm to his victim and perceives sexual activity as beneficial and unlikely to harm a person. Offenders rarely modify these implicit theories even when faced with evidence (behaviour) to the contrary. Instead, the offender may simply reinterpret or reject it. For example, a child's

friendly behaviour might be evidence to the offender that the child wants to have sex with him. Similar to Ward and Keenan's idea that the distortions of sexual offenders reflect their more general implicit theories about their victims, Marshall et al. (1999) stress, 'the distorting process thought to be characteristic of sexual offenders does not differentiate them from the rest of us; it is the content of their distortions, and the goals manifested by their behaviours, that differentiates them.' All sex offenders have a tendency to misread social cues by others and are poor at identifying emotions such as anger or fear in their victims. Both rapists and child molesters often perceive their victims as initiating sexual contact, and see their victims' actions as sexually provocative. Child molesters misread cues from children in several ways, and the better they know the victim the more likely this is to happen. Children are naturally affectionate towards adults, particularly those whom they know well. Child molesters view these naturally affectionate actions—such as sitting on an adult's lap—as sexual in nature and perceive the children as initiating sexual contact. They also perceive any sexual curiosity displayed by the child as a desire to know about sex, and they want to 'teach' the child through sexual experiences. These misperceptions reinforce the offenders' narcissistic beliefs and reduces the likelihood of any empathy for his victims.

Integrated Theory

Finkelhor (1984) is one of the leading theorists on child sexual abuse. He proposed a four-factor model of the preconditions to child sexual abuse, which integrate the various theories about why individuals begin to participate in sexually deviant behaviour. This organizational framework addresses the full complexity of child sexual abusers, from the motivation to offend (etiology of offending behaviour) to the rationalization of this behaviour (maintenance of behaviour). The primary focus of Finkelhor's model is on the internal barriers, or 'self talk,' comments and observations of sex offenders about the world around them. This self-talk allows offenders to break through barriers, which, until this time, had prevented them from acting out their feelings about perceptions of injustice, loneliness and other such stressors. Once these barriers are diminished, this defective thinking can lead to actions, which are the result of normal internal barriers being absent. In order to better explain this process, Finkelhor constructed an organizational framework consisting of four separate underlying factors that explain not only why offenders abuse, but also why the abuse continues.

Finkelhor coined the term "emotional congruence" to convey the relationship between the adult abuser's emotional needs and the child's characteristics. For example, if an abuser's self-perception is child-like (i.e., he has childish emotional needs); he may wish to relate to other children. Similarly, if an abuser suffers from low self-esteem and a low sense of efficacy in social relationships, he may be more comfortable relating to a child due to the sense of power and control. Sexual arousal, the second component of Finkelhor's theory, evaluates the reasons why children would elicit sexual arousal in an adult. Finkelhor looks to social learning theory in order to explain this phenomenon. One explanation is that the child sexual abuser was molested when he was a child. Through conditioning and imprinting, he comes to find children arousing later in adulthood. An alternate explanation is that the child sexual abuser's experience of being victimized as a child is not conditioned, but modelled by someone (i.e., his abuser) who finds children sexually stimulating. Blockage essentially deals with the abuser's ability to have his sexual and emotional needs met in adult relationships. Finkelhor looks to both psychoanalytic theory and attachment theory to explain this component. As stated previously, psychoanalytic theory describes child molesters as having intense conflicts about their mothers or 'castration anxiety' that makes it difficult or impossible to relate to adult women. With regard to adult attachments, child molesters have failed to develop the appropriate social skills and self-confidence necessary to form effective intimate relations with adults. Finkelhor further breaks down the theory of blockage to incorporate what he calls developmental blockages and situational blockages. Developmental blockages once again refer to psychoanalytic theory wherein an individual is psychologically prevented from moving into the adult sexual stage of development. Situational blockage refers to the event wherein an individual, who has apparent adult sexual interests, is blocked from normal sexual expression owing to the loss of a relationship or some other transitory crises. The final component, disinhibition, refers to the factors that help a child molester overcome his inhibitions so that he allows himself to molest a child. Finkelhor looks to cognitive-behavioural theories to explain this component. Specifically, he considers the influence of cognitive distortion in the facilitation of child molesting behaviour. Further, personality factors, such as substance abuse and stress, are viewed as entities that contribute to the lowering of inhibitions. Overall, this organizational framework describes who is at risk to offend. It is likely that individuals who offend have been able to cope with many of the above problems (e.g., developmental blockage) and opportunities (e.g., access to children) at different times.

However, it is the combination of these problems, in addition to some type of demand on their coping system that contributes towards an attitude supportive of sexual offending, thereby establishing a risk to offend. That risk increases the likelihood that a person may act out in a sexual fashion because his or her belief system has filtered out the normal inhibitions towards sexual offending. Unfortunately, the relief that is associated with sexual offending is reinforcing because it provides an emotional and physical response to coping in a way in which the offenders feel they have control, unlike much of the other parts of their lives.

Chart II: Summary of Theories Explaining Child Sexual Abuse

Theory	*Description of Theory*
Biological Theory	Concerned with organic explanations of human behaviour; physiological factors (e.g., hormone levels, chromosomal makeup) have an effect of sexual behaviour; androgens promote sexual arousal, orgasm, and ejaculation, as well as regulate sexuality, aggression, cognition, emotion and personality; abnormal levels of androgens lead to aggressive sexual behaviour.
Psychodynamic Theory	Sexual deviance is an expression of the unresolved problems experienced during the stages of development; the human psyche is composed of three primary elements: the id, the ego and the superego; sexual deviancy occurs when the id (pleasure principle) is overactive.
Behavioural Theory	Deviant sexual behaviour is a learned condition, acquired through the same mechanisms by which conventional sexuality is learned; it is acquired and maintained through basic conditioning principles.
Attachment Theory	Humans have a propensity to establish strong emotional bonds with others, and when individuals have some loss or emotional distress, they act out as a result of their loneliness and isolation.
Cognitive-Behavioural Theory	Addresses the way in which offenders' thoughts affect their behaviour; focuses on the way in which sex offenders diminish their feelings of guilt and shame by rationalizing it through excuses and justifications.
Integrated Theory	There are preconditions to child sexual abuse, which integrate the various theories about why individuals begin to participate in sexually deviant behaviour; addresses the motivation to offend and the rationalization of the behaviour; focus is on the inhibitions of the offenders (internal barriers) and how when these barriers are diminished, distorted thoughts can lead to deviant actions.

Types of Child Sexual Abusers

In the ongoing effort to develop an understanding of characteristics that would allow for classification of sex offenders into specific groups, many researchers have proposed typologies of offenders. These typologies, or classification schemes, utilize offender characteristics and/or victim-choice information, including interpersonal and situational characteristics, to outline a framework for analysis (Knight and Prentky, 1990; Simon et al., 1992; Schwartz, 1995).

The Fixated/Regressed Typology

In the 1970s, researchers began to classify offenders based upon their motivation for committing sexually deviant behaviour. One of the most basic classification schemes was proposed by Groth et al. (1982), who considered two issues: the degree to which the deviant sexual behaviour is entrenched and the basis for psychological needs. With regard to the first issue, Groth proposed the fixated-regressed dichotomy of sex offending. This is not simply a dichotomous distinction, but rather exists on a continuum. The fixated offender is characterized as having a persistent, continual and compulsive attraction to children. They are usually diagnosed with pedophilia, or recurrent, intense, sexually arousing fantasies of at least six months in duration involving pre-pubescent children (American Psychiatric Association, 1999). Finkelhor (1984) classifies these offenders as exclusively involved with children and points out that they are usually not related to their victims and are attracted to children from adolescence. According to Holmes and Holmes (2002), the offender has not fully developed and shows characteristics of a child. In particular, fixated offenders do not develop past the point where they find children attractive and desirable. The fixated offender's actions are typically premeditated in nature and do not result from any perceived stress. In addition, this type of offender is often unable to attain any degree of psychosexual maturity and, during adulthood, has had virtually no age appropriate sexual relationships. The fixated offender is more likely to choose victims who are male and not related to him (Abel and Rouleau, 1990; Simon et al., 1992). It is the fixated offenders who are most dangerous to society, constituting 'a public health problem' (Abel et al., 1994) as well as a 'criminal problem' (Freeman-Longo, 1996). These offenders develop relationships with vulnerable children (vulnerable in either an emotional or situational sense), and they typically recruit, groom and maintain the children for a continuing sexual relationship (Conte, 1991). The offenders delude themselves into believing they have established a caring, supportive role with the child and that the child is able to derive pleasure and educational experience from the interaction (Abel and Rouleau, 1995; Marshall and Barbaree, 1990b). Fixated offenders are particularly dangerous because their offenses often go unreported, and subsequently, many have been convicted for far fewer offenses than they actually committed (Abel and Rouleau, 1990; Abel et al., 1994). Offenders who abuse young boys are at the highest risk of recidivating and are also likely to commit the most offenses (Marques, Day, et al., 1994; Marques, Nelson et al., 1994). Abel and Rouleau's (1990) study of 561 male offenders who voluntarily sought treatment showed that the non-incestuous offenders in the sample who assaulted young boys averaged 281 offenses with an average of 150 victims. It is the strongly fixated offenders who have the most victims and the highest rate of recidivism and should consequently be considered the highest risk to the community. The regressed offenders' behaviour, on the other hand, usually emerges in adulthood and tends to be precipitated by external stressors. Gebhard et al. (1965) touched upon the role of external stressors as precursors to sexual offending. In this early classification system, the authors state that sexual offending is the product of environmental stressors and disordered childhood relationships. These two variables intersect in such a manner as to render the offender powerless to control his behaviour, thus culminating in an offensive act. At the time of the creation of this classification system, the authors were unable to specify childhood precursors to offending; however, there has been extensive research evaluating the nature of stressors. These stressors can be situational, such as unemployment, marital problems and substance abuse, or can relate to negative affective states such as loneliness, stress, isolation or anxiety. These stressors, according to Schwartz (1995), often lead to poor self-confidence and low self-esteem, thereby undermining the abusers confidence in them as men. Sexual involvement with children is not fixed, but is instead often a temporary departure from the offender's attraction to adults (Simon et al., 1992). This type of offender is more likely to choose victims who are female. Regressed offenders tend to victimize children to whom they have easy access, and as such, they often victimize their own children. It is difficult to establish accurate patterns of arousal for regressed offenders, and researchers (Freund, McKnight, Langevin et al., 1972; Quinsey, Steinman, Bergerson et al., 1975) have found that they have arousal pattern similar to that of 'normal' men. Arousal is generally measured through a penile plethysmograph (PPG) as the male is shown erotic material. The control group generally shows some level of arousal to photos of young children in erotic poses, and it is therefore difficult to differentiate between the two groups. This indicates that, as with rapists, the offender is not necessarily motivated by sexual needs alone. A distinction is made between a sex pressure offense and a sex-force offense. In a sex-pressure offense, the offender either entices or entraps his victim. In his pursuit for sexual gratification, the offender would prefer his victim to cooperate. However, should his victim resist, the offender usually will not follow through with the sexually abusive behaviour. In contrast, a sex-force offense is one wherein the offender uses either intimidation or physical aggression. When intimidation is used, the offender may be drawn to his victim primarily because the victim is easily overpowered and may present less resistance than an adult. The offender is using his

Chart III: Characteristics of Fixated and Regressed Offenders

Type of Offender	*Motivation*	*Primary Victim Preference*	*Risk of Reoffending*
Fixated Offender	• Having never developed an attraction to age appropriate partners, the fixated offender has a persistent, continual, and compulsive attraction to children. • Behaviour emerges in Adolescence. • Offenses are premeditated in nature and do not stem from Stressors. • Most likely to be diagnosed/ characterized with pedophila/ ephebophilia.	• Extra-familial • Female (prepubescent), male (pubescent/ adolescent). • Typically recruits vulnerable children and engages inextensive grooming in order to ensure the continuation of the abuse.	• Very high risk of Recidivism. • The risk of Recidivism increases according to the number of victims.
Regressed Offender	• Offending stems from stressors in the individuals environment which undermine self-esteem and confidence. • Behaviour emerges in adulthood. • Offending is a departure from the offender's attraction to adults. • Similar to rapists, the offender is not necessarily motivated by sexual needs alone.	• Intrafamilial, acquaintance. • Gender varies, depending on who is accessible. • Tend to victimize children to whom they have easy access	• Since they are not sexually fixated on children, they are at a lower risk of reoffending if treated. • Capable of feeling remorse for their actions.

victim purely as a means of sexual release. Those offenders who use physical aggression to overpower their victim, commonly known as "sadistic" offenders, must inflict pain in order to achieve sexual gratification. Fortunately, this type of offender is the rarest.

Simon et al., (1992) attempted to empirically validate the fixated-regressed typology. They sampled 136 consecutive cases of convicted offenders over a two-year period. They reviewed pre-sentence data that comprised a case history; MMPI results, pre-sentence reports and police report data. Application of the criteria defining fixated versus regressed status yielded a unimodal and continuous distribution of offenders rather than the bimodal (fixated/regressed) distribution predicted by Groth's theory. Based on the results of this study, Simon et al. suggested that Groth's fixated/regressed dichotomy was unable to account for all child sexual abusers and recommended using a modification of Groth's approach. This modification would entail the use of Groth's criteria along a continuum and rejecting the original dichotomy. The findings of Simon et al. identify a potential causal link between general criminality, anti-social behaviour and child molestation. These variables have been typically ignored by theories such as Groth's. A further contrast between Groth's classification system and Simon et al. is the suggested existence of at least three different age groups of child molesters (not two). The presence of these age clusters suggests that situational opportunities (i.e., marital discord and availability of a young, potential victim) may interact with the "stable" tendency of an individual with a past history of antisocial acts. This leads to a potential increase in the risk of child sexual abuse. Thus, molesters of different age groups may differ in terms of the predisposition to molest as well as the opportunity.

The FBI Typologies

The FBI also expanded on Groth's typologies to include seven sub-groups of offenders: regressed, morally indiscriminate, sexually indiscriminate, inadequate (these are situational offenders); seductive, fixated and sadistic (these are preferential). Four of these sub-groups (regressed, morally indiscriminate, sexually indiscriminate and inadequate) correspond to regressed offenders as described by Groth and three sub-groups (seduction, introverted and sadistic) correspond to Groth's description of fixated child molesters. The morally indiscriminate offender chooses his victim based on accessibility, whereas the sexually indiscriminate offender is driven by his desire to experiment with almost any type of sexual behaviour. The inadequate offender chooses his victim because he is socially inept and likely to perceive his victim as a vulnerable object through which he may satisfy his sexual curiosity. Those offenders who utilize seduction will groom their victim. However, the introverted offender does not have the social skills necessary to seduce a victim, thus they molest very young children. Chart IV summarizes the characteristics of these offender types.

Chart IV: The FBI Typologies of Situational and Preferential Offenders and their Seven Sub-groups

Type of Offender	*Characteristics of Offenders*
Situational offenders	
Regressed	Offenders have poor coping skills, target victims who are easily accessible, abuse children as a substitute for adult relationships.
Morally Indiscriminate	Offenders do not prefer children to adults and tend to use children (or anyone accessible) for their own interests (sexual and otherwise).
Sexually Indiscriminate	Offenders are mainly interested in sexual experimentation, and abuse children out of boredom.
Inadequate	Offenders are social misfits who are insecure, have low self-esteem and see relationships with children as their only sexual outlet.
Preferential offenders	
Seductive	Offenders "court" children and give them much affection, love, gifts and enticements in order to carry on a "relationship".
Fixated	Offenders have poor psychosexual development, desire affection from children, and are compulsively attracted to children.
Sadistic	Offenders are aggressive, sexually excited by violence, target stranger victims, and are extremely dangerous.

Source: Holmes and Holmes (1997).

The MTC: CM3 Typology

In their attempt to classify child molesters, Knight and Prentky (1990) employed deductive rational and inductive-empirical research strategies (simultaneously) to develop multi-dimensional typologies of offenders on two axes. Axis I address the degree to which an offender is fixated with children and is further broken down to consider the offender's level of social competence. Axis II evaluates the amount of contact an offender has with children and is analyzed according to the meaning (interpersonal or sexual) of that contact. This axis further evaluates the amount and type of physical injury involved in the contact. Through this system, which is known as the Massachusetts Treatment Center: Child Molester Typology, versions 3 [MTC: CM3], each offender is assigned a separate Axis I and Axis II typology. Knight and Prentky state that this classification system has already demonstrated reasonable reliability and consistent ties to distinctive developmental antecedents. In addition, the preliminary results of a 25-year recidivism study of offenders conducted by the authors indicate that aspects of this system have important prognostic implications. In 2001, Looman et al., attempted to replicate Knight and Prentky's research strategies with 109 child molesters in Canada. These child molesters were classified in accordance with the MTC: CM3 typology. Groups of molesters were compared on a number of meaningful variables, such as number of victims and sexual deviance. Results showed that it is possible to apply the MTC: CM3 child molester typology in a population outside of Massachusetts. All molesters, with the exception of the sadistic types, were classified into all sub-groups with an acceptable level of reliability. The authors claim that this exception may be due to the low number of offenders who fell into these sub-groups rather than difficulties with the classification system. Differences were found between groups on the phallometric assessments, with the high fixation-low social competence group having highest levels of deviance on the slide assessment for Axis I. Interestingly, the average deviance indices for all four levels of Axis I indicated at least a failure to differentiate appropriate from inappropriate stimuli in terms of sexual responding; however, the high fixation-low social competence group was the only one that demonstrated a clear sexual preference for children. The high fixation-low social competence group was also distinguished by their preferences for male victims and their higher levels of self-reported childhood sexual abuse. On Axis II, the low contact-high injury offenders displayed more deviant arousal on the female's sexual violence assessment than other groups. These offenders were also more intrusive in their offending and were more likely to use physical force. Although most Axis II groupings were equally likely to choose male as well as female victims, the exploitative group had a clear preference for female victims. Differences were not found for groups when rates of sexual and violent recidivism were examined although it was revealed that sadistic offenders committed a great number of violent offenses. Preferential child molesters (i.e., those in high fixation and high contact categories) were found to be more likely to exhibit deviant arousal, to have greater numbers of victims and to cause little physical harm. They were also more likely to commit new sexual offenses although this difference was not significant. Given that deviant sexual arousal is one of the best predictors of sexual recidivism, these individuals present as being higher risk and having higher treatment needs. Low contact-high injury offenders also had a greater number of victims and were more likely to display deviant arousal. They were more likely to target strangers, were more intrusive in their offending and were more likely to cause serious physical harm to their victims. With regard to implications for risk assessment, sadistic offenders had a greater number of violent offenses, indicating that these offenders may be at higher risk for violent non-sexual offenses. Also, low social competence offenders were more likely to reoffend in a non-sexual, non-violent manner.

Chart V: MTC: CM3 Classification of Child Molesters

Axis	*Description of Axis Measurement*
Axis I	• Assesses the extent to which the offender is fixated with children (on a continuum). • Measures the level of social competence of the offender.
Axis II	• Assesses the amount of contact the offender has with children (e.g., exclusively involved with extra familial children, abuses own children). • Meaning of the contact (sexual and interpersonal). • Amount and type of physical injury involved in the contact (including threats and use of force).

Other Typologies

Other researchers have used various forms of data in their attempt to differentiate types of child molesters. Baxter et al., (1984) evaluated the criminal records, personal histories, social sexual competence and physiological responses to erotic stimuli of incarcerated pedophiles, ephebophiles (those individuals with recurrent, intense, sexually arousing fantasies about adolescents) and rapists. Results indicated that there were significant differences among the groups in criminal and personal background. Pedophiles tended to be older, more poorly educated, more likely to be unmarried and less frequently involved in non-sexual crime. Social and social-sexual inadequacy was common to all groups as reflected by under-assertiveness, low self-esteem and negative attitudes. Baxter et al.,'s data provide a degree of support for the view of the pedophile as a sexual deviate. Pedophiles were somewhat older than other subjects and were more likely to be repetitive sexual offenders, with less non-sexual criminal involvement than rapists or ephebophiles. They were more likely to exhibit deviant sexual arousal, inasmuch as they responded much more to children than no pedophilic subjects. In comparison to erotic preference for children, pedophiles display a greater propensity in their inability to either inhibit responding to children or portray a clear erotic preference for adults.

Non-pedophilic subjects showed an attenuated response to children relative to adults while pedophiles did not. Although the findings of the present study are consistent with earlier reports that many pedophiles are married and have children of their own, they conflict with the reports indicating that pedophiles tend to exhibit strong sexual preferences for children. The authors suggest that this may be a result of the rather small sample from which the present data were obtained. Overall, choice of victim was clearly related only to sexual response patterns, and then only in the case of a prepubescent victim. Pedophiles and homosexual offenders responded more to male children than did heterosexual offenders.

Simkins (1993) conducted an exploratory investigation, the purpose of which was to compare sexually repressed and non-repressed child molesters on therapy progress and on a battery of personality and research instruments. From information obtained on psychosexual histories, 68 child molesters were categorized as repressed, non-repressed or exploitive. Results indicated that significantly larger portions of therapy failures were sexually repressed. There were also significant differences between repressed and non-repressed offenders on some of the special research scales of the MMPI, the Burt Rape Myth Scales, some of the Multiphasic Sexual Inventory Scales and Mosher's Sex Guilt Scale. Differences on these measures are consistent with the characteristics of intrafamilial child molesters reported in the clinical and research literature. The results of this investigation are, however, quite speculative due to the small sample size of the repressed group. It is also conceivable that differences in treatment effectiveness between repressed and non-repressed groups may be attributed to differences in social skills rather than to sexual repression. Danni et al. (2002) conducted a study for the purpose of differentiating three types of child sexual offenders—pedophiles, ephebophiles and incest offenders. In this study, 168 convicted sex offenders participated. Data was gathered from the pre-sentence investigation reports, which were used by the court for sentencing proceedings. Eight independent variables were found to significantly discriminate among the three types of sex offenders, almost 90.0% of the time. These variables were: sexually victimized as a child, pre-pubertal victim, seduction motive, age-appropriate relationships, stress, own child as victim, social facade and anger. Based on these results, the authors concluded that pedophiles are more likely to have experienced sexual victimization as a child, to prefer pre-pubertal sex partners and to be motivated to seduce their victims than non-pedophiles. The findings also illustrate that ephebophiles are more likely to have experienced external stress than non-ephebophiles, while incest offenders are more likely to have a higher level of perceived entitlement than non-incest offenders.

Ephebophiles were correctly classified in 92.9% of the cases and incest offenders were classified correctly in 100.0% of the cases. However, pedophiles were the most difficult to correctly classify (84.1%). The authors attribute this phenomenon to the fact that pedophiles' victims are typically young and are not always able to effectively verbalize or convey the things that happen to them. The forms of seduction utilized by the offender may confuse the victims. The authors conclude that the primary characteristic of pedophilia is the offender's own childhood sexual victimization. The unwillingness to disclose that information makes it less likely that a pedophile will be discovered. They purport that this manipulative behaviour is harder to detect. Laws et al. (2000) conducted a study that examined the extent to which the use of multiple measures of pedophilic interest improved on the diagnostic accuracy of any single measure. One hundred twenty-four males voluntarily consented to participate in an outpatient evaluation and treatment programme for child molesters. Of these, 56.0% were referred from the Florida Department of Corrections, 31.0% were referred from private practitioners, mental health clinics or other professionals (i.e., attorneys), and 13.0% were self-reported. All participants admitted to either a sexual attraction to children or to some inappropriate sexual activity with a child. The average age of the participants was 36.08 years (range = 18-74). Eighty-seven percent were Caucasian, 8.0% were African American and 5.0% were

Hispanic. About 26.0% were married or involved in a common-law relationship, 28.0% were separated or divorced and 46.0% had never married. Socio-economic status based on annual income showed that 14.0% were middle class, 20.0% were lower middle class and 66.0% were lower class.

Fifty-two men did not participate in the research due to various reasons, including (a) bisexual child molesters were excluded, (b) anyone who did not complete all three measures were excluded and (c) the attrition rate for the outpatient treatment project was quite high. The remaining 72 child molesters completed a self-report card-sort measure of sexual interest, as well as direct monitoring of penile response (using the PPG) when presented with erotic slides or audio material. The reliability of all measures was high. All three measures used to assess pedophilic interest (i.e., card-sort, PPG slides, PPG audio) significantly differentiated boy-object and girl-object child molesters. The card-sort measure showed the greatest classification accuracy and was the only measure to significantly improve accuracy once the other two modalities were considered. Consideration of all three measures proved classification accuracy (91.7%) greater than any single measure.

Identification and Evaluation of Treatment Needs of Sexual Offenders

Identification

It is rare for a child to speak directly about sexual abuse. Evidence of physical trauma to the genitals or mouth, genital or rectal bleeding, sexually transmitted disease, pregnancy, unusual and offensive odors, and complaints of pain or discomfort of the genital area can all be indicators. An aware medical practitioner may notice these symptoms during a physical examination. However, in most cases of sexual abuse, there are no physical indicators of the crime. It is rare to actually have positive medical findings upon medical examination, although such findings can provide powerful corroboration of a child's account of sexual abuse. Most often, children who are victims of sexual abuse exhibit emotional or behavioural characteristics that may indicate distress. The presence of any one of these indicators does not necessarily mean that the child is or has been sexually abused. Children with several of these symptoms, however, are often referred for mental health evaluations. Most disclosures from children are to trusted friends or adults in their life—the teacher, coach, pastor, grandparent or therapist.

The reaction of the adult to whom a child discloses sexual abuse can significantly impact the child's subsequent adjustment. It is important for the adult to be respectful, caring, and believing. A response involving panic, shock, or disbelief, or an overly emotional response can negatively impact the child. Children often feel badly and blame themselves for the sexual abuse. Therefore, a response in which the adult communicates that the abuse was not the child's fault and that disclosing the information was the right thing to do is recommended. Preparing the child for the potential aftermath of the disclosure is also important. For example, if the adult to whom the child disclosed is a mandated reporter, the local child protection agency or law enforcement will have to be notified. If the adult to whom the child disclosed is a non-offending parent, the parent must take steps to protect the child from further abuse, including reporting the abuse to the proper authorities. In some states (e.g., Texas), if a non-offending parent fails to report, sexual abuse charges can be filed against them as well.

The legal process can be especially intimidating, confusing, and frightening for children. Many aspects of the process (such as providing testimony and multiple interviews) can be overwhelming for children. It is estimated that the average number of interviews a child victim whose case is going through the court system undergoes is eleven. It is often said that during this time, a child can potentially be "re-traumatized". The pre-trial phase can be more distressful for the child than the disclosure phase because the pre-trial phase often involves ongoing investigation, multiple interviews, and protracted fear of perpetrator retaliation. Children report a number of courtroom related fears. Approximately 95% report being frightened to testify and many children report that the day they testified was the worst day of their lives. Other reported fears include retaliation by the perpetrator, being sent to jail, being punished for making a mistake, having to prove their innocence, crying on the witness stand, describing the details of the offense/s in front of strangers, and not understanding the questions which are being asked.

Evaluation of Treatment Needs of Sexual Offenders

In order to determine the treatment needs of an individual, an exhaustive assessment must first take place. During the assessment, clinicians will examine a broad range of variables in order to identify the factors that place an individual at risk of committing sexual abuse. While there is no universally accepted assessment paradigm, mental health professionals are likely to assess risk through actuarial and clinical means. Actuarial assessments seek to evaluate an individual through interpretation of standardized scores on various risk assessment instruments whereas clinical assessments are based upon the mental health professional's personal judgment and knowledge. Grubin (1997) argues that actuarial instruments provide little information pertaining to the causation and management of sexual offending and say nothing about the individual. While clinical assessments can provide greater detail, Grubin provides evidence that it is a paradigm essentially based upon 'untested and unsound theoretical foundations.' The available literature suggests that one possible solution to the shortcomings of these models is to utilize a hybrid of the two in order to render a comprehensive report. When interpreting risk factors, it is imperative that the mental health professional specifies both the static and dynamic factors applicable to the individual. Static factors involve variables that are stable over time whereas dynamic variables are subject to change. While numerous studies have evaluated static risk factors, the literature is practically void of studies devoted to the evaluation of dynamic factors (Hanson, 1998). Hanson and

Harris (2000) addressed this issue by providing evidence that dynamic factors can be broken down further into stable dynamic risk factors (those expected to remain unchanged for a substantial period of time) and acute dynamic risk factors (factors that change rapidly). In their study of 208 sexual offense recidivists and 201 non-recidivist sex offenders, the authors concluded that stable dynamic risk factors showed the greatest potential in differentiating the recidivists from the non-recidivists. Criminal lifestyle variables were found to be the strongest predictors of recidivism. However, these results must be interpreted with caution due to methodological limitations. Once the differentiation has been made between static and dynamic factors, research has illustrated that specific factors contribute to offending behaviour. Browne et al. (1998) found that in a sample of 98 sex offenders, treatment drop out was best predicted by having spent time in prison, having committed a violence related index offense, having committed non-contact offenses, unemployment, substance abuse and delinquent/disruptive behaviour during treatment. Hanson and Harris (2000) concluded that recidivists had poor social support, attitudes tolerant of sexual assault, anti-social lifestyles, poor self-management strategies and difficulties complying with supervision. The recidivists showed similarities with the non-recidivists concerning general mood, but the recidivists displayed more anger and subjective distress before reoffending. Prentky et al. (1997) provided evidence illustrating that the strongest predictors of sexual offense recidivism include the degree of sexual preoccupation with children, presence of paraphilias and the number of prior sexual offenses. The meta-analysis conducted by Hanson and Bussière (1998) illustrated that the best predictors of recidivism were sexual deviancy as measured by PPG, history of sex crimes, psychological characteristics, negative relationship with mother, and failure to complete treatment and the presence of depression and anxiety. In recent years, a variety of evaluative instruments have been developed in order to assess the risk of sex offender recidivism. Some of these instruments include the Sex Offender Risk Appraisal Guide (SORAG), Rapid Risk

Assessment of Sexual Offense Recidivism (RRASOR), Static-99 and the Minnesota Sex Offender Screening Tool-Revised (MnSOSTR). General recidivism tools such as the Violence Risk Appraisal Guide (VRAG) and the Psychopathy Checklist-Revised (PCL-R) has also shown promise in determining sex offender recidivism. Barbaree et al. (2001) concluded that when these instruments were cross validated on a sample of 215 sex offenders, the VRAG, SORAG, RRASOR and Static-99 were capable of predicting general, violent and sexual recidivism. MNSOST-R scores and guided clinical interviews were able to indicate general recidivism, but showed little sensitivity in discerning between serious or sexual reoffending. Out of all of these measures, the PCL-R, when used alone, was sensitive in predicting general and serious recidivism but was unable to predict sexual recidivism. According to Abel et al. (1994), screening tests for pedophilia have existed in various forms for a number of years. These screening tools have included interviews, questionnaires, and home visits and police reports. Institutional policies have also been developed in the hopes of managing child molestation (education/training, elimination of individual staff-child interactions), yet all of these methods suffer from various limitations. The Abel Screening Tool (1994) entails a questionnaire and slides depicting children, adolescents and adults. The individual then rates these images based upon on how sexually arousing they are.

A psycho-physiological hand monitor then records physiological responses. The efficacy of the instrument was established by comparing the responses of a self-selecting sample of "normal" participants to that of pedophiles that had molested pubescent males and prepubescent males/females. The Abel Screen displays high specificity (77.0%-98.0%), sensitivity (76.0%-91.0%) and efficiency (77.5%-96.9%) when applied in a setting that assumes a 5.0% prevalence rate of child molestation. The volumetric phallometer (sensitivity 86.7%; specificity 95.0%; and efficiency 94.6%) and circumferential plethysmograph (sensitivity 47.5%; specificity 100.0%; efficiency 97.4%) also display respectable sensitivity, specificity and efficiency, but evidence suggests that these instruments are much more intrusive, expensive and problematic than the Abel Screen.

The Violence Risk Appraisal Guide (VRAG) and the Sex Offender Risk Appraisal Guide (SORAG) are very similar in their content. Rice and Harris (1997) utilized the VRAG on a sample of 159 sex offenders in order to determine its predictive accuracy in assessing sexual recidivism. The results support use of the VRAG in predicting violence among high-risk offenders, and it performed well upon cross validation and follow-up when the two samples were combined. The authors claim that from a practical standpoint, the focus should be placed upon predictions of future violence, not necessarily a differentiation between sexual and non-sexual violence. Nunes et al. (2002) compared the predictive accuracy of the SORAG to the revised Static-99. When the instruments were evaluated independently of one another, evidence suggests that they did not provide any unique contributions and may be redundant. However, when phallometric scores were computed in conjunction with Static-99 scores, accuracy increased. The authors propose that this effect was not observed in the use of the SORAG because it targets only general deviant arousal. Static-99, one of the most recent and promising risk assessment instruments, consists of only static risk factors taken from the RRASOR and the Structured Anchored Clinical Judgment (SACJ). Hanson and Thornton (2000) combined the two scales in order to determine whether or not a hybrid would display greater predictive accuracy than the individual scales. These instruments were applied across four data sets, and it was concluded that while the RRASOR and the SACJ were nearly equivalent in their predictive accuracy of sexual recidivism, Static-99 showed the greatest accuracy. However, Sjöestedt and Långström (2001) provide evidence illustrating that the RRASOR and Static-99 should not be used as the only determinants of risk. Cross-validation of these two instruments on a sample of 1,400 Swedish sex offenders illustrated that both instruments displayed moderate predictive accuracy regarding short-term sexual recidivism. However, Static-99 was found to have greater predictive accuracy when it came to assessing violent recidivism, not sexual recidivism. Social scientists have undertaken the task of developing a risk assessment instrument to screen for the presence of ephebophiles within the clergy. Musser et al. (1995) found that the Millon Clinical Multiaxial Inventory (MCMI-II) was incapable of differentiating cleric sex offenders from mentally ill clerics. Cimbolic et al. (1999) attempted to create an ephebophile scale by combining 11 items from the MCMI-II with 16 items from the MMPI-2.When tested on a sample of 165 Catholic priests undergoing treatment, the authors concluded that a combination of the two scales displayed greater accuracy and increased the internal consistency of the MCMI-II items. However, the combined scale failed to identify many of the ephebophiles in the sample. The individual scales were capable of differentiating sexually abusive clerics from mentally ill clerics, but the authors urge that a multidimensional approach be utilized when evaluating sex offenders.

Intervention

Models of Treatment for Sexual Offenders who Abuse Children

Treatment for sexual offenders has changed drastically over the past half-century (Laws and Marshall, 2003). Even though earlier non-behavioural treatment approaches were important in establishing that child sex offenders could be engaged in treatment, John B. Watson and Alfred Kinsey were prominent in the development of behavioural treatment approaches in the early to mid-20th century. Kurt Freund developed penile pethysmography (PPG) in 1957 in response to the sexual preference hypothesis. Despite many criticisms of the PPG, it remains popular and continues to be widely used. The earliest behavioural approaches to treatment reflected the view that deviant sexual behaviour was a distorted manifestation for pedophilia and other paraphilias. Exhibitionists and child molesters were treated with electrical aversion; the modification of sexual fantasies was the target of efforts applied to sadists and voyeurs. However, limited information existed about the long-term effects on overt behaviour of these techniques. A combination of behavioural and cognitive behavioural treatments began to emerge in the late 1960s. This decade is also noted for the further development of phallometric evaluations in assessment and the associated focus on modifying sexual preferences, introduction of cognitive processes and the first description of more comprehensive treatment programmes. In the early 1970s, cognitive psychology began to penetrate the field of treating child sex offenders—social skills training, assertiveness, sexual dysfunctions and gender role behaviour. The first conference, at which sexual offender issues were discussed from a behavioural or cognitive behavioural perspective was in 1975—this subsequently became known as the Association for the Treatment of Sexual Abuse (ATSA). The most significant innovation of the 1980s was the adaptation of the relapse prevention model from an addictions perspective, as well as formulating social learning theories of sexual offending behaviour. Further, a wide variety of programmes described targets such as sexual preferences, sex education, victim empathy, social skills, self-esteem, substance abuse, and anger management and relapse prevention. Contemporary sex offender treatment programmes (both in the U.S. and internationally) employ a multidimensional approach that includes cognitive-behavioural techniques, relapse prevention strategies and psychopharmacology to treat child sex offenders. Although there is no "cure" for individuals who sexually molest children, the above treatment approaches appear to be successful with regard to reducing recidivism rates (Barbaree and Marshall, 1991; Eccles and Walker, 1998; Wood et al., 2000; Aytes et al., 2001).

(i) Cognitive-Behavioural Treatment and Relapse Prevention

Cognitive-behavioural treatment has emerged as the principal type of treatment used to modify deviant sexual arousal, increase appropriate sexual desires, modify cognitive distortions and improve interpersonal coping skills. As a comprehensive structured treatment approach, cognitive-behavioural treatment integrates cognitive restructuring methods and behavioural techniques. According to Nicholaichuk et al. (2002), this treatment approach is based on the premise that "cognitive and affective processes and behaviour are linked, and that cognitions, affect, and behaviour are mutually influential." Therefore, treatment typically includes targeting the following: (1) deviant sexual behaviour and interests, (2) a wide range of social skills/relational deficits, and (3) cognitive distortions, which permit the offender to justify, rationalize and/or minimize the offending behaviour (Marshall and Barbaree, 1990; McGrath et al., 1998).

(ii) Deviant Sexual Behaviour and Interests

Combinations of behavioural approaches are frequently used in an attempt to address deviant sexual behaviour/interests. These approaches include covert sensitization, aversion therapy and masturbatory satiation. The objective of these approaches is to reduce deviant sexual behaviour/fantasy while maintaining and/or increasing sexual arousal to appropriate stimuli (Abel et al., 1992; Becker, 1994; Marshall and Barbaree, 1990; Quinsey and Earls, 1990; McGrath et al., 1998). Covert sensitization involves the pairing of a negative consequence (aversive event) with the sexual arousal stimulus. An example of this technique would consist of having the offender imagine a paraphilic event in order to elicit arousal, and at that point, imagine the humiliation of getting arrested for the event while at work or at home with his family. Aversion therapy is similar to covert sensitization; however, the sexual arousal stimulus is paired with an aversive event (i.e., mild electric shock, sniffing a noxious odor such as ammonia, sniffing rotting meat or tissue or boredom/fatigue). The goal of both of these approaches is to teach the offender to associate negative consequences/events with sexually deviant arousal/thoughts. Masturbatory satiation requires the offender to masturbate to ejaculation while verbalizing an appropriate sexual fantasy. The offender then continues to masturbate for 50-120 minutes while verbalizing deviant sexual fantasies. Since masturbation is unlikely to result in orgasm during the given time period, it is hoped that the offender will learn to associate deviant fantasy with unsatisfactory sexual activity. Furthermore, sexual gratification becomes associated with appropriate sexual behaviour.

(iii) Social Skills/Relational Deficits

Cognitive-behavioural treatment seeks to enhance the offender's interpersonal functioning, which includes enhancing relationship skills, appropriate social interaction and empathy (Marshall, 1989; McFall, 1990; Seidman et al., 1994; Marshall et al., 1999). Social problem solving, conversational skills, managing social anxiety, assertiveness, conflict resolution, empathy and intimacy, anger management, self-confidence and the use of intoxicants are targeted (Laws and Marshall, 2003). Educational modules, which include role-playing of specific types of social interactions, behavioural assignments and presentations on various aspects of social skills are the techniques utilized to address these social difficulties. The inclusion of empathy-enhancement in treatment is based on the belief that the attitudes of sexual offenders towards their victims will change if they understand how the victim feels. The subsequent development of empathy will inhibit future sexual abuse since empathy is something that people learn, rather than an instinct. This is achieved in treatment through utilization of audio-visual methods and materials to demonstrate the pain associated with victimization. These methods include writing assignments, wherein the offender describes his sexual assault from the victim's view point, and the use of role-play wherein the offender plays the role of himself confronted by a peer as well as the role of his victim, respectively (Mulloy and Marshall, 1999).

(iv) Cognitive Distortions

Cognitive restructuring is an integral part of cognitive-behavioural treatment. As mentioned previously, child sex offenders construct internal rationalizations, excuses and cognitive distortions in order to maintain their sexually deviant behaviour. Therefore, it is paramount that an offender's cognitive distortions are challenged so that he can comprehend his faulty thinking and recognize it's distorted, self-serving nature (Marshall and Barbaree, 1990). Additionally, the clinician will present more socially appropriate and adaptive views, and the benefits of accepting such views are identified. This is achieved by examining the role of rationalizations, excuses and cognitive distortions from a non-sexual approach in the lives of average people, thereby normalizing the process while showing its hazards. Role-play is also utilized in which the therapist plays the role of the offender, elaborating on the cognitive distortions elicited throughout the offense process, while the offender plays various roles, including that of a victim's parent and/or an old friend, who supports his taking responsibility for his behaviour and admitting his distortions.

(v) The Relapse Process

The classical relapse prevention treatment approach was initially developed in response to the clinical difficulties associated with the treatment of addictive behaviours, such as alcoholism and drug dependency. This approach was subsequently altered for use in the treatment of sex offenders (Eccles and Marshall, 1999; Laws, 1999; Laws et al., 2000).

In the classical model of relapse prevention, a lapse, which is perceived as a momentary indulgence but not a relapse, involved an actual re-indulgence in the problem behaviour (i.e., drinking). However, in the sex offender model of relapse prevention, a lapse is defined as "offense precursor activities such as deviant fantasies, purchasing pornography or cruising for potential victims," and perceived as a relapse (Laws et al., 2000). Therefore, in the treatment of sex offenders, the relapse prevention approach pays considerable attention to behaviours that might lead to sex offending as opposed to the actual re-indulgence in the aberrant behaviour. Relapses are regarded as the culmination of a series of events and situations through which the offender proceeds prior to offending (Eccles and Marshall, 1999). The relapse process (sometimes called a cycle or a chain) is based on the offender's capacity to cope with high-risk situations. These situations are defined as a set of circumstances that threaten the offender's sense of self-control. In treatment, the relapse process begins with the offender declaring his intent to abstain from the deviant behaviour. Self-management skills and the anticipation of adaptive coping mechanisms are reinforced. As the offender encounters high-risk situations, his self-management skills and coping mechanisms are challenged. Should the offender successfully cope with this situation, his sense of self-management survives and abstinence remains intact. Conversely, should the offender fail to successfully cope with the situation, his sense of self-management decreases, and a tendency to passively yield to the temptation of the next high-risk situation ensues. Each time the offender fails to cope with a high-risk situation, he will engage in one of the behaviours involved in his relapse process (i.e., deviant fantasy, the purchase of pornography). However, at this stage, these behaviours are considered lapses as opposed to a relapse. Several factors, subsumed by a concept referred to as the 'Abstinence Violation Effect' (AVE), determine whether a lapse becomes a relapse. A major aspect of the AVE is a conflict between the offender's definition of himself as an abstainer and his recent indulgence in a behaviour that is part of his relapse process (e.g., self-deprecation, the expectation to fail, his need for immediate gratification). At this stage, if the offender does not use treatment effectively to cope with his beliefs and/or urges, and to regain his confidence in self-management, a relapse is inevitable (Pithers et al., 1983; Pithers, 1990; Eccles and Marshall, 1999; Launay, 2001). Ward and Hudson's (2000) self-regulation model expanded the original relapse prevention process to incorporate more comprehensive cognitive, affective and behavioural factors. Further, within Ward and Hudson's model, post offense factors are considered. The self-regulation model of relapse prevention contains nine phases (life event, desire for deviant sex or activity, offense-related goals established, strategy selected, high-risk situation entered, lapse, sexual offense, post offense evaluation and attitude towards future offending) and four pathways (avoidant-passive, avoidant-active, approach-automatic and approach-explicit). According to Ward and Hudson, an important aspect of this model is that the offender can 'exit the relapse process at any time by implementing appropriate coping strategies ... move back and forth between different points in the offense chain ... [and] remain at specific phases for a relatively long time before moving on to the next phase.' In 2002, Bickley and Beech evaluated the ability of the self-regulation model to classify sexual offenders. The sample consisted of 87 child abusers who ranged in age from 21 to 75. The majority of the participants (62.0%) had offended outside the family, 15.0% had offended inside the family, and 23.0% had offended both inside and outside the family. Of the participants, 36.0% had offended against boys, 33.0% against girls, and 31.0% had offended against both sexes. Fifty-three per cent of the sample had a previous conviction for a sexual offense. The participants were classified as belonging to one of the four pathway groups identified by Ward and Hudson's self-regulation model of sexual offense process. Results indicated that the profile of the 'fixated' child molester is consistent with the self-regulation model's description of an approach pathway. In contrast, the 'regressed' offender is consistent with Ward and Hudson's description of an avoidant pathway. Bickley and Beech concluded that the self-regulation model could be reliably employed in the classification of child molesters, with inter-rater agreement found in more than 80.0% of the sample. Furthermore, differences across the two group distinctions (i.e., avoidant *vs.* approach, active *vs.* passive) in both the psychometric and offense demographic data provided objective support for the validity of the framework.

(vi) Treatment Efficacy Studies

Most studies conducted on treatment efficacy focus on the rate of recidivism among offenders. In studying recidivism rates, researchers compare sex offenders who have participated in treatment to those who have not. Further, they consider specific variables such as the type of treatment implemented and whether or not an offender completed the treatment process. In a follow-up study conducted on 89 sex offenders in Ontario,

Looman et al., (2000) found that those offenders who participated in treatment had a sexual recidivism rate of 23.6%, whereas those offenders who did not participate in treatment had a sexual recidivism rate of 51.7%. Similarly, when 296 treated and 283 untreated offenders were followed for a six-year period; Nicholaichuk et al. (2002) found that convictions for new sexual offenses among treated sex offenders were 14.5% *versus* 33.2% for untreated offenders. Further, during the follow-up period, 48.0% of treated offenders remained out of prison as compared to 28.3% of untreated offenders. Time series comparisons of treated offenders and comparison samples also showed that treated offenders reoffended at significantly lower rates after ten years. In reviewing studies pertaining to the efficacy of a particular type of treatment, there is significant evidence that cognitive-behavioural treatment has emerged as the principle type of sex offender treatment targeting deviant arousal, increasing appropriate sexual desires, modifying distorted thinking and improving interpersonal coping skills (Marshall and Barbaree, 1990; Becker, 1994; Nicholaichuk et al., 2002; Craig, 2003). Further, Marshall and Anderson (2000) found that cognitive-behavioural treatment programmes that have an internal self-management relapse prevention component appear to be the most successful in reducing recidivism rates. Studies of the effects of treatment completion on recidivism have also supported the effectiveness of treatment (Hall, 1995; Hanson and Bussière; 1998). A retrospective study, conducted by McGrath et al. (2003), found that the reduction in the sexual recidivism rate among those offenders who participated in treatment was statistically, as well as clinically, significant. Treatment completers were almost six times less likely to be charged with a new sexual offense than were offenders, who refused, dropped out or were terminated from treatment.

(vii) Pharmacological Interventions

Physiologically, the androgen (hormone) testosterone is the major activator element of sexual desire, fantasies and behaviour, and basically controls the frequency, duration and magnitude of spontaneous erections. Given this, medications used to treat deviant sexual behaviour are aimed at the reduction of testosterone and/or totally suppressing testosterone action at the levels of the receptor (Rösler and Witztum, 2000). These medications include antiandrogens such as Cyproterone Acetate (CPA), Medroxyprogesterone (MPA or Depo-Provera) and Long-Acting Analogues of Gonadotropin-Releasing Hormone (GnRH) (Berlin, 1983; Bradford, 1990; Grubin, 2000; Rösler and Witztum, 2000). Further, given the compulsive nature of pedophilic behaviour, benefits with regard to the containment of such behaviour have been seen through treatment with selective serotonin reuptake inhibitors (SSRIs) such as Sertraline, Fluoxetine, Fluvoxamine, Desipramine and Clomipramine. Even though there are a number of studies on the efficacy of the above medications with regard to the treatment of sexually deviant behaviour, most studies conclude that a combination of medical and psychological treatment has proven to be the most beneficial.

Counselling for Sexually Abused Children

The term 'counselling' refers to a relationship between a counsellor and a person looking for help with a problem. These are some definitions of 'Counselling' formulated by professional bodies and leading figures in the field: The term 'counselling' includes work with individuals and with relationships which may be developmental, crisis support, psychotherapeutic, guiding or problem solving ... The task of counselling is to give the 'client' an opportunity to explore, discover and clarify ways of living more satisfyingly and resourcefully (BAC, 1984). Counselling denotes a professional relationship between a trained counselor and a client. This relationship is usually person-to-person, although it may sometimes involve more than two people. It is designed to help clients to understand and clarify their views of their life space, and to learn to reach their self-determined goals through meaningful, well-informed choices and through resolution of problems of an emotional or interpersonal nature (Burks and Stefflre, 1979: 14). A principled relationship characterized by the application of one or more psychological theories and a recognized set of communication skills, modified by experience, intuition and other interpersonal factors, to clients' intimate concerns, problems or aspirations. Its predominant ethos is one of facilitation rather than of advice giving or coercion. It may be of very brief or long duration, take place in an organizational or private practice setting and may or may not overlap with practical, medical and other matters of personal welfare. It is both a distinctive activity undertaken by people agreeing to occupy the roles of counsellor and client ... and an emerging profession ... It is a service sought by people in distress or in some degree of confusion who wish to discuss and resolve these in a relationship which is more disciplined and confidential than friendship, and perhaps less stigmatizing than helping relationships offered in traditional medical or psychiatric settings (Feltham and Dryden 1993: 6). Counselling abused children is challenging is that it can arouse many complex feelings within the counsellor. Anger with the child's parents, uneasiness over the child's acting out, or feelings of frustration and sadness are not uncommon for counsellors to face. Anxiety about protecting the children from further maltreatment may be a predominant theme for the counsellor. It is important for counsellors working with the sensitive issues of maltreatment to seek consultation, supervision, or even treatment for themselves when they become overwhelmed with feelings. Recognizing one's professional limitations can also be helpful. It is important to remember that counselling alone cannot protect children, and that any effective long-term intervention will require a concerted team approach and a community which cares enough to offer adequate resources for families. Children will be healed and protected as families are helped.

One of the primary purposes of counselling the maltreated child is to provide a safe place and safe relationship within which the child may experiment with new adaptations to a safer world, and in which the child's arrested development may become 'unstuck'. Counsellors cannot literally replace the requisite parental bonding, which helps children to grow and develop, but have an opportunity to help the child develop a trusting relationship with an adult.

The key to understanding the maltreated child is to look at the developmental stage rather than the chronological age. The counsellor will be able to identify adaptations which the child made to the maltreatment and teach the child more appropriate ways of interacting. Children often reveal in play the traumatic events of their earlier years. They may also show to the counsellor maladaptive behaviour, which puts them at risk of further maltreatment.

In the counselling relationship, working with maltreated children requires many techniques other than talking and listening. Using structured or unstructured plays situations and artwork, music or clay provides a safe way for children to release tension and express themselves. Younger children do well with dolls and dollhouses to act out family issues for the counsellor. Many maltreated children have not had normal play opportunities and benefit greatly from free play in the counsellor's office. Using puppets, reading stories, or acting out role-plays are ways in which abused children can try out new approaches to relationships.

Abused children also do well when counsellors work with them in groups. Younger children do well with developmental playgroups, while older children and youth can benefit from activity groups as well as treatment-oriented groups. Group counselling can be especially useful with children and youth who have been sexually abused by reducing their feelings of shame and differences and helping them to learn how to protect themselves (McFadden, 1989).

Child Sexual Abuse: Legislations in India

India has no law on child sexual abuse. If a child is abused and the overwhelming cultural bias for denial is overcome then a case can be filed for statutory rape, or 'outraging the modesty of the woman', in the case of girls and for 'unnatural sexual offence' in the case of boys.

There are no specific procedural provisions concerned with ensuring successful prosecution, and protecting the best interests of the child. Thus procedural innovations, such as the exceptions to the rule against hearsay; the use of expert testimony as proof of abuse and the appointment of a guardian *ad litem* to protect the interest of the child at all stages of the proceedings, have not yet been introduced.

Further, the inadequacy of the substantive law is itself quite apparent in the fact that rape is defined too narrowly. Besides, 'outraging modesty' as a concept is patriarchal. While 'unnatural sexual offence' is problematic *vis-à-vis* the rights of sexual minorities. Besides, one needs a law, which is sensitive to the issue of continuous sexual abuse as a phenomenon. The extent laws in the Indian Judicial System for sexual abuse are the following:

(i) Ages for Legal Purposes

Age of simple majority

The legal age of majority is eighteen (18) years for male and female persons.

Age of consent for sexual activity

The legal age at which a person is currently competent to consent to sexual intercourse is currently eighteen (18) years.

Age of consent for marriage

The legal age of consent for marriage is eighteen (18) years for female persons and twenty-one (21) years for male persons as per the Child Marriage Restraint Act, 1929.

However, recently there is a proposal from the Ministry of Law, Government of India to bring down the age of marriage for boys to 18 years with a view to maintaining uniformity in age. This proposal has generated good debate among the professionals in India.

(ii) Rape

Section 376(1) of the Indian Penal Code

> *'Whoever, except in the case provided for by sub-section (2), commits rape shall be punished with imprisonment of either description for a term which shall not be less than seven years but which may be for life or a term which may extend to ten years and shall also be liable to fine unless the woman raped is*

> *his own wife and is not under twelve (12) years of age, in which case, he shall be punished with imprisonment of either description for a term which may extend to two years or with fine or with both:*
>
> *Provided that the Court may, for adequate and special reasons to be mentioned in the judgment, impose a sentence of imprisonment for a term of less than seven years.*
>
> (2) *Whoever—*
>
> *(a)—(e) (...)*
>
> *(f) commits rape on a woman when she is under twelve (12) years of age; or*
>
> *(g) (...),*
>
> *—shall be punished with rigorous imprisonment for a term which shall not be less than ten years but which may be for life and shall also be liable to fine:*
>
> *Provided that the Court may, for adequate and special reasons to be mentioned in the judgment, impose a sentence of imprisonment of either description for a term of less than ten years.'*

(iii) Other Forms of Child Sex Abuse

Section 90 of the Indian Penal Code

'A consent is not such consent as is intended by any section of this Code,

> *if the consent is given by a person under fear of injury, or under a misconception of fact, and if the person doing the act knows, or has reason to believe, that the consent was given in consequence of such fear or misconception; or*
>
> *if the consent is given by a person who from unsoundness of mind, or intoxication, is unable to understand the nature and consequence of that to which he gives his consent; or*
>
> *unless the contrary appears from the context, if the consent is given by a person who is under twelve (12) years of age.'*

Misconception of fact—Consent given under a misconception is invalid if the person to whom the consent is given is aware of its existence. A consent given on the misrepresentation of fact is one given under a misconception of fact within the meaning of this section. An honest misconception by both the parties, however, does not invalidate the consent.

Section 377 of the Indian Penal Code

'Whoever voluntarily has carnal intercourse against the order of nature with any man, woman or animal, shall be punished with imprisonment for life, or with imprisonment of either description for a term which may extend to ten years, and shall also be liable to fine.'

Explanation: Penetration is sufficient to constitute the carnal intercourse necessary to the offence described in this section. Sex with a female under fifteen (15) years of age is considered rape, even if wedded.

Section 376B of the Indian Penal Code

'Whoever, being a public servant, takes advantage of his official position and induces or seduces, any women, who is in his custody as such public servant or in the custody of a public servant subordinate to him, to have sexual intercourse with him, such sexual intercourse not amounting to the offence of rape, shall be punished with imprisonment of either description for a term which may extend to five years and shall also be liable to fine.'

Section 376C of the Indian Penal Code

'Whoever, being the superintendent or manager of a jail, remand home or other place of custody established by or under any law for the time being in force or of a women's or children's institution takes advantage of his official position and induces or seduces any female inmate of such jail, remand home, place or institution to have sexual intercourse with him, such sexual intercourse not amounting to the offence of rape, shall be punished with imprisonment of either description for a term which may extend to five years and shall also be liable to fine.'

Section 376D of the Indian Penal Code

'Whoever, being on the management of a hospital or being on the staff of a hospital takes advantage of his position and has sexual

intercourse with any women in that hospital, such sexual intercourse not amounting to the offence of rape, shall be punished with imprisonment of either description for a term which may extend to five years and shall also be liable to fine.'

'Seduction of a person in custody', Section 9 of the Immoral Traffic Prevention Act, 1986

'Any person who, having the custody, charge or care of, or position of authority over, any person causes or aids or abets the seduction for prostitution of that person shall be punishable on conviction with imprisonment of either description for a term which shall not be less than seven years but which may be for life or for a term which may extend to ten years and shall also be liable to fine:

Provided that the court may, for adequate and special reasons to be mentioned in the judgment, impose a sentence of imprisonment for a term of less than seven years.'

There is no specific provision in the Indian law as regards to sexual abuse of children by parents or teachers. Such acts are covered by the general provisions relating to sexual abuse of children by their custodian, in whatever capacity they may be.

(iv) Child Prostitution

Sections 366A and 366B are intended to punish the export and import of girls for prostitution. Section 366A deals with Procuration of minor girls from one part of India to another. Section 366B makes it an offence to import into India, from any country outside India, girls below the age of twenty-one (21) years for the purpose of prostitution.

Section 366A of the Indian Penal Code

'Whoever, by any means whatsoever, induces any minor girl under the age of eighteen (18) years to go from any place or to do any act with intent that such girl may be, or knowing that it is likely that she will be, forced or seduced to illicit intercourse with another person

shall be punishable with imprisonment which may extend to ten years, and shall also be liable to fine.'

Explanation: This section required two things: (l) inducing a girl under eighteen (18) years to go from any place or to do any act, and (2) intention or knowledge that such girl will be forced or seduced to illicit intercourse with a person.

Where a woman, even if she has not attained the age of eighteen (18) years, follows the profession of a prostitute, and in following that profession she is encouraged or assisted by someone, no offence under this section is committed by such person, for it cannot be said that the person who assists a girl accustomed to indulge in promiscuous intercourse for money in carrying on her profession acts with intent or knowledge that she will be forced or seduced to illicit intercourse.

The word 'seduced' is used in the ordinary sense of enticing or tempting irrespective of whether the minor girl has been previously compelled or has submitted to illicit intercourse.

Section 366B of the Indian Penal Code

'Whoever imports into India from any country outside India or from the State of Jammu and Kashmir any girl under the age of twenty-one (21) years with intent that she may be, or knowing it to be likely that she will be forced or seduced to illicit intercourse with another person, shall be punishable with imprisonment which may extend to ten years, and shall also be liable to fine.'

Section 367 of the Indian Penal Code

'Whoever kidnaps or abducts any person in order that such person may be subjected, or may be so disposed of as to be put in danger of being subjected to grievous hurt, or slavery, or to the unnatural lust of any person, or knowing it to be likely that such person will be so subjected or disposed of, shall be punished with imprisonment of either description for a term which may extend to ten years, and shall also be liable to fine.'

Section 372 of the Indian Penal Code

'Whoever sells, lets to hire, or otherwise disposes of any person under the age of eighteen (18) years with intent that such person shall at any age be employed or used for the purpose of prostitution or illicit intercourse with any person or for any unlawful and immoral purpose, or knowing it to be likely that such person will at any age be employed or used for any such purpose, shall be punished with imprisonment of either description for a term which may extend to ten years, and shall also be liable to fine.'

For the purpose of this section 'illicit intercourse' means sexual intercourse between persons not united by marriage, or by any union or tie which, though not amounting to a marriage, is recognized by the personal law or custom of the community to which they belong or, where they belong to different communities, of both such communities, as constituting between them a quasi-marital relation.

This section applies to males or females under the age of eighteen (18) years. It applies to a married or an unmarried female even where such female prior to sale or purchase, was leading an immoral life. It also applies where the girl is a member of the dancing girl caste.

Section 373 of the Indian Penal Code

'Whoever buys, hires or otherwise obtains possession of any person under the age of eighteen (18) years with intent that such person shall at any age be employed or used for the purpose of prostitution or illicit intercourse with any person or for any unlawful and immoral purpose, or knowing it to be likely that such person will at any age be employed or used for any such purposes, shall be punished with imprisonment of either description for a term which may extend to ten years, and shall also be liable to fine.'

This section and section 372 conjointly punish both the giver as well as the receiver of a person less than eighteen (18) years for an immoral purpose. Both the sections relate to the same subject-matters.

The Immoral Traffic (Prevention) Act, 1986 [IT (P) Act]

Section 5; Paragraph 1 IT (P) Act, 1986

'Procuring, inducing or taking persons for the purpose of prostitution:

(l) Any person who—

(a) procures or attempts to procure a person whether with or without his consent, for the purpose of prostitution; or

(b) induces a person to go from one place, with the intent that he may, for the purpose of prostitution, become the inmate of, or frequent a brothel; or

(c) takes or attempts to take a person or cause a person to be taken away from one place to another with a view to his carrying on, or being brought up to carry on prostitution; or

(d) causes or induces a person to carry on prostitution,

shall be punishable on conviction with rigorous imprisonment for a term of not less than three years and not more than seven years and also with fine which may extend to two thousand rupees, and if any offence under this sub-section is committed against the will of any person, the punishment of imprisonment for a term of seven years shall extend to imprisonment for a term of fourteen years:

Provided that if the person in respect of whom an offence committed under this sub-section:

(i) is a child, the punishment provided under this sub-section shall extend to rigorous imprisonment for a term of not less than seven years but may extend to life; and

(ii) is a minor, the punishment provided under this sub-section shall extend to rigorous imprisonment for a term of not less than seven years and not more than fourteen years.'

'Detaining a person in premises where prostitution is carried out', Section 6 IT (P) Act, 1986

'(1) Any person who detains any other person, with or without his consent,

(a) *in any brothel; or*
(b) *in or upon any premises with intent that such person may have sexual intercourse with a person who is not the spouse of such person,*

shall be punishable on conviction, with imprisonment of either description for a term which shall not be less than seven years but which may be for life or for a term which may extend to ten years and shall also be liable to fine;

Provided that the court may, for adequate and special reasons to be mentioned in the judgment, impose a sentence of imprisonment for a term of less than seven years.

(2) Where any person is found with a child in a brothel, it shall be presumed, unless the contrary is proved, that he has committed an offence under sub-section (1).

(2A) Where a child or minor found in a brothel, is, on medical examination, detected to have been sexually assaulted, it shall be presumed, unless the contrary is proved, that the child or minor has been detained for purpose of prostitution or, as the case may be, has been sexually exploited for commercial purposes.

(3) A person shall be presumed to detain a woman or girl in a brothel or in or upon any premises for the purpose of sexual intercourse with a man other than her lawful husband, if such person, with intent to compel or induce her to remain there—

(a) *withholds from her any jewellery, wearing apparel, money or other property belonging to her; or*
(b) *threatens her with legal proceedings if she takes away with her any jewellery, wearing apparel, money or other property lent or supplied to her by or by the direction of such person.*

(4) Notwithstanding any law to the contrary, no suit, prosecution or other legal proceeding shall lie against such woman or girl at the instance of the person by whom she has been detained, for the recovery of any jewellery, wearing apparel or other property alleged to have been lent or supplied to or for such woman or girl, or to have been pledged by such woman or girl for the recovery of any money alleged to be payable by such woman or girl.'

(v) Child Pornography

Section 292 of the Indian Penal Code

'(1) For the purposes of sub-section (2), a book, pamphlet, paper, writing, drawing, painting representation, figure or any other object, shall be deemed to be obscene if it is lascivious or appeals to the prurient interest or if its effect, or (where it comprises two or more distinct items) the effect of any one of its items, is taken as a whole, such as to tend to deprave and corrupt persons who are likely, having regard to all relevant circumstances, to read, see or hear the matter contained or embodied in it;

(2) Whoever—

- *(a) sells, lets to hire, distributes, publicly exhibits or in any manner puts into circulation, or for purposes of sale, hire, distribution, public exhibition or circulation, makes, produces or has in his possession any obscene book, pamphlet, paper, drawing, painting, representation or figure or any other obscene object whatsoever; or*
- *(b) imports, exports or conveys any obscene object for any of the purposes aforesaid, or knowing or having reason to believe that such object will be sold, let to hire, distributed or publicly exhibited or in any manner put into circulation; or*
- *(c) takes part in or receives profits from any business in the course of which he knows or has reason to believe that any such obscene objects are, for any of the purposes aforesaid made, produced, purchased, kept, imported, exported, conveyed, publicly or in any manner put into circulation; or*
- *(d) advertises or makes known by any means whatsoever that any person is engaged or is ready to engage in any act which is an offence under this section, or that any such obscene object can be procured from or through any person; or*
- *(e) offers or attempts to do any act which is an offence under this section,*

shall be punished [on first conviction with imprisonment of either description for a term which may extend to two years, and with fine which may extend to two thousand rupees, and, in the event of a second or subsequent conviction, with imprisonment of either description for a term which may extend to five years, and also with fine which may extend to five thousand rupees.

Exception:

This section does not extend to—

(a) any book, pamphlet, paper, writing, drawing, painting, representation or figure:

(i) the publication of which is proved to be justified as being for the public good on the ground that such book, pamphlet, paper, writing, drawing, painting, representation or figure is in the interest of science, literature, art or learning or other objects of general concern, or

(ii) which is kept or used bona fide for religious purposes;

(b) any representation sculptured, engraved, painted or otherwise represented on or in—

(i) any ancient monument within the meaning of the Ancient Monuments and Archaeological Sites and Remains Act, 1958 (24 of 1958); or

(ii) any temple, or on any car used for the conveyance of idols, or kept or used for any religious purposes.

Section 293 of the Indian Penal Code

'Whoever sells, lets to hire, distributes, exhibits or circulates to any person under the age of twenty (20) years, any such obscene object as is referred to in the last preceding section, or offers or attempts to do so, shall be punished [on first conviction with imprisonment of either description for a term which may extend to three years, and with fine which may extend to two thousand rupees and, in the event of a second or subsequent conviction, with imprisonment of either description for a term which may extend to seven years, and also with fine which may extend to five thousand rupees.']

The Goa Children's Act

With sexual abuse of children becoming increasingly associated with the tourism trade, Goa formed a model law and proposed the establishment of a Children's Court. The idea of a Children's Court was first mooted in the Government of India Children Act, 1960, which is today a forgotten piece of law. The Goa Children Act, 2003 is a legislation against child sexual abuse, especially those related to tourism. The legislation has specifically made any such cases of abuse non-bailable offences under Section 2(a) of the Criminal Procedure Code, 1973. The fines and jail terms are also severe—Rs. 100,000 with imprisonment between one to three years for sexual assault and incest, and Rs. 200,000 with seven to 10 years jail term in case of a grave sexual assault. The setting up of a Children's Court to try all offences against children is a bold step prescribed by this law. A child-friendly court will help to minimize the double trauma that abused children are subject to in courts, which even adults find awesome and terrifying.

The Goa Children's Act is unusual because it does not merely recommend punitive measures against offenders. Instead, in dealing with child sexual abuse it attempts to place responsibility on different sections of society to play a role in protecting all children and preventing the abuse of any child. The hotel owners, the photo studios, cyber cafe operators, the police, the tourism department and all those involved in the travel and tourism trade are expected to keep their eyes open and fulfil their duties, sensitive to the situation of any child they may come across in the performance of their duties. Moreover, it also seeks to establish child-friendly court procedures, which will help to ensure that children are able to give evidence without being in the presence of the perpetrators of the crime.

Already there have been at least three cases booked under the Goa Children's Act. However, the rules of operation under the new law are yet to be formulated. The Goa Children's Act has also come in for severe criticism for its poor drafting, and the lack of legal insight into some of its provisions. The Act was passed in a great hurry to meet the growing problem of child abuse in the state, but ground realities have led it to rough weather. Activists in the legal community believe that the legislation may need drastic amendments to meet its objective.

When one looks at ways in which this form of abuse can be tackled, there are few pointers for the Indian context. This largely points at how the legal discourse has operated to consistently make invisible, the daily abuse that many children suffer. The question is; is there any legal response one can make to detect and prevent child sexual abuse? How does one conceptualize a legal response, which can detect and prevent it? Finally, what kind of legal institutions and processes can combat the deeply entrenched social and cultural beliefs regarding the sanctity of the family?

This is an important question, as studies prove that reported cases of abuse are but a tip of the iceberg. Hence, if the best interest of the child is to guide child abuse legislation, adequate attention must be given to the issue of detection and prevention. Otherwise the result would be what has been critiqued as 'expressive justice'. Unfortunately we have given little thought to this question, with a greater preoccupation centring on how to set up more child-friendly investigation and trial procedures.

If a mandatory-reporting law is passed, then the next question is, to which competent authority should such an abuse be reported? In India, under the present legal framework, the abused child would come under the definition of 'neglected child' under the Juvenile Justice Act, 1986. In which case the Police, or any other person or organization authorized by the State Gvernment, may take charge to bring him/her before the Juvenile Board. Though the State Government has the power to authorize persons and organizations to take charge of the juvenile in most cases it is the police who are the authority. In the case of a sensitive issue, like child sexual abuse, the police may not be the best authority to take charge. Hence, it would make sense to empanel a group of social workers, one of whom would go along with the police officer. This concept is already being worked on in most major cities in India through a network called Child.

The law must implement the concept of a social worker or a guardian *ad litem* involved right from the initial process of investigation, as this involvement of legal institutions and processes might be detrimental to the best interest of the child. This is especially so in the Indian context where child-friendly court procedures have not yet evolved. The child is victimized a second time through the lengthy process of trial, the trauma of facing the abuser in the court room, the long-term impacts on relationships with other family members, the repeated questioning during investigation asking for details of the abuse and the cross examination process.

Writings on child sexual abuse have tended to focus on children within the realm of criminal justice. What is needed however is legal intervention, to tackle the detecting and reporting of the phenomenon itself. This should be enforced through the enactment of compulsory reporting laws.

2

Literature Review, Objectives and Hypotheses

Literature review is an essential and very significant component of any research. It assists the researcher to conceptualize the problem in a better way by evincing various perspectives of the problem. It provokes cogitating on various aspects of the problem. Literature review also gives an idea to hypothesize the problem aright.

In the present study, findings of previous researchers on various aspects of child sexual abuse were reviewed. For the convenience of the readers the literature review has been classified and presented under the following broad heads:

(1) Substance/Alcohol Abuse and Child Sexual Abuse
(2) Physical Health and Child Sexual Abuse
(3) Eating Disorders and Sexual Abuse
(4) Social and Mental Health and Child Sexual Abuse
(5) Homosexuality and Child Sexual Abuse
(6) Family and Child Sexual Abuse
(7) Trafficking and Child Sexual Abuse
(8) Other Relevant Studies

Substance/Alcohol Abuse and Child Sexual Abuse

A study was conducted by Spak et al. (1998) of Gotenborg University regarding the prevalence of childhood sexual abuse (CSA) before the age of 18 years and life-time sexual abuse (LSA) in a Swedish female, general population, to analyze associations between Child Sexual Abuse and life-time Alcohol Dependence or Abuse (ADA), and to identify possible confounding factors. A total of 316 women participated in a structured face-to-face interview, which focused on substance use and on social, psychological and behavioural characteristics, including experiences of sexual abuse. Findings indicated that the prevalence of CSA and LSA was 9.8% and 13.9%, respectively. CSA increased the risk for life-time ADA and anxiety, but not for depression. When potential confounding factors (e.g. early background factors, depression and anxiety) were adjusted for, Child Sexual Abuse under 13 years of age still predicted ADA in multivariate analyses, but Child Sexual Abuse under 18 years of age did not. The study concluded that LSA, and especially Child Sexual Abuse under 13 years of age, are factors that should be considered in treatment of women with ADA and in psychiatric treatment of women.

Women who are sexually abused during childhood are at increased risk for drug abuse as adults, according to NIDA-supported research conducted at the Medical College of Virginia Commonwealth University in Richmond. Using data gathered from interviews of 1,411 adult twins, Kendler et al., (2000) and his colleagues assessed the association between three levels of childhood sex abuse (non-genital, genital, and intercourse) and six adult disorders—major depression, generalized anxiety disorder, panic disorder, Bulimia Nervosa, alcohol dependence, and drug dependence. Women who experienced any type of sexual abuse in childhood were roughly three times more likely than unabused girls to report drug dependence as adults.

The study by Moran et al. (2004) was aimed to investigate associations between four categories of maltreatment and substance use among adolescents. All 10th through 12th graders (n=2187) at six public high schools in a rural Oregon county filled out an anonymous survey that included questions about their experience of emotional, sexual and physical abuse and their use of a variety of substances. Substance use was subsequently categorized as: (1) tobacco use, (2) alcohol use and (3) illicit drug use. Experience of maltreatment was subsequently categorized as: (1) no type of maltreatment, (2) emotional abuse, (3) physical abuse, (4) sexual abuse and (5) sexual and physical abuse. Outcomes suggested that all types of maltreatment, including emotional abuse, are related to significantly higher levels of substance use and should be considered serious risk factors for substance use during adolescence. Results also indicated that the strength of association between maltreatment and substance use varies by type of maltreatment. Youth who have experienced both physical and sexual abuse are at especially high risk of substance use. Further statistical comparisons of the magnitude effects of different types of maltreatment on substance use indicated a linear trend with the effects of emotional abuse being sufficiently lower than those of physical or sexual abuse, and the effects of the combination of physical and sexual abuse being significantly higher than the other types.

A study on drug abuse and its relationship to sexual abuse of street children by Sahil, an NGO in Pakistan (2003), showed a strong link between the above two parameters. All hundred and eighty children who were interviewed were drug addicts, and out of them hundred and sixty-two children were sexually abused. The study shows a relationship between drug abuse and child sexual abuse in two ways. Children may see drug use as a solution to their problems, or they take drugs to forget that they have been involved in sex work. Young people may see drug use as a solution to their problems, rather then as a problem in itself (ESCAP, 2003). Even though using drugs may lead to serious problems, many children and youth still use drugs because it either adds something to their lives or helps them to feel that they have solved their problems however fleeting this feeling might be. The influence of friends and peers in introducing drugs to the respondents was more significant than the fact that there were family members involved in drug abuse.

Wyatt et al. (2005) examined the patterns of substance abuse and barriers to health care among HIV-positive Black women with histories of childhood sexual abuse (CSA).

Baseline data on a community sample of 75 Black HIV-positive women were analyzed to assess and identify drug use, alcohol use, participation in an alcohol or drug treatment programme, and communication skills with providers. Findings indicated that substance use is a significant health problem, with 83.0% of the participants having used at least one substance regularly and 28.0% having engaged in regular injection drug use. Barriers to health care included confidentiality issues, poor financial resources, difficulty getting an appointment, excessive waiting to see a health care provider and obligation to care for others. Contrary to past research, poor communication between the participants and the providers did not seem to be a barrier to health care utilization for these women.

Physical Health and Child Sexual Abuse

Sexual abuse appears to increase risk for a range of physical health problems. In a comprehensive study of a population-based sample of women in Los Angeles, Golding (1994) showed convincingly that women who report being abused as a child or as an adult are found later in life to have higher than usual levels of physical problems, including ongoing pain (in several body sites), gastro-intestinal symptoms (vomiting, diarrhoea, food intolerance), excessive menstrual bleeding, and some neurological symptoms (e.g. fainting, paralysis and walking difficulties). In addition, there may be elevated rates of chronic physical disability and diabetes.

In Norway, Schei and Bakketeig (1989) found that traumatic events might have a cumulative effect on women, each experience increasing the likelihood of developing chronic pelvic pain or other somatised symptoms. In the USA, Leserman et al. (1997) found that a history of sexual abuse 'statistically explained' one quarter of all of the variation in physical health status among women attending a gastro-enterology clinic (i.e. sexual abuse was one of the most important background factors). Although these studies suggest quite serious long-term physical consequences of sexual abuse, they did not distinguish between events occurring in childhood or as an adult.

A recent study from France has found some evidence for ongoing physical problems among children who have been raped (Choquet et al., 1997). Among a nationally representative sample of more than 8,000 public school students, those who reported rape experiences had higher rates of gastro-intestinal problems (vomiting) and general malaise (dizziness, tiredness) than their peers who had not been raped. Among adult female survivors of child sexual abuse, chronic back pain and a range of problems in respiratory, gastro-intestinal, neurological and gynaecological functions have been reported (Pecukonis, 1996). It is unclear whether these problems reflect direct physical effects, or indicate a more general psychosomatic disorder.

There are several plausible explanations of how child sexual abuse could lead directly or indirectly to physical health problems in both children and adults (Golding, 1994). The most direct effects arise through STI and concurrent physical abuse. Indirectly, child sexual abuse clearly is a major life stress for many people, and as with other serious trauma, the resultant stress could reduce immune responses that could increase vulnerability to diseases (Koss et al., 1990). A history of child sexual abuse often increases the risk of detrimental health-related behaviours such as smoking, heavy drinking and illicit drug abuse (Choquet et al., 1997; Epstein et al., 1998; Holmes, 1997). Further, given that family break-up and poorer economic circumstances often follow incidents of child sexual abuse; individuals may find themselves with fewer of the economic and social resources that are necessary for promoting and maintaining physical health (Golding, 1994).

In a study by Oppong et al. (2006), the authors sought to determine whether a history of sexual abuse influences success after gastric bypass surgery. Presurgical self-report questionnaires collected information, including sexual abuse history and previous psychiatric hospitalization, and 27.0% reported a history of sexual abuse. A history of sexual abuse correlated with (non-significantly) less loss of excess weight at 12 and 24 months after surgery. No significant difference in excess-weight loss was detected among those with history of sexual abuse. In conclusion, it can be said that such abuse histories should not preclude surgery for these kinds of patients.

The link between child sexual abuse and risk for HIV infection has been proposed by several authors (Paone, 1991; Rosenfeld, 1993; Zierler, 1995), and recent research strongly confirms that association. Large, prospective, multisite studies of cohorts of women with and at high behavioural risk for HIV have uncovered striking data by conducting structured interviews with participants. Of 771 women enrolled in HIV Epidemiology Research Study (HERS) sites in Baltimore, Detroit, and the Bronx, 43.0% had been sexually abused as children and 45.0% had been sexually abused as adults (Vlahov, 1996).

In the Women's Interagency HIV Study (WIHS), data from 1560 women enrolled in New York City, Chicago, Washington, DC, and Los Angeles revealed that 40.0% reported a history of childhood sexual abuse (Cook, 1997). For these women, a history of sexual abuse, physical abuse or domestic abuse was highly correlated with engaging in risk behaviour for HIV. In particular, childhood sexual abuse was significantly associated with: use of IV drugs; exchange of sex for drugs, money or shelter; higher number of sexual partners; and having had a sexual relationship with a person at high risk for HIV. Additionally, childhood sexual abuse was significantly related to adult domestic violence as well as adult sexual abuse.

Lindegren et al. (1998) carried out a study on HIV and sexual abuse of children. Sexual transmission of Human Immunodeficiency Virus (HIV) is the predominant risk exposure among adolescents and adults reported with HIV infection and Acquired Immuno Deficiency Syndrome (AIDS). Although perinatal transmission accounts for the majority of HIV infection in children, there have been reports of HIV transmission through sexual abuse of children. They characterized children below 13 years of age who may have acquired HIV infection through sexual abuse. In this study, all reports by state and local health departments to the national HIV/AIDS surveillance system of children with HIV infection not AIDS (n = 1507) and AIDS (n = 7629) through December 1996 were reviewed for history of sexual abuse. Information was ascertained from data recorded on the case report form as well as investigations of children with no risk for HIV infection reported or identified on initial investigation. For children with a possible history of sexual abuse, additional data were collected, including how sexual abuse was diagnosed; characteristics of the perpetrator(s) (i.e., HIV status and HIV risks); and other possible risk factors for the child's HIV infection. Of 9136 children reported with HIV or AIDS, 26 were sexually abused with confirmed (n = 17) or suspected (n = 9) exposure to HIV infection; mean age of these children at diagnosis of HIV infection was 8.8 years (range, 3 to 12 years). There were 14 females and 3 males who had confirmed sexual exposure to an adult male perpetrator at risk for or infected with HIV; of these, 14 had no other risk for HIV infection, and 3 had multiple risks for HIV infection (i.e., through sexual abuse, perinatal exposure, and physical abuse through drug injection). The other 9 children (8 females, 1 male) had no other risk factors for HIV infection and were suspected to have been infected through sexual abuse, but the identity, HIV risk, or HIV status of all the perpetrator(s) was not known. All cases of sexual abuse had been reported to local children's protective agencies. Sexual abuse was established on the basis of physician diagnosis or physical examination (n = 20), child disclosure (n = 15), previous or concurrent non-congenital sexually transmitted disease (n = 9), and for confirmed cases, criminal prosecution of the HIV-infected or at-risk perpetrator (n = 8). For the 17 children with confirmed sexual exposure to HIV infection, 19 male perpetrators were identified who were either known to be HIV infected (n = 18) or had risk factors for HIV infection (n = 17), most of whom were a parent or relative. Results indicate that these 26 cases highlight the tragic intersection of child sexual abuse and the HIV epidemic. Although the number of reported cases of sexual transmission of HIV infection among children is small, it is a minimum estimate based on population-based surveillance and is an important and likely under recognized public health problem. Health care providers should consider sexual abuse as a possible means of HIV transmission, particularly among children whose mothers are HIV-antibody negative and also among older HIV-infected children. The intersection of child abuse with the HIV epidemic highlights the critical need for clinicians and public health professionals to be aware of the risk for HIV transmission among children who have been sexually abused, and of guidelines for HIV testing among sexually abused children, and to evaluate and report such cases.

Cohen et al. (2000) of CORE Center, Cook County Hospital carried out a study, the purpose of which was to determine the prevalence and effect of domestic violence and childhood sexual abuse in women with HIV or at risk for HIV infection. Participants included those with HIV or at risk for HIV infection enrolled in the Women's Interagency HIV Study. Childhood sexual abuse; all physical, sexual, and coercive violence by a partner; HIV serostatus; demographic data; and substance use and sexual habits were assessed. The results showed that life-time prevalence of domestic violence was 66.0% and 67.0%, respectively, in 1288 women with HIV and 357 uninfected women. One quarter of the women reported recent abuse, and 31.0% of the HIV-seropositive women and 27.0% of the HIV-seronegative women reported childhood sexual abuse. Childhood sexual abuse was strongly associated with a life-time history of domestic violence and high-risk behaviours, including using drugs, having more than 10 male sexual partners and having male partners at risk for HIV infection, and exchanging sex for drugs, money, or shelter. The concluding data support the hypothesis of a continuum of risk, with early childhood abuse leading to later domestic violence, which may increase the risk of behaviours leading to HIV infection.

Gutman et al. (1991) of the Duke University Medical Center carried out a study to figure out HIV transmission by child sexual abuse. During 1987-1989, 14 (14.6%) of the 96 children who tested positive for the Human Immunodeficiency Virus (HIV) and were followed up by the Duke University (Durham, NC) pediatric Acquired Immuno Deficiency Syndrome team, were confirmed to have been sexually abused. Every sexually abused child was evaluated for each of five modes of HIV transmission, and in nine children the pathway was identified. Four of the study children acquired HIV from child sexual abuse and in six, abuse was a possible source. Transmission by child sexual abuse was the most frequent of the proven modes of acquisition of HIV in this population. The other proven modes of acquisition were vertical transmission (n = 3) and HIV-contaminated blood transfusion (n = 2). Twelve males were identified (n = 8) or suspected (n = 4) of being perpetrators. Three knew themselves to have HIV at the time of an assault and eight were aware that the child had HIV at the time of an assault. There was no indication from any child that "safe sex" precautions had been observed. Children with HIV infection had multiple risk factors for abuse or neglect. The sociological descriptors of the lives of the 14 abused children showed multiple known risk factors for sexual abuse that also overlapped with known risk factors for or sequelae of the acquisition of HIV infection. These included drug abuse and alcoholism in the home, prostitution of a parent, lack of parenting, poverty, and chronic illness of the child. They advocated in this study that prevention efforts should recognize that children as well as adults are at risk for sexually transmitted HIV infection.

Rodgers et al. (2004) aimed to study the unique contribution of five types of maltreatment (sexual abuse, physical abuse, emotional abuse, physical neglect, emotional neglect) to adult behaviours as well as the additive impact of exposure to different types of childhood maltreatment. Two hundred and twenty-one women recruited from a VA primary care clinic completed questionnaires assessing exposure to childhood trauma and adult health behaviours. Regression models were used to test the relationship between childhood maltreatment and adult health behaviours. Results showed that sexual and physical abuse appears to predict a number of adverse outcomes; when other types of maltreatment are controlled, however, sexual abuse and physical abuse do not predict as many poor outcomes. In addition, sexual, physical and emotional abuse and emotional neglect in childhood were all related to different adult health behaviours. The more types of childhood maltreatment participants were exposed to the more likely they were to have problems with substance use and risky sexual behaviours in adulthood. The study indicates that it is important to assess a broad maltreatment history rather than trying to relate specific types of abuse to particular adverse health behaviours or health outcomes.

Lysaker et al. (2005) cross-sectional research suggests reported childhood abuse in schizophrenia spectrum disorders is linked with graver symptom levels and social dysfunction. To examine this, biweekly ratings of positive and emotional discomfort symptoms were compared along with weekly accounts of hours worked over 4 months of rehabilitation of 12 participants with schizophrenia or schizoaffective disorder and childhood sexual abuse history and 31 with schizophrenia or schizoaffective disorder and no childhood sexual abuse history. Repeated-measures ANOVA revealed the abuse group had consistently higher levels of both symptom components and poorer participation in vocational rehabilitation. A time by group effect was observed for hours of work, with the abuse group working increasingly fewer hours over time. Participants reporting abuse also were more likely to perform poorly on a test of executive function and to have particularly higher levels of hallucinations and anxiety over time.

Lysaker et al. (2005) carried out a study to explore the associations of anxiety-related symptoms with reported history of childhood sexual abuse in schizophrenia spectrum disorders. Data were gathered on trauma history, PTSD symptoms, social anxiety, and state and trait anxiety from 45 men with a SCID-I-confirmed diagnosis of schizophrenia or schizoaffective disorder and 11 with a SCID-I-confirmed diagnosis of PTSD with no history of psychosis. Participants with schizophrenia spectrum disorders (schizophrenia group) were divided into those with and without history of childhood sexual abuse. Analysis of variance comparing the childhood sexual abuse (N=21) and non-abused (N=19) schizophrenia groups and the PTSD group on all anxiety assessments revealed that the sexually abused schizophrenia group had significantly higher levels of dissociation, intrusive experiences, and state and trait anxiety than the non-abused schizophrenia group. When compared with participants with PTSD and no psychosis, the sexually abused schizophrenia group had significantly lower levels of state anxiety, anxious arousal, intrusive experiences, and fearful social avoidance.

Eating Disorders and Sexual Abuse

A study was carried out by Rorty et al. (1994) focusing on childhood sexual, physical and psychological abuse in Bulimia Nervosa. This study sought to determine if rates of childhood sexual, physical, psychological, and multiple abuse (i.e. abuse in more than one form) differed between women with a life-time history of Bulimia Nervosa and women with no history of eating disorders. Subjects were 80 women, aged 18-35, with a life-time history of Bulimia Nervosa (40 women who had recovered for a year or more and 40 women currently suffering from Bulimia Nervosa) and 40 women who had never had an eating disorder or related difficulties. The cohort was obtained primarily by newspaper advertisement. Subjects participated in structured diagnostic interviews and completed paper-and-pencil questionnaires related to abusive experiences in childhood. Results showed that women in the Bulimia Nervosa group reported higher levels of childhood physical, psychological, and multiple abuses. Contrary to expectation, rates of sexual abuse did not distinguish the groups, except in combination with other forms of abuse. The higher rates of psychological, physical and multiple abuses found among women with a life-time history of Bulimia Nervosa, than among comparison subjects, underscore the importance of examining the full range of possible abusive experiences in women with eating disorders, rather than focusing simply on sexual abuse.

Researchers, Sullivan et al. (1995) tried to understand the significance of a history of childhood sexual abuse in Bulimia Nervosa. In this work carried out in Christchurch, New Zealand, Childhood Sexual Abuse (CSA) was found to have occurred to a substantial minority of women with Bulimia Nervosa. A study of 87 bulimic women in a clinical trial resulted in forty-four per cent reporting a history of CSA. Bulimic women with CSA reported earlier onset of bulimia, greater depressive symptoms, worse global functioning and more suicide attempts, and were more likely to meet criteria for bipolar II disorder, alcohol and drug dependence, conduct disorder and avoidant personality disorder. The study concluded that although those with CSA had greater co-morbidity, it was not an important modifier of bulimic symptoms.

In a study using 786 women identified as bulimics (n=3), sub-clinical bulimics (n=37), and normal subjects (n=719) by scores on the Bulimia Test—Revised (BULIT-R, Thelan et al., 1991). Hastings and Kern (1994) sought to determine if a significant association exists between bulimia and childhood sexual abuse (CSA). In addition to investigating this association, the authors also examined the relationships between family environment, CSA, and bulimia. The authors reported that subjects were given three questionnaires in counter-balanced order to assess bulimia, CSA, and family environment. These questionnaires were: (1) the Bulimia Test—Revised (BULIT-R Thelan et al., 1991); (2) the Child Sexual Abuse Questionnaire (Walters, Smolak, and Sullins, 1987); and (3) the Family Environment Scale (FES), Form R (Moos & Moos, 1984). After conducting a series of chi-square Analyses and One-way Analyses of Variance (ANOVAs), the authors found that bulimia was associated with self-reports of significant sexual abuse during childhood and/or adolescence. Furthermore, they reported that the severity of the abuse was related to the severity of the bulimia. As for their investigation of family environment, the authors' results indicated that CSA and family variables combined in an additive manner to increase the risk of bulimia. However, the authors suggest that biological, personality, and contextual factors are still important factors in the etiology of bulimia as 38.0% of the normals reported CSA and/or dysfunctional family environments without reporting symptoms of bulimia.

Using college undergraduates is a common and convenient method of sample selection. Such samples have several limitations; however, results from such studies are nonetheless important in determining the nature of the relationship between childhood sexual abuse and the development of eating disorders. Miller et al. (1993) used a sample of 144 female undergraduates to determine possible relationships between CSA and adolescent onset of Bulimia Nervosa while also investigating family functioning in women diagnosed with bulimia. The authors' primary hypothesis was that adolescents diagnosed as bulimic would report a higher incidence of CSA than non-bulimic adolescents. The following research protocols were administered to each subject: (1) Background information sheet on the subject and the subject's family; (2) Bulimic Investigatory Test, Edinburgh (BITE; Henderson and Freeman, 1987); (3) Sexual Life Events Questionnaire (SLEQ; Finkelhor, 1979); (4) Dissociative Experiences Scale (DES; Bernstein and Putnam, 1986); and (5) Childhood Family Mealtime Questionnaire (CFMQ; Miller et al., 1993). The authors' main hypothesis was tentatively supported with the bulimic group reporting more incidents of sexual abuse with a family member or relative after the age of 12 while also reporting more incidents of sexual abuse with an adult before the age of 12. The authors suggest that elevated sexual abuse rates among bulimic women may explain why bulimics tend to report negative feelings regarding their bodies. The authors also found that the bulimic who reported sexual abuse dissociate significantly more than non-abused bulimic women; thus, the authors further suggest that binge-purge cycles may serve to provide a form of psychological dissociation and/or emotional numbness. As in most studies, not all bulimics reported histories of sexual abuse and some non-bulimics did report sexual abuse; thus, it appears that there are other operating factors outside the experience of sexual abuse that ultimately lead to the development of an eating disorder. The authors also examined events that occurred during mealtimes and found that bulimia may be more likely to develop in women who have experienced a combined pattern of sexual abuse and food-related stress and control.

Wonderlich et al. (1996) used 38 women involved in an incest treatment programme at a family service centre to examine the hypothesis that victims of CSA would show greater levels than control subjects (27 subjects receiving treatment at the same family service centre, but with no history of CSA) of each of the DSM-III-R diagnostic criteria for Bulimia Nervosa. Furthermore, the authors predicted that victims of CSA would present with higher levels of other tension-reducing behaviours (e.g., alcohol and cigarette use, self-mutilation, and suicidal gestures) than the control subjects. Their second hypothesis was that the magnitude of the emotional reaction to CSA is correlated with the development of eating disorders with the level of post-traumatic stress disorder symptomatology being correlated with the presence of bulimic behaviour. Subjects were given the following questionnaires: (1) Eating Disorders Questionnaire (EDQ); (2) Eating Disorders Inventory (EDI); and (3) Response to Childhood Incest Questionnaire (RCIQ). Consistent with their prediction, the authors found that the CSA subjects reported more bulimic behaviour than the control subjects. Furthermore, their prediction that CSA subjects would display more tension-reducing behaviours was also supported, with incest victims displaying significantly more substance use, cigarette smoking, self-mutilation, and suicidal gestures than the control subjects. The authors suggest that these findings, along with the increased level of bulimic behaviour, are consistent with the idea that CSA individuals engage in many self-destructive behaviours, which potentially reduce emotional distress associated with their abuse. Furthermore, the authors found that the presence of bulimic behaviour was also associated with reported symptoms of posttraumatic stress disorder. They suggest that dieting, bingeing, and purging may be efforts to manage emotional states associated with memories of their abuse. The authors further suggest that eating disturbance is linked to the affective reactions, associated with the abuse. They conclude that their data provide support for the notion that bulimic behaviours are involved in affective regulation instead of being reactions to thoughts and memories of abuse.

Eating disorders are often seen more prevalently in psychiatric populations suffering from various types and degrees of psycho-pathology. Early researchers hotly debated whether CSA was an actual risk factor for the development of eating disorders. Pope and Hudson (1992) concluded that there was no evidence to suggest CSA as a risk factor for Bulimia Nervosa. Considerable debate arose about the methodology of the early studies and the associated conclusions (e.g. Wooley, 1994). Psychologist Susan Wooley observed that, for a long time, differential prevalence (i.e., higher rates of CSA among eating-disordered subjects than among women without eating disturbances) was the primary criterion used to judge whether CSA might influence the onset or maintenance of an eating disturbance (Wooley, 1994). Unfortunately, as a result of this debate, clinicians were alienated from researchers. Clinicians wanted to offer informed, quality care to patients with eating disorders whose CSA or other trauma appeared closely intertwined with their eating problems, while researchers denied that the connection existed.

New research has turned the tide of this debate. In 1994, Marcia Rorty and her colleagues found elevated rates of parental psychological abuse among women with Bulimia Nervosa when compared to non-bulimic women. Well-designed national studies by Dansky, Brewerton, Wonderlich, and others have supported the idea that CSA is indeed a risk factor for the development of bulimic pathology among women. Wonderlich and his colleagues found that CSA was a non-specific risk factor for Bulimia Nervosa, particularly when there is psychiatric comorbidity. They also found some indication that CSA is more strongly associated with bulimic disorders than with restricting anorexia, but CSA did not appear to be associated with severity of the disturbance. Fairburn and his colleagues (1997) also provided evidence that both sexual abuse and physical abuse in childhood represent global risk factors for Bulimia Nervosa. According to these researchers, both factors also increase the chance that a woman will develop a variety of psychiatric problems, including mood and anxiety disorders.

A study conducted by Smolak and Murnen (2002) to examine the relationship between eating disorders and child sexual abuse had two specific goals. The first being to assess the magnitude and consistency of the relationship between Child Sexual Abuse (CSA) and Eating Disorders (ED). The second was to examine methodological factors contributing to the heterogeneity of this relationship. Meta-analysis was used to examine both questions. Fifty-three studies were included in the analysis. The results showed that a small, significant positive relationship between CSA and ED emerged. The relationship was marked by heterogeneity. Effect sizes were largest when CSA was the grouping variable, the Eating

Disorders Inventory (EDI) or the Eating Attitudes Test (EAT) was used as the measure of eating disorders, and non-clinical groups were compared with clinical samples.

Another community-based study by Romans et al. (2001) in New Zealand examined how some women who have experienced Childhood Sexual Abuse (CSA) develop an Eating Disorder (ED), whereas others develop depression and anxiety, and others show no adverse psychological sequel. A two-stage random community sampling strategy was used to select two groups of women: (1) women with CSA prior to age 16 years and (2) a comparison group of women reporting no abuse. Both groups completed the Parental Bonding Instrument (PBI), the Present State Examination, and additional ICD-10 eating disorders questions. Information on the nature and frequency of the CSA was obtained at interview. CSA women with ED (CSA+ED) were compared with CSA women without ED (CSA-noED) and with CSA women with anxiety and/or depression (psychiatric comparison group). Higher rates of EDs in women who have experienced CSA were confirmed in this study. Belonging to a younger age cohort, experiencing menarche at an early age, and high paternal over control on the PBI independently increased the risk of developing an ED in women who had experienced CSA. Low maternal care was specifically associated with the development of anorexia nervosa, whereas early age of menarche differentiated women with Bulimia Nervosa. Younger age and early age of menarche also differentiated the CSA+ED women from the psychiatric comparison group. It was inferred from this study that early maturation and paternal over control emerged as risk factors for ED development in women with CSA. Although these variables are also risk factors in the general population, women with CSA may be vulnerable to ED development because these risk factors are particular domains of concern that emanate from experiences of CSA.

Social and Mental Health and Child Sexual Abuse

Common sense and accumulated experience in legal and clinical services clearly indicate that many victims of child sexual abuse suffer both acute and chronic psychological and social problems. This is confirmed by a wealth of published research. What follows is a brief summary of the major findings from some recent studies.

Fearfulness and anxiety-related symptoms have been frequently described as short-term and long-term effects in sexually abused children. The primary symptoms include sleep disturbances, insomnia and nightmares, phobic avoidance, generalized worry, oversenstivity and poor concentration (McLeer et al., 1998; Mullen et al., 1993). In a recent study in Philadelphia of 142 sexually abused children aged 6 – 16 years who had not been referred to clinical mental health services, McLeer et al. (1998) found these children to have significantly more worry/over-sensitivity, poor concentration and higher physiological anxiety than were present either in control children or in clinically-referred children with no history of sexual abuse.

Severe cases of abuse are strongly predictive of Post-Traumatic Stress Disorder (PTSD). Goodwin (1985) described post-traumatic symptoms in child victims of incest (e.g. fear, startle reactions, reenactment of the trauma, flashbacks and depressive symptoms). Goodwin also compared adult rape victims with sexually abused children and found that the children displayed more severe and longer lasting symptoms than did the adults, because the children experienced more frequent sexual assaults during a more prolonged period. Studies designed to explore more fully the PTSD symptoms of sexual abuse in children revealed the most frequently observed symptoms to be:

- acting as if the traumatic event was happening again,
- avoidance behaviour and phobias, and
- aggressive behaviour (McLeer et al., 1998).

PTSD (sometimes referred to as rape trauma syndrome for victims of sexual assault) can be divided into two phases: the acute phase and the long-term phase, best described as disorganization and reorganization respectively. The immediate response may last for hours or days (acute phase) and is characterized by a distortion or paralysis of the individual's coping mechanisms. Outward responses vary from complete loss of emotional control to an apparently well-controlled behaviour pattern. The signs may include generalized pain throughout the body; eating and sleep disturbances; physical symptoms such as vaginal discharge, itching, and rectal pain; and emotional complaints such as depression, anxiety and mood swings. In the days and weeks that follow, non-specific anxiety is often expressed in the form of a variety of complaints such as musculo-skeletal problems, headaches and insomnia. The delayed phase (or organizational phase) is characterized by rationalization regarding the assault and the need to continue with daily activities and work. It is characterized by flashbacks, nightmares, phobias, and a need for reorganization of thought processes, as well as gynecologic and menstrual complaints. This delayed phase may occur months or years after the event and may involve major lifestyle adjustment. Often, victims present for health services without disclosing their experience and are unaware of its potential complications (McLeer et al., 1998). An adolescent may present to a health or social service, for example, with depression and multiple phobias, acting-out behaviours including running away, truancy or promiscuity. It has been estimated that between 32.0% and 80.0% of victims of sexual abuse suffer from PTSD (Kilpatrick et al., Edmonds & Seymour 1992; American Academy of Paediatrics Committee on Adolescence 1994). A complicating factor is that PTSD can also follow other forms of abuse, and it is often difficult to ascertain whether it arises specifically from the sexual abuse (Roth et al., 1997).

Dissociation, or alteration in consciousness resulting in impairment of memory or identity, has been observed in children traumatized by sexual abuse (Bucky and Dallenberg, 1992; Dancu et al., 1996). Signs of early dissociation in children are forgetfulness with periods of amnesia, excessive fantasizing and day-dreaming, trance-like states, sleep-walking, the presence of an imaginary companion, and blackouts. Dissociative problems appear to be greatest among people with the most severe abuse, including forced sexual intercourse as a child and repeated episodes of assault (Briggs and Joyce 1997; Draijer and Langeland, 1999); children and adults presenting with multiple personality disorder, the most extreme form of dissociation, often are victims of severe physical or sexual abuse (Beitchman et al., 1992).

Dalenberg and Palesh (2004) conducted a research to determine the relationship between violent trauma, child abuse history and dissociative symptoms in a Russian population. Three hundred and one undergraduate students from Moscow State Linguistics University participated in the study and completed the Dissociation Continuum Scale, the Violence History Questionnaire, the Traumatic Event Survey (TES) and a demographic measure. It was found that scores on dissociation and its sub-factors were significantly higher in the Russian sample compared to the normative US group. The best predictors for dissociation were experiencing a violent trauma, child abuse history and/or the experience of a fearful event. Those participants with a prior child abuse history were more symptomatic after adult trauma than those with no such history. They concluded that relationship between trauma/abuse and dissociation is unlikely to be a result of suggestion by therapists or media exposure, since the correlation appears in a Russian population who are relatively unexposed to these suggestive sources. The validity, reliability and structure of the dissociation measure were relatively similar in American and Russian samples.

Disturbances in sexual behaviour are among the most striking and dramatic symptoms observed in sexually abused children. Sexual hyper-arousal (such as compulsive masturbation and promiscuity) and sexually aggressive behaviour, with a tendency to repeat and re-enact the sexual victimization, have been frequently described in the literature. Many victims appear to be unable to differentiate between affectionate and sexual relationships (Green, 1993). Among adults, it has been reported that as many at 45.0% of victims may encounter orgasmic failure; 38.0% will have prolonged abstinence from sexual activity; 35.0% will have altered sexual response; and 25.0% will have altered emotional response

(Dupre et al., 1988). Such problems are commonly found in studies of women attending counselling or mental health clinics (Beitchman et al., 1992). Although early studies of the general, non-clinical, population did not find excess sexual dysfunction among people with a history of child sexual abuse (Greenwald et al., 1990; Fromuth and Burkhart, 1989), a recent national survey in the USA has found significant negative effects (Laumann et al., 1999). Specifically, problems in achieving and maintaining sexual arousal were much more common in female child sexual abuse victims than in other women, while males suffered from an excess of erectile dysfunction, premature ejaculation and low sexual desire in comparison with those who had not been victims of adult–child contact.

Recent studies have documented an association between a history of Child Sexual Abuse (CSA) and high-risk sexual behaviours among adolescents. For example, findings from the 1997 Massachusetts Youth Risk Behaviour Surveillance Survey indicated that among 1,610 sexually experienced girls and 831 sexually experienced boys in the 9th through 12th grades, 30.2% of the girls and 9.3% of the boys disclosed a sexual contact against their will. Sexually abused girls were significantly more likely than those without such a history to report early sexual activity, to report multiple partners, and to have been pregnant (Raj et al., 2000). Fergusson et al. (1996) also examined the extent to which exposure to CSA was associated with increased rates of sexual risk-taking behaviours among 520 young women (aged 18) in New Zealand. Retrospective reports of CSA indicated that females who experienced sexual abuse (intercourse) were 4.4 times more likely to engage in sexual activity and be pregnant, 9.3 times more likely to have had five or more sexual partners, and 6.6 times more likely to have had sexual intercourse before age 16. The association remained significant even after controlling for other adverse childhood experiences. Further, Brown et al. (2000) conducted a study of 208 adolescent patients who attended psychiatric day schools and residential programs, and found that more than half reported a history of sexual abuse. Those with a history of sexual abuse were three times more likely than their peers to report inconsistent condom use. They demonstrated significantly less condom self-efficacy, less knowledge of HIV, less impulse control, less frequent purchase and use of condoms, and significantly higher rates of sexually transmitted diseases (STDs), compared to adolescents without a history of sexual abuse.

A number of hypotheses have been offered to explain how a history of sexual abuse leads to sexual risk-taking behaviour. For example, Finkelhor and Browne (1985) proposed a model that describes how children who have experienced CSA learn inappropriate sexual behaviours. The processes can be analyzed in terms of four factors: traumatic sexualization, betrayal, stigmatization, and powerlessness. Children who are given a variety of incentives, such as affection, attention, and gifts, in return for sex develop distorted sexual morals. They also learn to associate sexuality with shrine and guilt because of messages about the sexual behaviour from the abuser or others who learned about the abuse. These processes interrupt normal sexual development and lead to inappropriate sexual behaviours. Difficulty establishing and maintaining relationships may also be a common experience for sexual abuse victims. Many have difficulties with issues of control, anger, shame, trust, dependency and vulnerability (Drossman, 1992). In a population-based sample of 720 Australian women, Fleming et al. (1999) found women with a history of child sexual abuse to have poorer self-esteem and problems with intimate relationships, and these were most severe for women who had had childhood experiences of forced sexual intercourse, compared with other forms of sexual abuse.

Some child sexual abuse victims also have difficulty later in life when they become parents. Banyard (1997) demonstrated that childhood sexual abuse may be a risk factor for more negative views of parenting and greater use of physical punishment strategies, even after accounting for differences in family-of-origin relationship quality. Zuravin and DiBlasio (1992) found that experiencing childhood sexual abuse was one factor that distinguished adolescent mothers who had been reported for neglect of their children from those who had not. In a later study, Zuravin et al. (1996) found that the severity of childhood sexual abuse was associated with an increased likelihood of having a child who experienced some form of maltreatment. Of course, such effects may be the result of the relationship between abuse and higher rates of depression or other psychopathology, lower self-esteem, problematic family relationships (in which incest might have occurred) and fewer social supports (Banyard, 1997).

Depression and low self-esteem are common among women and men with a history of child sexual abuse (Brayden et al., 1995; Miller et al., 1995; Roosa et al., 1999), although the nature of the link between abuse and depression has not been precisely defined. A sense of betrayal, exploitation, stigmatization, badness, shame, guilt and helplessness may become incorporated into the child's self-image, and might, in turn, relate to levels of depression (Finkelhor and Browne, 1985). Depression might also relate to the level of support within the family, good support acting as a buffer against poor emotional outcomes (Runtz and Schallow, 1997). The nature of the post-disclosure crisis (such as parental separation, placement of sibling in foster care etc.) may also affect the extent of depression experienced after the event.

A study of 547 young women in south-east Queensland by Donald (1998) found that those who reported ever having been forced into sexual contact also reported higher levels of depression, lower body image and self-esteem, higher rates of illicit drug use and poorer general physical health than young women who did not report abuse.

Conway et al. (2004) aimed to address the hypothesis that adults reporting sexual abuse are more likely to exhibit a general tendency to ruminate on sadness. The relations between reported abuse, rumination on sadness and dysphoria were also examined. Undergraduate students (101 women and 100 men) reported on childhood and adult sexual abuse and instances of intimidation, as well as completing the Rumination on Sadness Scale [Journal of Personality Assessment 75 (2000) 404] and the Beck Depression Inventory Results showed that participants who reported more abuse were more likely to report rumination on sadness. Both reports of abuse and of rumination were linked to dysphoria. Overall, casual modelling indicated that two models were equally effective in accounting for the data: (a) victimization leads to dysphoria, with this relation being partly mediated by rumination and (b) victimization leads to dysphoria, which in turn leads to rumination. Both models are also consistent with prior research. For men considered separately, both models were found equally effective. For women, model A best accounted for the data. It is safe to conclude from this study that one of the pathways by which victimization may lead to depression in adulthood is by encouraging the development of a tendency to ruminate on sadness. Alternatively, victimization may lead to depression by other means and the experienced depression or dysphoria may foster rumination.

Homosexuality and Child Sexual Abuse

Sheila Alexander-Reid carried out a research on available literature of sexual orientation and child sexual abuse. She noted that studies show that there is no connection to homosexuality and child sexual abuse. Dr. Carole Jenny reviewed 352 medical charts, representing all of the sexually abused children seen in the emergency room or child abuse clinic of a Denver children's hospital during a one-year period (from July 1, 1991 to June 30, 1992). The molester was a gay or lesbian adult in only 2 of the 269 cases in which an adult molester could be identified, less than 1percent of the cases (Jenny et al., 1994).

Groth and Birnbaum (1978) found that none of the 175 adult males in their sample—all of whom were convicted in Massachusetts of sexual assault against a child—had an exclusively homosexual adult sexual orientation.

In one review of the scientific literature, noted authority Dr. A. Nicholas Groth wrote: "Are homosexual adults in general sexually attracted to children and are preadolescent children at greater risk of molestation from homosexual adults than from heterosexual adults? There is no reason to believe so. The research to date all points to there being no significant relationship between a homosexual lifestyle and child molestation. There appears to be practically no reportage of sexual molestation of girls by lesbian adults, and the adult male who sexually molests young boys is not likely to be homosexual (Groth and Gary, 1982, p.147). The heterosexual partner of a relative is more likely to sexually abuse children than someone who is gay. A 1994 study found that "a child's risk of being molested by his or her relative's heterosexual partner is 100 times greater than by someone who might be identified as a homosexual. (Jenny et al., Are Children at Risk for Sexual Abuse by Homosexuals? 94 Pediatrics 41; July 1994; study of 269 sexually abused children when an adult offender was identified.)

A sexual abuser who molests a child of the same sex is usually not considered homosexual. McConaghy (1998) cautioned against confusing homosexuality with pedophilia. He noted, "The man who offends against prepubertal or immediately post pubertal boys is typically not sexually interested in older men or in women".

'It is meaningless to speak of fixated molesters in these terms—as heterosexual or homosexuals—they are attracted to children, not to men or women' (Groth and Birnbaum, 1978).

The experts agree that there is no link to homosexuality and child abuse.

The American Psychological Association, the National Association of Social Workers, the American Academy of Child Psychiatrists and the Child Welfare League of America all have policy statements stating there is no correlation between homosexuality and child abuse. When asked about this question, the American Psychiatric Association wrote to the Senate stating: "While we are all concerned by the issue of sexual abuse, there is no credible evidence that lesbians and gay men are more likely to commit such offenses than others. Gay men and lesbians do not pose any particular threat to youth and should not be singled out or discriminated against in any manner.

A study of the sexual behaviour of men in the United States based on the National Survey of Men (a nationally representative sample comprised of 3,321 men aged twenty to thirty-nine, published in *Family Planning Perspectives*), found that "2.0% of sexually active men aged twenty to thirty-nine...had any same-gender sexual activity during the last ten years. Approximately 1.0% of the men (1.3% among whites and 0.2% among blacks) reported having had exclusively homosexual activity.

A study of 457 male sex offenders against children reported in the *Journal of Sex and Marital Therapy* found that "approximately one-third of these sexual offenders directed their sexual activity against males."

The *Archives of Sexual Behaviour* also noted that homosexual pedophiles are significantly over represented in child sex offence cases: The best epidemiological evidence indicates that only 2.0 4.0% of men attracted to adults prefer men (Billy et al., 1993); in contrast, around 25.0-40.0% of men attracted to children prefer boys (Gebhard et al., 1965; Mohr et al., 1964). Thus, the rate of homosexual attraction is 6 to 20 times higher among pedophiles.

A study of male child sex offenders featured in *Child Abuse and Neglect* found that 14.0% targeted only males, and a further 28.0% chose males as well as females as victims, thus indicating that 42.0% of male pedophiles engaged in homosexual molestation.

Family and Child Sexual Abuse

Csorba et al. (2006) carried out a descriptive, cross-sectional study on 52 sexually abused girls under the age of 18, the aim of which was to analyze the characteristics of intrafamilial female child sexual abuse and to explore common features that may be utilized as targets for possible methods of prevention. The results of the study indicate that 86.0% of the victims were pupils, 50.0% of them were between 11 and 14 years of age. The perpetrator was the victim's father in 44.0%, and the stepfather in 40.0%. The abuse occurred on multiple occasions in 52.0%. The occurrence rate of assault was the highest in the summer season (58.0%), mostly in the afternoon (42.0%) and it took place almost exclusively at home (98.0%). The mother accompanied the victim in 38.0% of the cases and the police in 40.0%. Vaginal penetration was the type of abuse in 75.0%, and sexual perversion in 25.0% of the cases. Only nine cases were reported to the police and as a result of legal proceedings, five perpetrators have been sentenced. It can be concluded from the study that the majority of crimes takes place within the family and are disclosed after multiple episodes. The small proportion of reported sexual assaults is the consequence of the lack of harmony between the Hungarian conditions of emergency care and the criminal law. Prevention calls for attention at all levels of child education, observation at off-school times, early involvement of health professionals, applying standardized medical guidelines and the modification of jurisdiction.

Mathoma et al. (2006) conducted a study, which sought to explore the phenomenon of child sexual abuse by investigating the knowledge and perceptions of parents regarding this problem in Botswana and Swaziland. Respondents of the study included 8 men (1 from Swaziland and 7 from Botswana) and 10 women (3 from Swaziland and 7 from Botswana) who were parents aged between 26 and 70 years. The results of the study showed that the respondents acknowledged the prevalence of child sexual abuse in Botswana and Swaziland and further demonstrated their knowledge of the predisposing factors, perpetrators of the problem, and effects of sexual abuse on children. They placed major emphases on community involvement in fighting against the problem; appropriate education of children, parents, families, and community members about child sexual abuse; and improvement on the laws that protect children against sexual abuse to successfully curb the problem.

The cross-sectional study conducted by Kim et al. (2005) aimed to identify the prevalence of incest among Korean adolescents and to determine the family problems, perceived family dynamics, and psychological consequences associated with incest in South Korea. A total of 1,672 adolescents (1,053 student adolescents and 619 delinquent adolescents) were selected for this study. The results showed a 3.7% prevalence of incest in the tested Korean population. Families in which incest occurred were characterized by higher levels of problems, such as psychotic disorders, depression, criminal acts, and alcoholism among family members. Adolescent incest victims showed significantly more dysfunctional and unhealthy family dynamics and expressed significantly higher maladaptive and problematic psychological patterns than non-victimized adolescents. The study also identified some of the family problems and dysfunctional family dynamics may associate with intrafamilial child sexual abuse in Korea.

Trafficking and Child Sexual Abuse

Deb (2002) remarked that the cases of child sexual abuse are either not reported or under-reported especially in the developing countries owing to social stigma, lack of intervention agencies and/or lack of justice. It has been estimated that in the general population, 1-in-3 girls are sexually abused before the age of 18. For boys, the odds are 1-in-8. The average age of child sexual abuse: eleven, although some psychopaths have been known to strike upon children much younger. However, it has tremendous negative impact on over all mental and social development of the children. Deb reviewed various aspects concerning this issue like definitions, etiology, prevalence/incidence, consequences, and legal measures available in India to combat this social problem and suggests prevention and intervention methods in the light of Indian scenario.

Deb (2005) stated that child trafficking has become a serious social problem in some parts of India. West Bengal is one of the badly affected States. Especially at risk are the girl children of rural areas from poor and poorly connected families. Improvement of the rural economy (to lessen the lure of monetary inducement that poor families face) and creating awareness in rural areas, along with the involvement of Panchayat members and the local administration as well as NGOs, are preventive measures that need to be urgently promoted. In addition, awareness about the issue should be created among the law enforcement agencies and legal measures enacted to prosecute perpetrators.

Deb (2005) carried out a study on covering trafficked children with a view to understanding the socio-economic profile of the young trafficked women in West Bengal, substance abuse among them and their HIV status as very few studies were carried out on this issue. A group of 35 young trafficked women were covered in the study and they were interviewed by a semi-structured questionnaire. In addition, in-depth interview and case study methods were also adopted for data collection. Findings revealed that majority of the young trafficked women (82.9%), mostly illiterate (57.1%) and semi-literate (42.9%) with more than two siblings (91.4%), were aged between 18-20 years. Parents', mostly illiterate and very poor, were involved in agriculture as labourers and some of them work as vegetable sellers. After trafficking, only 28.6% have had contact with their family and occasionally parents visit them in the rehabilitation homes. However, most of the parents did not know that their girl child was involved in prostitution after trafficking. About 89.0% of the trafficked women had a history of sexual abuse in early life. After coming into flesh trade about 80.0% became dependent on different types of substances while 20.0% became pregnant accidentally. Four of them (11.4%) were also tested HIV positive. Findings suggest awareness campaign about the child trafficking in the rural areas should be organised on regular basis and in this process all the Panchayat Members and senior community leaders like school teachers, Police and local administrators should be involved. In addition, for improving the rural economy, awareness about Government welfare programmes should be created and NGOs should come forward to help poor people to enjoy the benefits of the Government programmes.

Deb and Sen (2005a) conducted a study with a view to understanding the extent of psychological trauma experienced by the young trafficked women. The history of physical and sexual abuse and HIV status was also explored. A group of 35 young trafficked women aged between 14-22 and working as prostitutes were covered in the study. Data were collected by the Trauma Symptom Inventory (TSI) by John Briere (1991). The study was carried out in West Bengal, India during July-

December 2004. Analysis of the background data pointed toward low literacy, large family size, low family income, low general awareness level and young age as vulnerability factors for trafficking. The TSI results indicated that close to half the sample (42.9%) experienced post-traumatic stress, sexual difficulties and self-dysfunction, while 29.0% experienced dysphoric mood. A significant difference was found between the trafficked and the non-trafficked sample on the clinical scales of depression, intrusive experiences, sexual concerns and dysfunctional sexual behaviour ($p < .01$). The findings suggest comprehensive rehabilitation of the trafficked women with special emphasis on need of mental health.

In a study covering 35 trafficked children and young women carried out by Deb et al. (2005) found that trafficking is usually conducted through offers of false marriages and jobs, or through outright abduction and sale. In almost all the districts and even some villages, the traffickers, who have a strong network, engage agents, who include: another person who herself is a victim of trafficking, unemployed persons, drug addicts/alcoholics or aged women with no income. Sometimes, these agents work under compulsion and/or they are blackmailed into abetment. Since poverty and illiteracy are the prime factors contributing to trafficking, income-generating and literacy programmes should be arranged for needy families. Local NGOs also need to take the initiative to raise awareness levels in Panchayats in order to check trafficking. Training programmes and workshops need to be organized too, for the local administration, Panchayat members and police officers.

Chatterjee et al. (2006) aimed at investigating the short and long-term problems faced by the trafficked children. A group of 41 female trafficked children, in the age group of 10-18 years was covered in the study and they were selected following incidental sampling technique from the rehabilitation Home of 'Sanlaap' (an NGO) and from the Observation Home for Girls. Data were collected from the trafficked children following an in-depth interview method. Further, for better realization of the objective, detailed case studies have been developed. Findings highlighted the problems encountered by the trafficked children, which can be broadly categorized as mental, physical and social. HIV/AIDS—the dreaded disease was found out among 6 out of 41 trafficked children covered in the study. Among the mental dispositions depression, loneliness and loss of interest disturb nearly every child. To top if all they feel the discrimination in the social sphere which encompasses two broad areas namely stigmatization and family rejection. A further analysis of the after effects were clubbed into two dimensions, namely short-term and long-term problems of which minor health problems and settlement in future are the dominant ones respectively. Findings also revealed that family members had developed a negative attitude towards these children and generally do not come to visit them. Authorities of the welfare agencies should initiate dialogue with the family members of all trafficked children for merger with the family. Identified parents of the trafficked children should be counseled to change their neglecting attitude towards these children. So far as rehabilitation is concerned, trafficked children are receiving some vocational training in Sanlaap. However, in the Government. Observation Home similar activities should be arranged after identification of their skills, interest and demand of the market.

Other Relevant Studies

Rellini et al. (2006) conducted a study to understand psychophysiological sexual arousal in women with a history of child sexual abuse on the basis of literature that suggested that Child Sexual Abuse (CSA) survivors with Post Traumatic Stress Disorder (PTSD) have higher baseline Sympathetic Nervous System (SNS) activity than healthy controls and also research that suggested that the SNS plays a critical role in female physiological sexual arousal. The impact of SNS activation through intense exercise on sexual arousal in women with CSA and PTSD were examined and physiological and subjective sexual arousal in women with CSA (n=8), women with CSA and PTSD (n=10), and healthy controls (n=10) during exposure to non-erotic and erotic videos were measured. After exercise, women with CSA and women with CSA and PTSD showed no significant differences in the physiological sexual response compared with no exercise, which was different from the increased physiological sexual response after exercise observed in control women.

Lalor's (2004) article reviews the English-language literature on child sexual abuse in sub-Saharan Africa (SSA). The focus was on the sexual abuse of children in the home/ community, as opposed to the commercial sexual exploitation of children. English language, peer-reviewed papers cited in the Social Sciences Citation Index (SSCI) were examined along with reports from international and local NGOs and UN agencies. Few published studies on the sexual abuse of children had been conducted in the region, with the exception of South Africa. Samples were predominantly clinical or University based. A number of studies accounted that approximately 5.0% of the sample reported penetrative sexual abuse during their childhood. The most frequent explanations for the sexual abuse of children in SSA include rapid social change, AIDS/HIV avoidance strategies and the patriarchal nature of society. Child sexual abuse is most frequently perpetrated by family members, relatives, neighbours or others known to the child. To conclude it could be remarked that there was nothing to support the widely held view that child sexual abuse is very rare in SSA—prevalence levels were comparable with studies reported from other regions. The high prevalence levels of AIDS/HIV in the region expose sexually abused children to high risks of infection. It is estimated that, approximately 0.6-1.8% of all children in high HIV-incidence countries in Southern Africa will experience penetrative sexual abuse by an AIDS/HIV infected perpetrator before 18 years of age.

Martin et al. (2004) made a cross-sectional study of gender specific relationships between self-reported child sexual abuse and suicidality in a community sample of adolescents. Students aged 14 years on average (N=2485) from 27 schools in South Australia completed a questionnaire including items on sexual abuse and suicidality and measures of depressions (Centre for

Epidemiological Studies Depression Scale), hopelessness (Beck Hopelessness Scale) and family functioning (McMaster Family Assessment Device General Functioning Sub-scale). The results of the study indicated that in boys, self-report sexual abuse is strongly and independently associated with suicidal thoughts, plans, threats, and deliberate self-injury and suicide attempts after controlling for current levels of depression, hopelessness and family dysfunction. In girls, the relationship between sexual abuse and suicidality is mediated fully by depression, hopelessness and family dysfunction. Girls who report current high distress about sexual abuse, however, have a threefold increased risk of suicidal thoughts and plans, compared to non-abused girls. Boys who report current high distress about sexual abuse have 10-fold increased risk for suicidal plans and threats and 15-fold increased risk for suicide attempts, compared to non-abused boys. Fifty-five percent (n=15) of sexually abused boys attempted suicide versions versus 29.0% (n=17) girls. The study depicts that a history of sexual abuse should alert clinicians, professionals and careers in contact with adolescents to greatly increased risks of suicidal behaviour and attempts in boys, even in absence of depression and hopelessness. Distress following sexual abuse, along with depression and hopelessness indicate increased risk of suicidal behaviour in girls as well as boys.

A study was conducted by Roberts et al. (2004) to investigate links between child sexual abuse (occurring before 13 years), later mental health, family organization, parenting behaviours and adjustment in offspring. A sample of 8292 families of Avon, England met inclusion criteria for identifiable family type and completed self-report data on prior sexual assault. Further data were collected on life-course variables, socio-economic variables, psychological well-being, relationship quality, parent-child relationship quality and children's adjustment. After adjustment for other childhood adversity, prior child sexual abuse was associated with a range of outcomes in adulthood, including current membership of a non-traditional family type (single mother and stepfather) poorer psychological well-being, teenage pregnancy, parenting behaviours and adjustment problems in the victim's offspring later on. The relationship of child sexual abuse with aspects of the parent-child relationship in later life and with the offspring's adjustment difficulties were mediated in part by mother's mental health-chiefly anxiety. To summarize the findings indicated that child sexual abuse has long-term repercussions for adult mental health, parenting relationships and child adjustment in the succeeding generation.

Schultz et al. (2003) conducted a research regarding emotional closeness with perpetrators and amnesia for child sexual abuse. In order to address this issue, 240 female participants completed questions about CSA, the Dissociative Experience Scale (Bernstein and Putnam, 1986), Perceived Emotional Closeness with Perpetrator Scale (Schultz, Passmore, and Yoder, 2000), and the Gudjonsson Suggestibility Scale 2 (GSS 2) (Gudjonsson, 1987). Eighty-two (36.0%) reported CSA and 37.0% of these indicated memory disturbances for the CSA. Participants reporting memory disturbances also reported significantly higher numbers of perpetrators, chemical abuse in their families, and closer relationships with the perpetrator(s) than participants reporting no memory disturbances.

Whealin's (2002) study describes the occurrence of childhood unwanted sexual attention and explores its relation to child sexual abuse (CSA). Three hundred fifteen university women (mean age=19.5) completed the Exposure to Sexual Attention Scale, a 200-item inventory which assesses various forms of UWSA received prior to age 18. Findings suggested that non-contact UWSA is a pervasive experience across settings for girls, with 98.7% reporting UWSA during childhood. Those reported most often to perpetrate UWSA (e.g., other students, adult strangers, child strangers, and other children) were also most often reported as sexual abusers. Emotional reactions by women to both UWSA and CSA were predominantly negative, although significantly greater levels of fear reactions were reported by the CSA group when compared to the UWSA group. Overall findings suggested that UWSA is an almost universal experience for girls that cause significant anger and fear.

Hiebert-Murphy, D. (2001) carried out a study to explore partner abuse among women in families in which a child has disclosed child sexual abuse. 102 mothers completed a measure of partner abuse and the Coping Responses Inventory. Results suggested that, like women in the general population, mothers of children who have been sexually abused have often experienced partner abuse. As expected, physical abuse in a current relationship was found to be related to the use of avoidance strategies in dealing with the sexual abuse disclosure.

Deb's (2005) study of a group of 120 migrant child labourers working in households, tea stalls, garages and shops in South Kolkata reveals that an overwhelming number of the children are abused, in some way or the other—physically, mentally, or sexually. In-depth probing revealed that 42.5% working children (37.3% boys and 51.1% girls) were victims of mental torture while 32.5 and 10.8%, respectively, were abused physically and harassed sexually. Both physical abuse and sexual harassment were more prevalent among girl children. Of those with health problems, a good number of them remain untreated. In some cases, abuse and neglect become fatal. Law enforcement agencies should be very strict against the perpetrators, who badly abuse and maltreat helpless children. Simultaneously, the community should be sensitized to this issue. In this regard, Non-Governmental Organizations (NGO) should take initiative to for creating social awareness.

Justification of the Study

Literature review indicates that a number of studies were carried on different dimensions of child sexual abuse in the developed countries. However, very few studies have been carried out in the developing countries especially in India in this regard. Findings of previous studies revealed that sexually abused children undergo severe psychological problems like stress, anxiety, depression and so on. They require mental support and special care to overcome their psychological problems and in this regard, care givers especially parents, guardians and counsellors can play a vital role. Since not much is known about the impact of sexual abuse on mental disposition of children in the context of the Indian society, the necessity of the study was reinforced. The findings of the present study would be an eye opener to other researchers. It is expected that findings of the present study would clearly indicate what sort of mental health problems sexually abused children suffer from and the role of support services on mental disposition of sexually abused girl children. Findings of the present study would also guide the local health service providers especially counselors to deal with sexually abused children properly and would also help to guide their family members.

Objectives

Broad Objective

To study the impact of sexual abuse on mental disposition of children.

Specific Objectives

- To study the demographic and socio-economic background of sexually abused girl children.
- To study the level of depression among sexually abused girl children.
- To study the level of aggression among sexually abused girl children.
- To understand the emotional and social adjustment capability of sexually abused girl children.
- To study the personality pattern of sexually abused girl children.
- To understand the experience of the counselors in dealing with the sexually abused girl children.
- To understand the nature of care and support services available for sexually abused girl children.

- To understand the perception of the sexually abused girl children about the nature of care and support services.
- To suggest need-based psychosocial rehabilitation measures for sexually abused girl children.

Hypotheses

(i) Level of depression of sexually abused and non-sexually abused girl children differs significantly, irrespective of age group.

(ii) Level of depression of sexually abused girl children aged between 13-15 years and 16-18 years differs significantly, irrespective of effectiveness of counselling as perceived by the subjects.

(iii) Level of depression of sexually abused girl children who received counselling and perceived it to be beneficial and those who did not receive counselling and/or did not perceive it to be beneficial differs significantly, irrespective of age group.

(iv) Level of aggression of sexually abused and non-sexually abused girl children differs significantly, irrespective of age group.

(v) Level of aggression of sexually abused girl children aged between 13-15 years and 16-18 years differs significantly, irrespective of effectiveness of counselling as perceived by the subjects.

(vi) Level of aggression of sexually abused girl children who received counselling and perceived it to be beneficial and those who did not receive counselling and/or did not perceive it to be beneficial differs significantly, irrespective of age group.

(vii) Emotional adjustment of sexually abused and non-sexually abused girl children differs significantly, irrespective of age group.

(viii) Emotional adjustment of sexually abused girl children aged between 13-15 years and 16-18 years differs significantly, irrespective of effectiveness of counselling as perceived by the subjects.

(ix) Emotional adjustment of sexually abused girl children who received counselling and perceived it to be beneficial and those who did not receive counselling and/or did not perceive it to be beneficial differs significantly, irrespective of age group.

(x) Social adjustment of sexually abused and non-sexually abused girl children differ significantly, irrespective of age group.

(xi) Social adjustment of sexually abused girl children aged between 13-15 years and 16-18 years differs significantly, irrespective of effectiveness of counselling as perceived by the subjects.

(xii) Social adjustment of sexually abused girl children who received counselling and perceived it to be beneficial and those who did not receive counselling and/or did not perceive it to be beneficial differs significantly, irrespective of age group.

(xiii) Personality disposition of sexually abused and non-sexually abused girl children differs significantly, irrespective of age group.

(xiv) Personality disposition of sexually abused girl children aged between 13-15 years and 16-18 years differs significantly, irrespective of effectiveness of counselling as perceived by the subjects.

(xv) Personality disposition of sexually abused girl children who received counselling and perceived it to be beneficial and those who did not receive counselling and/or did not perceive it to be beneficial differs significantly, irrespective of age group.

Operational Definition

Sexual Abuse: 'Any sexual activity or experience imposed on a child that results in emotional, physical or sexual trauma' (Sandra Butler, 1985). In the present study, sexual abuse of children included touching of private parts, fondling, penetration and rape.

Mental Disposition: In the present study the dimension of mental disposition, which was explored, include depression, aggression, emotional and social adjustment and personality (viz. introversion/extroversion, self-concept, independence/dependence, temperament and anxiety) of the sexually abused institutionalized girl children.

Depression: The term depression is used in everyday language to describe a range of experiences from a slightly noticeable and temporary mood decrease to a profoundly impaired and even life-threatening disorder.

Aggression: The term 'aggression' is a mode of frustration (Chauhan and Tiwari, 1971). "Frustration is a state of affairs against which the affected individual's energies are more or less strongly mobilized which he seeks to eliminate or, if possible entirely to avoid, if happiness may fairly be said to represent the ultimate goal of all human endeavour, frustration as its anti-thesis." (Mowser, 1938).

Adjustment: Adjustment is derived from the Latin word *ad-juxtare*, derived from *juxta*, and it means regulating, adapting or settling. Adjustment is an index of integration between needs and satisfaction and is related to achievement, social acceptance, age, sex, economic security and moral standards (Chauhan, Tiwari and Khatter, 1972). By the process of adjustment, an individual experiences several facts and events, by which he tries to shape and reshape his personality.

Emotional Adjustment: Emotional adjustment is a prerequisite for social adjustment (Schneider, 1951). Emotionally well-adjusted people are quick to establish affectionate relationship with others.

Social Adjustment: Social adjustment refers to the change in habitual conduct or behaviour, which an individual must make in order to fit into the community in which he lives (Warren, 1934).

Personality Disposition: Personality implies the pattern of collective character, behavioural, temperamental, emotional, and mental traits of a person. Personality cannot be measured through one factor or dimension. It has multi-dimensional factors. In this study, five personality dimensions were measured, viz., extroversion-introversion, high self-concept, low-self-concept, independence-dependence, temperament and anxiety.

Context of the Study

Child abuse and neglect is a deep-rooted cultural problem in India. It is prevalent in all sections of the society. Even in the 21st century children are killed in the name of religion. In the recent past, media has reported a number of such cases. In one such case in rural Orissa, India occurred in 1996 lower court had given a verdict for life imprisonment to father who sacrificed his son before god image being guided by some religious belief. However, this issue is yet to be recognized in India. Corporal punishment of children is still regarded as a method of behaviour modification of children.

A large number of children across the globe are sexually abused. Global statistics say that one in every third child is either sexually abused and/or harassed. In India situation could be similar and even worse. In fact, in the developing countries there is no system of maintaining record on child abuse and neglect in general and child sexual abuse in particular. Hence, it is very difficult to make any clear statement about the magnitude of the problem.

According to Oates (1996), sexual abuse of children means involvement of dependent, developmentally immature children and adolescents in sexual activities, which they do not fully comprehend and to which they are unable to give informed consent. Sexual abuse includes touching, fondling and penetration.

Broadly there are two forms of sexual abuse of children, i.e. rape and incest. 'Rape' is defined as any sexual behaviour imposed on a child by a stranger, and 'incest' defined as any sexual behaviour imposed on a child by a member of either the immediate or extended family. The extended family includes people whom the child or family has known for a significant length of time and whom they trust, such as fathers, stepfathers, uncles, siblings and other family members, as well as friends, neighbours, teachers, doctors and members of religious communities. Broadening the concept of incest beyond close blood relations is very important. It helps underscore the special harm caused by any sexual activity between a person in a position of status, trust and authority, and a child in a position of dependency. However, sexual abuse can be physical, verbal or emotional (*Source*: ESCAP-HRD, United Nations, 2002).

Abuse may be a single incident, or it may take place over a period of years. Both boys and girls are equally potential to be the victim of sexual abuse. Earlier, parents were scared of leaving their little daughters alone, but now even boys are not safe. They are equally vulnerable. But cases of sexually abused boys are rarely reported in India. Disadvantaged boys, i.e. children living in slums or on roadsides are more vulnerable to sexual abuse. There is also little recognition of the sexual abuse of boys, which is covered under Section 377 (sodomy) of the IPC. There is no law specifically dealing with the rape of boys in India.

There is a misconception among some communities in the rural areas that if any elder person suffering from Sexually Transmitted Diseases (STDs) they will be free from this disease if they have sex with a minor aged girl. Driven by this wrong notion sometimes illiterate people abuse children sexually and the children become the victim of STDs.

Symptoms of Sexually Abused Children: Sexual abuse may surface through a broad range of physical, behavioural and social symptoms. Indicators, taken separately, may not be symptomatic of sexual abuse. The symptoms that follow are a guide and should be examined in the context of other behaviours or situational factors which are mentioned below (*Source*: UCDAVIS Children's Hospital):

Disclosure: Direct or indirect statement to a parent, friend, teacher or other trusted adult.

Physical Symptoms: Sexually transmitted disease, genital discharge or infection, physical trauma, pain with urination, general pain, or bleeding.

Sexual Behaviours: Detailed and age inappropriate understanding of sexual behaviour by younger children; inappropriate or aggressive sexual behaviour with peers or toys; excessive curiosity about sexual matters or genitalia; prostitution of promiscuity.

Behavioural Indicators: Regressive behaviour (wetting/soiling, thumb sucking); psychosomatic complaints (headaches/stomach aches); depression; fears; nightmares or sleep disturbances; repressed anger/hostility; low self-esteem; suicide attempts; poor social skills; rebellious, runaway, or delinquent behaviour; school problems; alcohol/drug abuse.

In this regard researchers carried out a number of studies in different parts of the globe. Findings of some of the studies are given below:

Swanston et al. (2003) made an effort to understand the psychological adjustment of 103 sexually abused children in Sydney after nine years as compared to non-abused young people of similar age and gender to assess group differences and examine potential risk factors. At intake, data on the nature of the index sexual abuse, demographics and the family environment were collected by clinicians. A comparison group, of similar age and gender, was selected from schools in the catchment area of the CPUs. Six years after presentation for the abuse, records of the statutory child protection authority were checked to determine any further notifications for abuse and/or neglect. Nine years after intake, 49 of the abused young people and 68 of the non-abused young people and/or their parents were interviewed and assessed. The sexually abused young people performed more poorly than non-abused young people on psychometric tests of depression ($p=.001$), self-esteem ($p<.001$), anxiety ($p<.001$), behaviour (Child Behaviour Checklist: $p=.01$; Youth Self Report: $p=.01$; Young Adult Self Report: $p<.001$), and despair ($p=.001$). They were also more likely to have a history of bingeing ($p=.002$), self-inducing vomiting ($p=.02$), smoking cigarettes ($p=.01$), and using amphetamines ($p=.002$), ecstasy ($p=.002$) and cocaine ($p=.004$). Potential risk factors were in two groups, family and child. Family factors: family functioning, parental drug/alcohol problems, mother's sexual abuse history, mother's depression and socio-economic status. Child factors: despair and hopefulness, number of negative life events, ratings of their father's care, previous notifications for child sexual abuse and placements in out-of-home care by the statutory child protection authority. In the presence of other risk factors, child sexual abuse was a significant predictor of self-esteem, behaviour and bingeing. Rather than focusing only on the individual's child sexual abuse, treatment may also need to address the family's functioning and the individual's feelings of despair.

In another study Sandnabba et al. (2003) explored the sexual behaviours of 2- to 7-year-old children through reports of day-care personnel. The results suggest that child sexual behaviour reported by day-care personnel may provide useful information about the development of children's sexuality.

Walrath et al. (2003) examined multiple empirically based perspectives (i.e., child, caregiver, and clinician) of behaviour and functioning as they contribute to the clinical and psychosocial profile of children (aged 5 to 17.5 years) with reported histories of sexual abuse. The findings indicate that the profile of children entering into Comprehensive Community Mental Health Services with reported histories of sexual abuse, as compared to those without such histories, is complex and best understood via multiple perspectives. Caregiver, child and clinician rated information, when taken together, provide a comprehensive clinical and psychosocial profile around which to plan and implement individualized service plans.

Collin-Vezina and Cyr (2003) carried out a secondary study to understand the issue of inter-generational transmission of child sexual abuse (CSA). In light of the research reviewed, it seems that the transmission of CSA is far from inevitable, since one-third of sexually abusive men and half of sexually abused children's mothers mentioned having been sexually abused in their childhood. Because of the retrospective method used in many studies, causal links could not be established. Authors suggested that more studies on CSA transmission are needed to understand the mechanisms that are involved in that cycle, as well as to develop effective strategies to treat and prevent CSA.

Lamb et al. (2003) attempted to determine whether child witnesses of sexual abuse were more or less informative about the alleged incidents than alleged victims when interviewed similarly. These results confirm that young children can be informative witnesses about events that they have either experienced or witnessed.

Incidences of Child Abuse and Neglect: It is very difficult to project the incidence rate and magnitude of various forms of child abuse and neglect in India, as there is no systematic system of maintaining record like in the developed countries and also very few population-based studies are carried out on this issue.

Reported cases gives some idea about various forms of crimes committed against children especially sexual abuse in India during 1992-1996 (Table 2.1). In India cases of sexual abuse/harassment are not reported owing to negligence, perceived harassment in the police department and in the court and threat from the perpetrators. In addition, fear of social discrimination and boycott also inhibit the victim party to report the case to police. Hence, the figures in Table 2.1 are definitely an underestimation of actual incidence. Figures in Table 2.1 shows that maximum number of child rape cases was reported followed by kidnapping/abduction and exposure/abandonment.

Table 2.1: Incidence of Crime Committed Against Children in India During 1992-1996

Incidence Variation / *Crime Head*	*Percentage*						
	1992	*1993*	*1994*	*1995*	*1996*	*1995 over 1992*	*1996 over 1995*
Child rape (up to 16 years)	3113	3393	3986	4067	4083	31.2	0.4
Kidnapping and Abduction	521	485	864	726	571	9.6	–21.3
Procuration of Minor girls	—	—	206	107	94	—	–21.1
Selling of girls for prostitution	—	—	34	17	6	—	–64.7
Buying of girls for prostitution	—	—	4	19	22	—	15.8
Abetment of Suicide	—	—	7	9	11	—	+22.2
Exposure and Abandonment	—	—	491	570	554	—	–1.8
Infanticide	—	—	131	139	113	—	–18.7
Foeticide	—	—	45	38	39	—	2.6
Child Marriage Restraint Act	—	—	53	57	89	—	56.1

Source: Crime in India, 1996, p.96 (Figures not available).

In an Indian study carried out by Pagare (2003) in an observation home in Delhi it was found that 38.1% of boy children were sexually abused. On clinical examination, among the sexually abused children (n=72) physical and behavioural signs were noticed in 23.8% and 16.3% respectively. In case of sexual abuse the most common perpetrators of sexual abuse were strangers. Sexual abuse was found to be significantly associated with domestic violence (p=0.016), solvent/ inhalant use (p=0.0002) and working status (p=0.017).

In another study carried out in south Kolkata among migrant child labour, the authors found that 11.0% of girl children working as maid-servants were subjected to victims of sexual abuse and/or harassment (Deb and Mitra, 2002).

Findings also revealed that sexually abused children may also develop or learn sexualized behaviours that put them at risk of continued abuse by the same perpetrator or new abuse by different perpetrators (Dodge et al., 1990, Friederich, 1988).

A history of childhood sexual abuse was found in studies of prostitutes (Fields, 1981; Silbert and Pines, 1983), child molesters (Groth and Burgess, 1979), rapists and physically abusing parents (Finkelhor and Browne, A., 1986). Finkelhor reported a connection between homosexuality in male adults and child sexual abuse (Finkelhor, 1984). Steele and Alexander (1981) found that sexually abused individuals generally showed impaired personal and emotional functioning like depression, poor self-esteem, feelings of isolation and stigma, fear of man, hostility towards parent and a higher incidence of eating disorders in their adulthood.

A recent longitudinal cohort study in Christchurch, New Zealand found significant associations between sexual abuse during childhood and subsequent mental health problems such as depression, anxiety disorders and suicidal thoughts and behaviour (Fergusson et al., 1996). This apart, a variety of symptoms, behavioural changes, and diagnosis sometimes occur in sexually abused children (Wolfe, 1999; Briere and Elliott, 1994).

3

Method

Geographical Coverage

The present study was confined to Kolkata Metropolitan City and its suburbs.

Target Group

The present study covered three categories of respondents, viz.

- Sexually abused girl children aged between 13-18 years.
- Sexually non-abused girl children aged between 13-18 years.
- Counsellors of sexually abused girl children.

Study Tools

The present study is an accumulation of both qualitative and quantitative data. In order to achieve the objectives of the present study, following study tools were used after local adaptation. For qualitative data:

- Background Information Schedule developed by Dr. Sibnath Deb and Aparna Mukherjee (2004).
- Structured Questionnaire for ascertaining sexual abuse of children developed by Dr. Sibnath Deb and Aparna Mukherjee (2004).
- Semi-structured Questionnaire for counsellors developed by Dr. Sibnath Deb and Aparna Mukherjee (2004).

For quantitative data the following study tools were used:

- Beck Depression Inventory developed by Aaron T Beck (1994) and locally adapted by Aparna Mukherjee and Dr. Sibnath Deb (2004).
- Aggression Scale developed by Roma Pal (1981) and locally adapted by Aparna Mukherjee and Dr. Sibnath Deb (2004).
- Social Adjustment Inventory developed by Roma Pal (1985) and locally adapted by Aparna Mukherjee and Dr. Sibnath Deb (2004).
- Multi-dimensional Personality Inventory developed by Km. Manju Agarwal (1988) and locally adapted by Aparna Mukherjee and Dr. Sibnath Deb (2004).

Short Description of the Study Tools

Background Information Schedule

The Background Information Schedule was developed by Mukherjee, Aparna and Deb, Sibnath (2004) to gather information about socio-economic and familial background of the sexually abused children. In addition, the schedule was designed to gather information regarding the history of abuse, reporting of sexual abuse to appropriate authorities and reaction of the family members about such incident along with future ambition, vocational training of the children living in the rehabilitation homes and their perception about the benefits of support services provided to them. This schedule has six broad sections, viz.,

Section 1: **Socio-Economic and Demographic Information:** This section focuses on the demographic and socio-economic profile of the subject like age, number of siblings, type of family, size of family, educational background of parents, occupation of parents, monthly income and living environment (rural or urban area). Section one consists of ten items in aggregate.

Section 2: **History of Abuse:** This segment consists of six items and is designed to gather data about the age when the child was abused, relationship with the perpetrator, if any, situation when abused, undergone medical treatment, if any, after the abuse, frequency of sexual abuse and the outcome of sexual contact, if any.

Section 3: **Reporting:** This part comprises of five items wherein emphasis is given to the reporting of the incident to suitable authorities like law enforcement officials or local non-governmental organizations and the reasons thereof for not reporting the incident to them.

Section 4: **Reaction of Family Members and Future Aspiration:** This section stresses on the reaction of the family members about the unfortunate incident and also attempts to gather data regarding contact of the family members with the child living in the shelter along with periodicity of contact, if any, or the reason for not keeping in touch with the inmate. It also seeks to know the future aspiration of the child. This part has five items in total.

Section 5: **Skill Building and Perception about the Home:** This division again constitute of five items dealing with the issue of vocational training the child might have received or is currently learning in her stay at the shelter. It also attempts to retrieve information regarding the child's perception of the home and the behaviour of the staff therein.

Section 6: **Attitude towards Counselling Services:** This section comprises of items, which endeavours to retrieve information about counselling services and their positive or negative impact on the inmates.

Sexual Abuse Screening Questionnaire

The questionnaire was developed by Mukherjee, Aparna and Deb, Sibnath (2004) to achieve some knowledge regarding the past sexual experiences of the respondent's to gauge their suitability for the study.

Semi-structured Questionnaire for Counsellors

The semi-structured questionnaire was developed by Mukherjee, Aparna and Deb, Sibnath (2004) to gather information from the counselors about their perceived problems in dealing with sexually abused victims and their suggestions thereof to improve the condition of the shelter inmates.

Beck Depression Inventory II

Description: The Beck Depression Inventory—Second Edition (BDI-II) is a 21 item self-report instrument for measuring the severity of depression in adults and adolescents. This version of the inventory (BDI-II) was developed for the assessment of symptoms corresponding to criteria for diagnosing depressive disorder listed in the American Psychiatric Association's Diagnostic and Statistical Manual of Mental Disorders—Fourth Edition (DSM-IV: 1994). The BDI-IA replaced the original instrument (BDI) that had been developed by Beck, Ward, Mendelson, Mock and Erbaugh (1961). For the new, revised version (BDI-II), four items (weight loss, body image change, somatic preoccupation and work difficulty) were dropped and replaced by four new items (agitation, worthlessness, concentration difficulty and loss of energy) in order to index symptoms typical of severe depression or depression warranting hospitalization. Two items were changed to allow for increases as well as decreases in appetite and sleep. Many of the statements (or alternatives) used in rating the other symptoms were reworded. Unlike the BDI-IA, the BDI-II constitutes a substantial revision of the original BDI.

Response Mode: There are four possible responses to the 21 groups of statements. The respondents were asked to read each item carefully and circle the number of the statement, which they think is most appropriate for them.

Scoring: The BDI-II is scored by summing up the ratings of all the 21 items. Each item is rated on a 4-point scale ranging from 0 to 3. If a respondent has made multiple endorsements for an item, the alternative with the highest rating is used. The maximum total score is 63 and the lowest score is 0. For the purpose of the present study the English version of the questionnaire was translated into facile Bengali language and used after ascertaining the face validity by three experts. Scoring was done following the scoring rationale of the inventory.

Reliability: An estimate of the stability of BDI-II over time was based on the responses of a sub-sample of 26 Philadelphia outpatients who were administered the BDI-II at the times of their first and second therapy sessions, approximately 1 week apart. The test-retest correlation of .93 was significant ($p < .001$). The first session mean BDI-II total score of 20.27 (SD=10.46) and the second session mean BDI-II total score of 19.42 (SD=10.38) were comparable {paired t (25) =1.08. not significant}.

Validity: BDI-II was developed especially to assess the depressive symptoms listed as criteria for depressive disorders in DSM-IV. For content validity, items were reworded and new items added so as to assess the DSM-IV criteria for depression more fully.

Several different types of analyses were conducted to estimate the convergent validity of BDI-II. BDI-IA and BDI-II were administered during initial evaluation on 191 outpatients of two American states. The order of the presentations was counterbalanced and atleast one other instrument was given between administrations of the two versions of the BDI. The correlation between BDI-IA and BDI-II was .93 ($p < .001$). The mean BDI-IA and BDI-II scores were 18.92 (SD=11.32) and 21.88 (SD=12.69), respectively. The mean BDI-II score was 2.96 points greater than that of the BDI-IA {paired t (190) =8.56, $p < .001$}.

84 out of 127 Philadelphia outpatients were mailed the BDI-IA to complete at home approximately one week before their intake evaluations. The correlation between the total scores on the take-home BDI-IA forms and the BDI-II forms, which were completed during the initial intake, was .84 ($p < .001$). The mean BDI-IA and BDI-II total scores were 18.15 (SD=9.99) and 21.63(SD=11.50), respectively. Again, the mean BDI-II total score was significantly greater than the mean BDI-IA total score {paired t (83) =3.65, $p < .001$}.

Evidence of the factorial validity of BDI-II is provided by the intercorrelations among the 21 BDI-II items, which were first calculated from the responses of the sample of psychiatric outpatients (N=500). The intercorrelation for the matrix was .95, a value that was considered to be 'marvelous'.

Steps Followed for Local Adaptation of the Test

The Socio-cultural admissibility of the test was ascertained by following the below mentioned steps:

Step I: Items of the test were translated into local Bengali language and was checked by three experienced researchers.

Step II: The Bengali version of the test of B.D.I. II was retranslated into English to ascertain whether the meaning of the test items remained the same.

Aggression Scale

Description: The term 'Aggression' is a mode of frustration (Chauhan and Tiwari, 1972). 'Frustration is a state of affairs against which the effected individual's energies are more or less strongly mobilized which he seeks to eliminate, or, if possible entirely to avoid, if happiness may fairly be said to represent the ultimate goal of all human endeavour, frustration as its anti-thesis' (Mowser, 1938). The present scale is based on Chauhan and Tiwari's Frustration Scale or alternatively it can be said that the present scale is the extended form of Chauhan and Tiwari's Frustration Scale in which aggression has been taken as a mode of frustration. The items in the scale are related to reactionary attitudes, irritation, drive for dominance, love for fighting, anger behaviour, aggressive tendency against existing traditional social customs and rules, preference for fighters and for counter behaviour, appreciation for rebellion and competitiveness. Operationally defined, all the items of this Aggression Scale are matters of behaviour in daily life. It comprises of 30 items overall and is designed to measure the level of aggression in an individual.

Response Mode: Each of the item has six alternate answers (multiple choice) graded on a six-point scale on the positive dimension and zero point on the negative dimension. The possible responses against each statement are 'very much', 'much', 'ordinary', 'less', 'very less' and 'not at all'. The subject is instructed to put a tick (√) mark against the response, which is best suited for him/her.

Scoring: The maximum score of this scale is 150 and the minimum score is 0. Low score indicates no or very less aggression while high score points to very high aggression. High scoring individuals are extremely frustrated and are generally rebellious. Individuals with low score are perceived to be calm and quite satisfied with the way they lead their lives. The English version of this questionnaire was translated into comprehensible Bengali language and three experts were consulted to ascertain the face validity. Scoring was done following the scoring rational of the scale.

Reliability: To obtain the reliability co-efficient, the scale was administered to 300 subjects both male and female belonging to rural as well as urban localities. The split-half reliability was calculated by odd-even method. The correlation coefficient was .82, which shows the scale is highly reliable. The test-retest reliability of this scale was calculated by administering this scale twice on a sample of 200 subjects (not included in the above sample). The reliability coefficient was found out to be .78.

Validity: The validity of the scale was checked through the administration of both the present scale and Chauhan and Tiwari's Frustration Scale (only aggression scores were calculated) to a sample of 100 students in an interval of 15 days. The validity coefficient was .74, which shows that the present scale is valid for the measurement of aggression.

Since the present scale is available in both English and Hindi, to check the form reliability, both versions of the scale was administered to a group of 100 students who knew both the languages. The validity coefficient of the both test was .78, which shows that Hindi as well as English version of the scale is valid for the measurement of aggression.

Steps Followed for Local Adaptation of the Test

Step I: English version of the questionnaire was translated into easy Bengali language and the Bengali version of the questionnaire was retranslated again into English to ensure proper and meaningful translation of the test items. The translation was checked by three subject experts. Translation from English to Bengali and retranslation from Bengali to English concurred, i.e. the meaning of the different items of the questionnaire of the two versions remained the same. This process was followed for ascertaining the face validity of the questionnaire.

Step II: Test-retest method was followed to ascertain the reliability of the scale. The questionnaire was administered to sexually abused girl children after 30 days of first administration of the test and the reliability coefficient was found to be .78.

Social Adjustment Inventory

Description: The concept of adjustment has its origin in biology and is derived from Darwin's concept of evolution during mid-eighteenth century. Subsequently it was adopted by the psychologists who renewed its definition as "an index of integration between needs and satisfaction and is related to achievement, social acceptance, age, sex, economic security and moral standards" (Chauhan, Tiwari and Khatter, 1972).

The individual adjusts both socially as well as emotionally with his environment since these are very important aspects of human life. Social adjustment refers to the "change in habitual conduct or behaviour which an individual must make in order to fit into the community in which he lives" (Warren, 1934). Emotional adjustment is viewed as a prerequisite for social adjustment. Schneider (1951) pointed out that emotionally well-adjusted individuals promptly establish affectionate relationship with others. To stress the importance of both, the present inventory includes social as well as emotional adjustment items.

Items for this purpose were selected after careful examinations from other available standard inventories and were modified, where felt necessary. Though, in the preliminary form there were 80 items, only 60 of them were retained after the pilot study which was pretested on 197 subjects.

The present inventory is a beneficial device to evaluate social adjustment of adolescent people. Two types of scores, e.g., emotional and social adjustment can be obtained from this inventory.

Response Mode: Each of the items has two responses 'yes' and 'no'. The subject is instructed to put a tick (√) mark against the answer, which is best suited for him/her.

Scoring: The maximum score of this inventory is 120 and the minimum score is 60. The subject gets a score of 2 if the answer is 'yes' and a score of 1 for answering 'no'. Low score in emotional adjustment items, indicate good adaptation while high score points exactly to the opposite. Alternatively, low score in social adjustment items; indicate poor social adaptation while high score points to the contrary.

The inventory has no specific time limit but usually it takes about 30 to 45 minutes for completion.

For the purpose of the present study the English version of the questionnaire was translated into easy Bengali language and applied after ascertaining the face validity by three experts. Scoring was done following the scoring rationale of the inventory. It should be noted here that in case of emotional adjustment items, the rational was the higher the score, the poorer the adjustment and lower scores are indicative of better emotional adjustment whereas in case of social adjustment items, higher score indicates better social adjustment and lower score suggests poor social adjustment.

Reliability: To determine the reliability of the inventory, it was administered to 300 pupils of Intermediate and College, of both sexes, in equal number and split-half reliability was calculated. The reliability coefficient was .82. For the test-retest reliability, the inventory was administered twice within an interval of 1 month, to the 100 students of B.A., again of both the sexes and the correlation coefficient was .87.

Validity: The present inventory along with Tiwari and Srivastava's Adjustment Inventory were administered to a group of 150 undergraduate and post-graduate students to determine the validity of emotional and social adjustment scales. The validity of the two inventories (only two scales) was .77 and .80 respectively.

Steps Followed for Local Adaptation of the Test

Step I: English version of the questionnaire was translated into easy Bengali language and the Bengali version of the questionnaire was retranslated again into English to ensure proper and meaningful translation of the test items. The translation was checked by three subject experts. Translation from English to Bengali and retranslation to English concurred i.e. the meaning of the different items of the questionnaire of the two versions remained the same. This process was followed for ascertaining the face validity of the questionnaire.

Step II: Test-retest method was followed to ascertain the reliability of the scale. The questionnaire was administered to sexually abused girl children after 30 days of first administration of the test and the reliability coefficient was found to be .76.

Multi-dimensional Personality Inventory

Description: The term 'Personality' refers to the total functions of an individual who interacts with his/her environment. The purpose of the measurement of personality is to describe a person in terms of traits. In the present study Multi-dimensional Personality Inventory was used to understand the personality dispositions of sexually abused girl children along with the normal population.

The Multi-dimensional Personality Inventory was developed and standardized by Km. Manju Agarwal in 1988. The inventory measures six dimensions of personality like extroversion-introversion, self-concept, dependence-independence, temperament, adjustment and anxiety. Each dimension has twenty items. Hence there are altogether 120 items in the inventory.

Response Mode: The response is recorded against three mode of response like 'yes', 'sometimes' and 'no'. The subject is instructed to put a tick (√) mark against the answer, which is best suited for him/her.

Scoring: The subject gets a score of 3 if he/she answered 'yes', score of 2 for answering 'sometimes' and 1 for answering 'no'. Thus, the maximum score in each dimension is sixty and minimum score is twenty. There is no specific time limit for the completion of the inventory but generally the subject is asked to complete it as early as he/she can.

For the purpose of the present study the English version of the questionnaire was translated into easy Bengali language and applied after ascertaining the face validity by three experts. Out of the six dimensions, only five were chosen for the study, barring adjustment. Scoring was done following the scoring rationale of the inventory.

Reliability: For ascertaining the reliability coefficient of the inventory, it was administered to a sample of 600 students. The Split-half reliability Coefficient was computed for the six sub-scales as well as for the total score.

Table 3.1: Showing Split-half Reliability Coefficient of the Inventory

Sub-Scale	*Correlation Coefficient*
Extroversion-introversion	.82
Self-concept	.84
Dependence-independence	.78
Temperament	.87
Adjustment	.79
Anxiety	.86
Total	.74

The Test-retest reliability of the inventory was also calculated by administering it on a sample of 100 students in an interval of 20 days. The Test-retest reliability coefficient is given below:

Table 3.2: Showing Test-Retest Reliability Coefficient of the Inventory

Sub-Scale	*Correlation Coefficient*
Extroversion-introversion	.72
Self-concept	.81
Dependence-independence	.69
Temperament	.72
Adjustment	.84
Anxiety	.71
Total	.74

Validity: For ascertaining the validity, the scale was administered to a group of 100 students. The validity coefficient of the inventory is given below:

Table 3.3: Showing Validity Coefficient of the Inventory

Sub-Scale	*Correlation Coefficient*
Extroversion-introversion	.84
Self-concept	.72
Dependence-independence	.82
Temperament	.76
Adjustment	.69
Anxiety	.84

Steps followed for local adaptation of the test: The test was locally adapted by Bhattacharjee, Anjana and Deb, Sibnath (2004).

Selection of Sample

The steps, which were followed for selection of sample, are as follows:

Step I: First, a list of Government shelter and private shelters were prepared in Kolkata. From the said two lists four shelters, following one Government shelter and three private shelters were selected randomly.

Government Shelter: Sundarbhai Mulchand Home, Liluah, Howrah

Private/Non-Governmental Shelters: The following three non-governmental organizations were covered in the study for selection of sample:

- All Bengal Women's Union, Elliot Road.
- 'Sneha', a shelter of Sanlaap, Narendrapur.
- Child Care Home, Salt Lake.

Step II: From the said four shelters, altogether 120 sexually abused children were covered in the study. They were selected from the Government shelter and three Private shelters following purposive sampling technique.

Step III: A group of 120 normal children were covered in this study and they were selected randomly from four schools situated in close proximity to the shelters for comparison of data with sexually abused children. Normal sample were matched in terms of gender and age.

Step IV: In addition, a group of 7 counselors were covered in the study to gather their views about the problems encountered by them in dealing with the sexually abused children and they were selected following convenience sampling technique. In short, the sample structure is given below:

Table 3.4: Sample Structure

Respondents	*Sample Size*
Sexually abused children	120
Normal population (matched group)	120
Counsellors	7
Total	247

Data Collection

First, permission from the authorities of one Government shelter and three non-governmental shelters was obtained and then a tentative time schedule was developed in consultation with the authorities of the said shelters for data collection.

Data were collected from the sexually abused children following face-to-face interview method.

At the outset, rapport was established with the sexually abused children after conversing with them about their likings, distastes and avocations and then the objectives of the study and how the findings could be beneficial for similar people were explained to them so that they feel at ease and relaxed while sharing necessary personal information and/or responding to different items of the psychological tests.

In case of any confusion regarding the suitability of the subject for the study, concerned counsellors of the different shelters were consulted. Altogether 120 sexually abused children were selected to participate in the study.

Data from normal population was taken from four schools, situated in close proximity to the shelters, following the same rules as was done with the shelters. All the respondents were briefed about the objectives of the study and data were collected from those who willingly agreed to participate in the study. Self-administration method for data collection was employed in case of school subjects.

For collection of data from the counselors, they were approached, while they attended to their regular duties.

Data Analysis

Data collected from the sexually abused children and normal population were checked and edited so that any gap or confusion identified at the preliminary stage could be clarified. The filled in data sheets were subjected to in-house thorough editing and scrutiny. Finally, the data from the data sheets were entered with accuracy and precision in the computer for computation.

Statistics is the science of methodology for the collection, systematic presentation, mathematical analysis and interpretation of data and for drawing inferences about the explored property in the relevant population.

For statistical analysis of the data, Minitab statistical package was used. In case of quantitative data, descriptive statistics like measures of Central Tendency and dispersions were carried out and then 't'-test was applied for verification of the research hypotheses.

For analysis of qualitative data content analysis was carried out.

Ethical Issues Considered

Success of any study counts upon unconditional and enthusiastic cooperation from the respondents. If the respondents are not willing to participate in the study voluntarily they might provide slipshod response, which could mislead the overall findings of the study. In order to ensure the quality of data and also for ethical purposes the following steps were adopted:

The following ethical issues were taken into account while contacting and obtaining data from children:

- Objectives of the study were briefed to all the study subjects and their informed consent was obtained.
- Date and time of the interview/data collection was decided as per the convenience of the study subjects.
- Subjects were assured about the confidentiality of the imparted information.
- Subjects were informed of their choice to withdraw themselves at any point during the study period, if they so wished.

Problems Encountered

While carrying out any study, each and every researcher confronts some difficulties and they find out the solutions to achieve their objectives accordingly. It is important to delineate the problems encountered by any investigator so that future researchers can gain knowledge from the same and accordingly adopt proper measures for conducting similar studies hereafter more effectively.

In this study the main problems encountered by the investigator include:

- Sustaining the interest of some of the sexually abused children for data collection.
- Some of the respondents, both normal and abused children became restless after giving data for one/two tests. In cases like this, the researcher had to fix up another date as per the convenience of the respondents.
- Sometimes it was difficult to convince the general population for voluntary participation in this research work.
- Non-availability of respondents despite the appointment was another constraint. Some of the respondents did not turn up on the date of appointment.
- Sometimes the researcher had to wait for long hours to meet the children in the shelters because they had their diurnal routine to follow.
- Sometimes it was very difficult to make some illiterate subjects understand the meaning of the statements.

Limitations of the Study

For some researchers, collecting data from adequate number of samples and obtaining the consent for wilful participation in the study requires much effort and patience along with perseverance. In this study, too, the researcher was confronted with the same problem. The study was carried out covering 120 sexually abused children only. To reconfirm the verified hypotheses another study with a more macroscopic sample is recommended. Lack of other comparison groups may also be considered as a methodological limitation of this study.

4

Interpretation of Results

In order to achieve the objectives of the present study, data were collected from 120 sexually abused and 120 non-sexually abused girl children, and 7 counsellors of the various shelters. After thorough scrutiny and editing of the data, necessary statistical treatment were done for verification of the hypotheses. Data were fractioned under four broad segments as follows:

Section I: Demographic and Socio-economic Information,

Section II: Mental Dispositions of the Sexually Abused Girl Children,

Section III: Future Aspiration, Skill Building and Perception about the Home,

Section IV: Perception of Counselors in Dealing with Sexually Abused Children.

SECTION I: DEMOGRAPHIC AND SOCIO-ECONOMIC INFORMATION

Data pertaining to demographic and socio-economic information of the sexually abused girl children have been provided in Table 4.1. Children usually belonged to two age groups, viz.13-15 years (37.5%) and 16-18 years (62.5%).

As far as educational background is concerned, a large number of children were found to be illiterate while 29.2% and 26.6% of them attended primary school and pursued secondary education respectively.

Table 4.1: Demographic and Socio-economic Information (N=120)

Parameters	*Characteristics*	*Mode of Response*	
		Frequency	*Percentage*
Age	• 13-15	45	37.5
	• 16-18	75	62.5
Education	• Illiterate	53	44.2
	• Below Primary	35	29.2
	• Below Secondary	32	26.6
Marital Status	• Married	24	20.0
	• Single	96	80.0
Number of Siblings	• Single Child	11	9.2
	• One	13	10.8
	• Two	15	12.5
	• More than two	81	67.5

Base: All Respondents who were Sexually Abused.

Most of victimized children, i.e., about 67.5% had more than two siblings while 12.5% and 10.8% had two and one siblings respectively. So far as marital status is concerned, 20.0% were married while the rest 80.0% were single.

Table 4.2 provides requisite information about the family of the sexually abused girl children. It can be seen here that 93.3% of them came from a nuclear family while 6.7% from a joint family.

Family size variations were also evident from the data. Majority of the family had members ranging between 4-6. Some families (37.5%) also had more than 7 members while the rest 19.2% of the family tended to be below 4.

With regard to parent's education, about 38.3% of the respondent's fathers and 70.8% of their mothers were illiterate. About 33.3% and 19.2% of them, i.e., fathers and mothers respectively studied up to primary level of education. Only a few (19.2% of the fathers and 8.4% of the mothers) had had the opportunity to study further up to the secondary level. Minute percentage (4.2%) of the fathers and less than one per cent mothers could manage to pass the Madhyamik Examination while 17.0% of the fathers and 0.8% of the mothers passed the Higher Secondary Examination. Only 3.3% of the fathers profited from graduate education while none of the mothers seemed to have attained that level.

Table 4.2: Information about the Family (N=120)

Parameters	*Characteristics*	*Mode of Response*	
		Frequency	*Percentage*
Family Type	• Joint	8	6.7
	• Nuclear	112	93.3
Family Size	• Below 4	23	19.2
	• 4-6	52	43.3
	• 7 & above	45	37.5
Father's Education	• Illiterate	46	38.3
	• Up to Primary	40	33.3
	• Up to Secondary	23	19.2
	• Passed Secondary Exam	5	4.2
	• Passed H.S.	2	1.7
	• Graduate	4	3.3
Mother's Education	• Illiterate	85	70.8
	• Up to Primary	23	19.2
	• Up to Secondary	10	8.4
	• Passed Secondary Exam	1	0.8
	• Passed H.S.	1	0.8
Father's Occupation	• Service	30	25.0
	• Business	34	28.3
	• Casual Worker	6	5.0
	• Unemployed	8	6.7
	• Others	42	35.0
Mother's Occupation	• Service	33	27.5
	• Business	2	1.7
	• Housewife	60	50.0
	• Casual Worker	11	9.2
	• Others	14	11.7
Total Monthly Income	• Less than Rs.1000	55	45.8
	• Rs.1001-2000	33	27.5
	• Rs.2001-3000	16	13.3
	• Rs.3001 and above	16	13.3
Place of Living	• Rural	55	45.8
	• Urban	40	33.3
	• Semi-Urban	25	20.8

Base: All Respondents who were Sexually Abused.

Parent's occupations were wide-ranging, as it has been observed from the data overhead. A quick glance at the column of father's occupation gives us a rough sketch depicting that 25.0% of them were engaged in some service, 28.3% were involved in small-scale business while 5.0% were casual workers. About 6.7% turned out to be unemployed while 35.0% were involved in other chores like farming.

Half of the mothers (50.0%) were house-wives and 27.5% were appointed in some service like Ayah, Anganwadi worker etc. About 1.7% owned a business while 9.2% were casual workers, viz., daily labourers in construction sites and 11.7% mostly assisted their husbands in farming.

Monthly income of the family of the respondents lied mostly below Rs.1000 (45.8%). For about 27.5% of the family, income ranged between Rs.1001-Rs.2000. About 16 (13.3%) families had their income in the range of Rs.2001-Rs.3000 while the same percentage was applicable for the Rs.3001 and above category.

Majority of the respondents dwelt in rural areas, while 33.3% had their home in the urban areas. About one-fifth (20.8%) of the children domiciled in the semi-urban area.

Nearly 45.8% of the respondents stated that they were sexually abused between the ages 14-17 years while 37.5% were sexually abused between 10-13 years. The rest 16.7% were sexually victimized at a very young age, i.e., between 6-9 years.

As far as the perpetrators of the abuse are concerned, nearly 55.8% were strangers while 29.2% were relatives. The rest 15.0% belonged to the 'other' category, which constituted mostly of known local acquaintances.

About 73.3% of the respondents stated that they were mostly abused after being drugged and sold to brothels in various major cities like Mumbai, Delhi, Pune and Kolkata and some of them also mentioned that they ran away from their home because they were lured with better job prospects in big cities and were consequently entrapped in this vicious cycle. More than one-fifth (24.2%) of them were abused when nobody was at home while 2.5% averred that they were sexually abused while going to somebody's place or coming back from school.

Table 4.3: History of Abuse (N=120)

Parameters	*Characteristics*	*Mode of Response*	
		Frequency	*Percentage*
Age at the time of first abuse	• 6-9	20	16.7
	• 10-13	45	37.5
	• 14-17	55	45.8
Perpetrator	• Relative	35	29.2
	• Stranger	67	55.8
	• Others	18	15.0
Situation when abused	• Nobody was at home	29	24.2
	• While going to some-body's place/coming from school	3	2.5
	• Others (lured with good job prospects and marriage and so on)	88	73.3
Frequency of Sexual Abuse	• Once	37	30.8
	• Twice	2	1.7
	• Thrice & above	81	67.5
Whether examined by a doctor and received treatment eventually after rehabilitation?	• Yes	118	98.3
	• No	2	1.7
Whether pregnant as an outcome of abuse?	• Yes	8	6.7
	• No	112	93.3

Base: All Respondents who were Sexually Abused.

More than half of the respondents (67.5%) were subjected to sexual torture more than three times while a small number of them (1.7%) mentioned that they were sexually abused only twice. Nearly one-third (30.8%) of the respondents had to undergo this savage act only once.

Virtually all (98.3%) of the ill-treated children were examined by the doctor and received further treatment after being rehabilitated while only 1.7% did not have the privilege of medical aid and assistance. Pregnancy resulted in 6.7% of the respondents as a consequence of sexual abuse.

Table 4.4 yields the most important aspect of child sexual abuse, i.e. reporting of the case to the Police and other competent authorities. It can be seen here that the majority

(98.3%) of the abuse was not reported to the Police while only two families reported the incidence to them and received some kind of police assistance. This statistic is a big cause for concern. More than half of the respondents (54.2%) stated that they did not report the incidence to the Police because of social stigma, which includes ostracization. About one-third (33.3%) of the cases went unaccounted for because the family members dreaded harassment as an aftermath of the report. About 12.5% of the respondents mentioned that their family was threatened by the perpetrator to suppress the issue in hand.

A big role can be played by the NGOs in assisting these helpless victims but the stark reality is that there exists not enough organizations that work in this domain. As a result, about 92.5% of the cases were not reported to the NGOs while only 7.5% of the cases were reported.

Table 4.4: Reporting of Abuse (N=120)

Parameters	*Characteristics*	*Mode of Response*	
		Frequency	*Percentage*
Whether the incident was reported to the police?	• Yes	2	1.7
	• No	118	98.3
If no, why wasn't the incident reported to the police?	• Because of perceived harassment	40	33.3
	• Threatened by the perpetrator	15	12.5
	• Social stigma	63	52.5
Whether the incident was reported to the NGO?	• Yes	9	7.5
	• No	111	92.5
If no, why wasn't the incident reported to the NGO?	• There is no NGO in the locality	16	13.3
	• Social stigma	2	1.7
	• Others (the victims are rescued by the Police and sent directly to the shelters)	93	77.5

Base: All Respondents who were Sexually Abused.

Table 4.5: Reaction of Family Members to the Incident (N=120)

Reaction of the family members to the incident	*Mode of Response*	
	Frequency	*Percentage*
• Discriminated	9	7.5
• Not discriminated	55	45.8
• Others (e.g. not established contact with the family members after abuse/ victimization)	56	46.7

Base: All Respondents who were Sexually Abused.

As seen from Table 4.5, most (45.8%) of the respondents were not discriminated by their immediate families while only 7.5% experienced otherwise. About 46.7% of the respondents were still in the process of establishing contacts with their families with the support of the social and legal workers in the shelters they are put up in. This process often takes long mostly because of incomplete address provided by the respondents.

Table 4.6: Contact with Family Members, if any, after the Incident (N=120)

Contact with Family Members	*Mode of Response*	
	Frequency	*Percentage*
• Yes	54	45.0
• No	66	55.0

Base: All Respondents who were Sexually Abused.

Table 4.6 depicts data regarding contact with family members. About 55.0% were still unable to establish liaison with their family while the rest (45.0%), seemingly fortunate ones had had some kind of involvement with their family. It is crucial to note here that one of the non-discriminated abused girl child decided not to have any sort of correspondence with the family because she did not wish to return to her previous non-salubrious milieu and lead a life of indignity, again.

Table 4.7 indicates that 31.7% of the respondents have their parents or other family members visiting them once every month. About 9.2% stated that their family members did not have a fixed schedule to visit them, and but did so occasionally while 4.2% stated that they had the opportunity to see their family members once or twice a year.

Table 4.7: Periodicity of Contact with Family Members (N=54)

Periodicity of Contact with Family Members	*Mode of Response*	
	Frequency	*Percentage*
• Once a month	38	31.7
• Once or twice a year	5	4.2
• No fixed time	11	9.2

Base: Respondents who have Contact with their Family Members.

Out of a total of 120 sexually abused girl children who were interacted with for the purpose of the study, only 58.3% perceived counselling to be beneficial while the rest 41.7% perceived it to be not that facilitative, as is discernable from Table 4.7a.

Table 4.7a: Perception of Sexually Abused Girl Children about Counselling Benefit (N=120)

Perception about Counselling	*Mode of Response*	
	Frequency	*Percentage*
• Beneficial	70	58.3
• Not beneficial	50	41.7

Base: All Respondents who were Sexually Abused.

SECTION II: MENTAL DISPOSITIONS OF THE SEXUALLY ABUSED GIRL CHILDREN

Beck Depression Inventory

In order to understand the level of depression of the sexually abused children and for comparison of the same with the normal population, i.e., school going girl children of the same age group who did not experience sexual abuse in life, 'Beck Depression Inventory'—a standardized psychological tool was used after local adaptation. The distributions of measures of central tendency and deviations have been provided in Table 4.8.

Table 4.8: Central Tendency Measures and Deviations of Data Collected Through Beck Depression Inventory

Sample Group	*Central Tendency Measures*			*Deviations*	
	Mean	*Median*	*Mode*	*SD*	*SK*
Sexually Abused (N=120)	24.20	24.00	33.00	10.30	0.301
Non-Sexually Abused (N=120)	16.50	15.00	18.00	8.20	0.646

Base: All Respondents.

The mean value of the sexually exploited children with regard to depression was found to be 24.20, which were more than the mean value of non-sexually abused with respect to the same attribute, i.e.,15.00. The standard deviation scores of the above mentioned dimension of the victim children was 10.30 while in the case of non-sexually abused it was 8.20.

On further exploration of the data according to the scoring rational of the tool, it was found out, that of the 120 sexually abused girl children, 38 (31.7%) were severelly depressed while another 45 (37.5%) were moderately depressed (Fig. 4.1).

Data with regard to level of depression among sexually abused and non-abused girl children have been provided in Table 4.8a.

A comparative picture of data with regard to level of depression among sexually abused and non-abused girl children have been drawn in Fig. 4.2 in order to facilitate visual presentation of the same data.

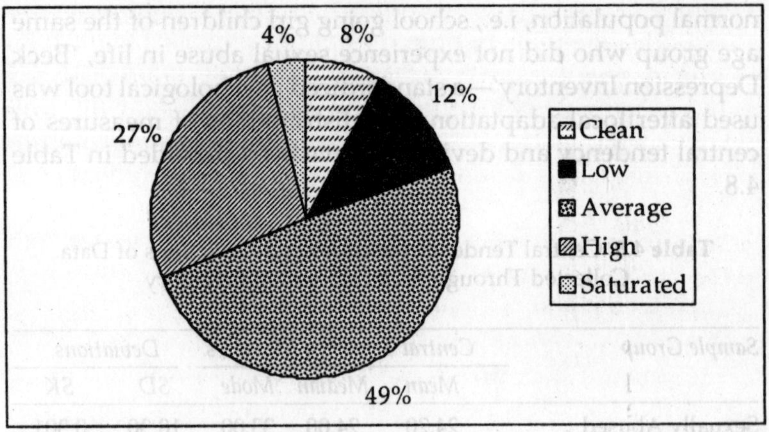

Fig. 4.1: Level of Depression among Sexually Abused Girl Children

Table 4.8a: Comparison of Depression of Sexually Abused and Non-Sexually Abused Girl Children

Sample Group	*Level of Depression (Score Range)*			
	Minimal (0-13)	*Mild (14-19)*	*Moderate (20-28)*	*Severe (29-63)*
Sexually Abused (N=120)	19 (15.83)	18 (15.00)	45 (37.50)	38 (31.67)
Non-Sexually Abused (N=120)	48 (40.00)	39 (32.50)	24 (20.00)	9 (7.50)

Base: All Respondents.

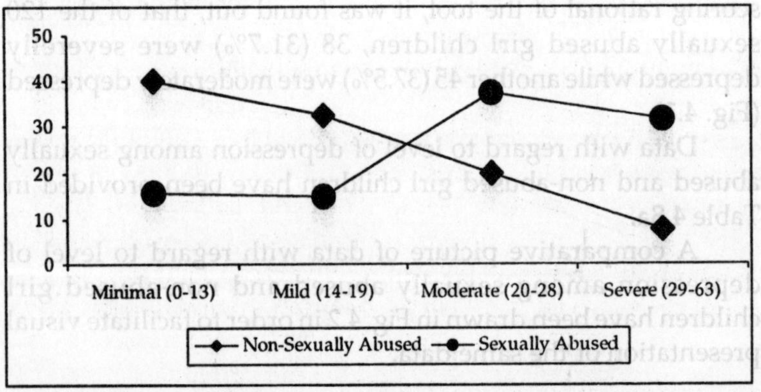

Fig. 4.2: Comparative Picture of Level of Depression among Sexually Abused and Non-Sexually Abused Girl Children

Further item-wise qualitative analysis of the data collected through Beck Depression Inventory revealed that the sexually abused girl children reported being mostly affected by pessimism, guilty feelings, self-dislike, worthlessness, concentration difficulty and loss of interest in sex.

The data were then processed properly for the verification of the first hypothesis i.e.,

> *'Level of depression of sexually abused and non-abused girl children differs significantly, irrespective of age group'.*

In order to verify the above hypothesis, 't'-test was applied for comparing the means and standard deviations as displayed in Table 4.9. It has been observed that 'p' value is less than 0.05 in case of depression.

Hence, at given 0.05 level of significance, it may be concluded that the first hypothesis, i.e., *'level of depression of sexually abused and non-abused girl children differs significantly, irrespective of age group'*, is retained.

It is evident from the data that sexually abused girl children were more prone to depression than their normal counterparts (Table 4.9).

Table 4.9: Comparison of Depression of Sexually Abused and Non-Sexually Abused Girl Children

Sample Group	*Sample Size*	*Mean*	*S.D.*	*t* (Test Statistic)*	*'p' Value*	*Level of Significance 'α'*
Sexually Abused	120	24.20	10.30	6.37	0.00	0.05
Non-Sexually Abused	120	16.50	8.20			

Base: All Respondents.

The data were then processed again for the verification of the second hypothesis, i.e.,

> *'Level of depression of sexually abused girl children aged between 13-15 years and 16-18 years differs significantly, irrespective of effectiveness of counselling as perceived by the subject'.*

To affirm the above hypothesis, 't'-test was applied for comparing the means and standard deviations as displayed in Table 4.10. It has been observed that 'p' value is more than 0.05 in case of the personality variable, viz., depression of different age groups namely 13-15 years and 16-18 years of sexually abused girl children.

Hence, it may be stated that the second hypothesis i.e., *'level of depression of sexually abused girl children aged between 13-15 years and 16-18 years differs significantly, irrespective of effectiveness of counselling as perceived by the subjects'*, has been rejected.

Table 4.10: Comparison of Depression of Different Age Groups of Sexually Abused Girl Children

Sample Group	*Sample Size*	*Mean*	*S.D.*	*t* (Test Statistic)*	*'p' Value*	*Level of Significance 'α'*
13-15 years	45	24.58	9.58	0.33	0.742	0 .05
16-18 years	75	23.90	10.80			

Base: All Respondents who were Sexually Abused.

For verification of third hypothesis as given below, the data were processed accordingly and are presented in Table 4.11.

'Level of depression of sexually abused girl children who received counselling and perceived it to be beneficial and those who did not receive counselling and/or perceived it to be not beneficial differs significantly, irrespective of age group'.

It has been observed that the sexually abused girl children who benefited from counselling and those who did not profit from the same differed significantly ($p< .05$) (Table 4.11). Hence, it may be stated that the third hypothesis i.e., *'level of depression of sexually abused girl children who received counselling and perceived it to be beneficial and those who did not receive counselling and/or did not perceive it to be beneficial differs significantly, irrespective of age group'*, is retained. From the mean score of depression, it may be stated that the victim children who gained considerably from adequate counselling possessed lower levels of depression as compared to their counterparts i.e., those who did not benefit as much from the same.

Table 4.11: Comparison of Depression of Sexually Abused Children who Benefited and/or Not Benefited from Counselling

Sample Group	*Sample Size*	*Mean*	*S.D.*	*t* (Test Statistic)*	*'p' Value*	*Level of Significance 'α'*
Benefited from counselling	70	20.14	9.43	-5.70	0.00	0 .05
Not benefited from counselling	50	29.82	8.77			

Base: All Respondents who were Sexually Abused.

Aggression

Data with regard to 'aggression' of the sexually abused children and for comparison of the same with the non-sexually abused girl children were collected by 'Aggression Scale'—a standardized psychological test that was further locally adapted. The distributions of measures of central tendency and deviations have been provided in Table 4.12.

Table 4.12: Central Tendency Measures and Deviations of Data Collected through Aggression Scale

Sample Group	*Central Tendency Measures*			*Deviations*	
	Mean	*Median*	*Mode*	*SD*	*SK*
Sexually Abused (N=120)	76.30	76.00	70.00	19.80	-4.9
Non-Sexually Abused (N=120)	66.20	64.50	69.00	17.00	0.363

Base: All Respondents.

The mean value of the sexually exploited children with regard to aggression was found to be 76.30, which was more than the mean value of non-sexually abused girl children with respect to the same attribute i.e., 66.20.The standard deviations of the scores of the above mentioned dimension of the [former group was 19.80 while in the case of later group it was 17.00].

From the scoring rational of the psychological tool, it was noted, that 5 (4.2%) of the sexually abused girl children belonged to saturated aggression category while more than one-forth (26.7%) were highly aggressive in nature (Fig. 4.3).

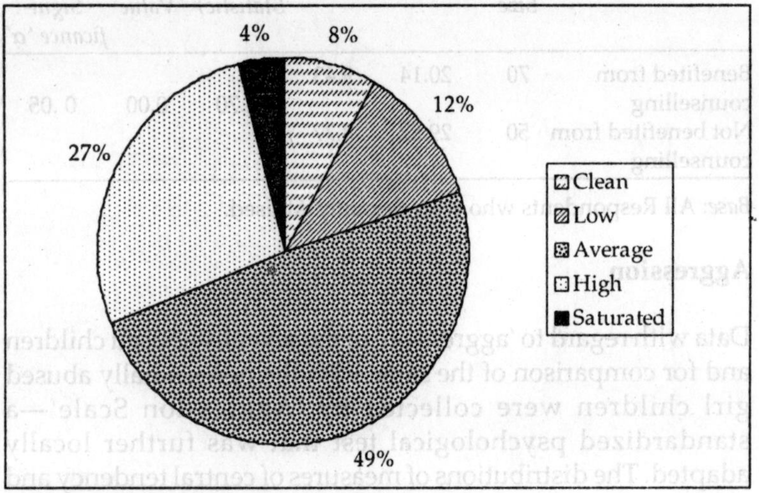

Fig. 4.3: Level of Aggression among Sexually Abused Girl Children

Data with regard to level of aggression among sexually abused and non-abused girl children have been provided in Table 4.12a.

A comparative picture of data with regard to level of aggression among sexually abused and non-abused girl children have also been drawn in Fig. 4.4 in order to facilitate visual presentation of the same data.

Further, item-wise qualitative analysis of the data of Aggression Scale revealed that sexually abused girl children reacted more aggressively to some of the statements of the study tool. For example,

'How much do I agree in tit for tat?'

'How much anger do I experience when people do not work according to me?'
'How much anger do I experience in arguments with other people?'
'How much anger do I experience when people do not consider my opinion?'
'How much anger do I experience when someone is late in returning my things?'

Table 4.12a: Comparison of Aggression of Sexually Abused and Non-abused Girl Children

Sample Group	*Level of Aggression (Score Range)*				
	Saturated (107 & above)	*High (90-106)*	*Average (61-89)*	*Low (46-60)*	*Clean (45 & below)*
Sexually Abused (N=120)	5 (4.17)	32 (26.67)	60 (50.00)	14 (11.67)	9 (7.50)
Non-Sexually Abused (N=120)	1 (.83)	16 (13.33)	56 (46.67)	35 (29.17)	12 (10.00)

Base: All Respondents

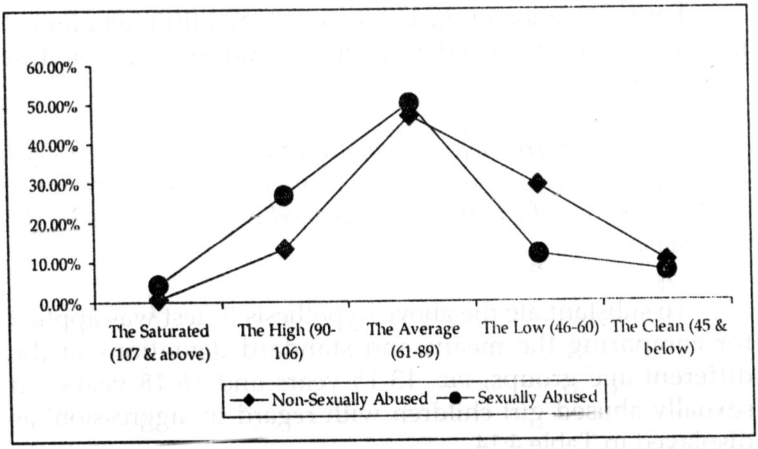

Fig. 4.4: Comparative Picture of Level of Aggression among Sexually Abused and Non-Sexually Abused Girl Children

The data were then processed properly for the verification of the fourth hypothesis, i.e.,

'Level of aggression of sexually abused and non-abused girl children differs significantly, irrespective of age group'.

Data in Table 4.13 shows that 'p' value is less than 0.05 in case of 'aggression'. Therefore, it may be stated that given a 0.05 level of significance, the fourth hypothesis i.e., *'level of aggression of sexually abused and non-abused girl children differs significantly, irrespective of age group'*, has been retained.

Table 4.13: Comparison of Aggression of Sexually Abused and Non-Sexually Abused Girl Children

Sample Group	*Sample Size*	*Mean*	*S.D.*	*t* (Test Statistic)*	*'p' Value*	*Level of Signi-ficance 'α'*
Sexually Abused	120	76.30	19.80	4.25	0.00	0 .05
Non-Sexually Abused	120	66.20	17.00			

Base: All Respondents.

For verification of the below mentioned fifth hypothesis, the data were processed accordingly and are presented in Table 4.14.

'Level of aggression of sexually abused girl children aged between 13-15 years and 16-18 years differs significantly, irrespective of effectiveness of counselling as perceived by the subjects'.

To substantiate the above hypothesis 't'-test was applied for comparing the means and standard deviations of the different age groups, *viz.* 13-15 years and 16-18 years old sexually abused girl children with regard to 'aggression' as displayed in Table 4.14.

From Table 4.14, it has been observed that aggression level remained the same more or less for both the age groups (p> .05). Therefore, the fifth hypothesis i.e., *'level of aggression of sexually abused girl children aged between 13-15 years and 16-18 years differs significantly, irrespective of effectiveness of counselling as perceived by the subjects'* is rejected. It is relevant to state here that the mean value of 13-15 years old sexually abused children were more than their 16-18 years old counterparts.

Table 4.14: Comparison of Aggression of Different Age Groups of Sexually Abused Girl Children

Sample Group	*Sample Size*	*Mean*	*S.D.*	*t* (Test Statistic)*	*'p' Value*	*Level of Significance 'α'*
13-15 Years	45	78.80	18.60	1.09	0.280	0 .05
16-18 Years	75	74.80	20.50			

Base: All Respondents who were Sexually Abused.

For verification of sixth hypothesis as given below, the data were processed accordingly and is presented in Table 4.15.

> *'Level of aggression of sexually abused girl children who received counselling and perceived it to be beneficial and those who did not receive counselling and/or did not perceive it to be beneficial differs significantly, irrespective of age group'.*

For confirmation of the above hypothesis, 't'-test was applied. It has been observed that sexually abused girl children who gained from counselling and who did not, differed significantly (p< .05) (Table 4.15). Hence, it may be stated that the sixth hypothesis is retained.

From the mean score of aggression, as seen below, it may be stated that the children who benefited from counselling and guidance were less aggressive in nature as compared with their counterparts, i.e., the children who did not profit from counselling.

Table 4.15: Comparison of Aggression of Sexually Abused Girl Children who Benefited and/or Not Benefited From Counselling

Sample Group	*Sample Size*	*Mean*	*S.D.*	*t* (Test Statistic)*	*'p' Value*	*Level of Significance 'α'*
Benefited from counselling	70	70.10	16.30	–4.35	0.00	0 .05
Not benefited from counselling	50	85.00	21.20			

Base: All Respondents who were Sexually Abused.

Emotional Adjustment

In order to understand the 'emotional adjustment' among the sexually abused children and for comparison of the same with the non-sexually abused girl children 'Social Adjustment Inventory' was used after local adaptation. There are two broad dimensions of the scale i.e.,

- Emotional Adjustment
- Social Adjustment

It is relevant to mention here that the scoring rational of emotional adjustment items and social adjustment items are diametrically opposite in nature. In case of emotional adjustment, the higher the score, the poorer the adjustment whereas lower score indicates good emotional adjustment. Again, in case of social adjustment higher scores suggest better social adjustment while lower score indicates just the opposite i.e., poor social adjustment. The distributions of measures of central tendency and deviations of Emotional Adjustment scores have been provided in Table 4.16.

Table 4.16: Central Tendency Measures and Deviations of Emotional Adjustment Scores

Sample Group	*Central Tendency Measures*			*Deviations*	
	Mean	*Median*	*Mode*	*SD*	*SK*
Sexually Abused (N=120)	47.10	47.00	47.00	5.50	–3.4
Non-Sexually Abused (N=120)	43.00	42.00	46.00	4.80	0.313

Base: All Respondents.

The mean value of the sexually exploited children with regard to emotional adjustment was found to be 47.10, which was more than the mean value of non-sexually abused girl children with respect to the same attribute, i.e., 43.00.The standard deviations of the scores of the above mentioned dimension of the abused children was 5.50 while in case of non-sexually abused children it was 4.80.

It has also been observed that out of 120 sexually abused girl children, 73 (60.8%) possessed poor emotional adjustment capability since their score lies above the Mid-Value. The mid point/mid-value was calculated using the formula Mid-Value= (Lower Limit + Upper Limit)/2, which in this case was 45 (Fig. 4.5).

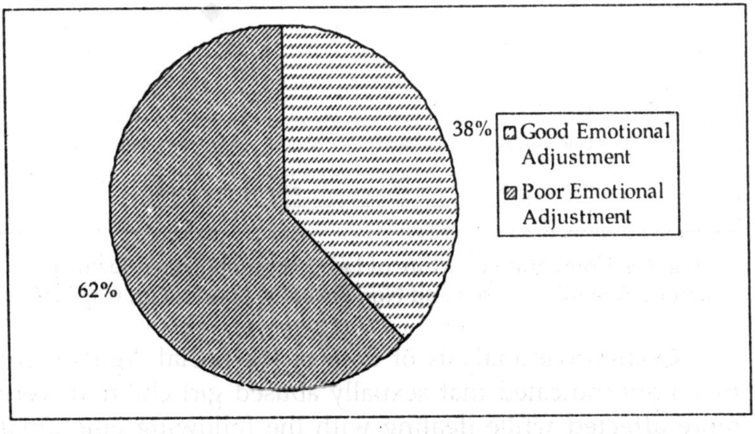

Fig. 4.5: Level of Emotional Adjustment among Sexually Abused Girl Children

Data with regard to emotional adjustment of sexually abused and non-abused girl children have been provided in Table 4.16a.

Table 4.16a: Comparison of Emotional Adjustment of Sexually Abused and Non-abused Girl Children

Sample Group	*Level of Emotional Adjustment (Score Range)*	
	Good Emotional Adjustment (30-45)	*Poor Emotional Adjustment (46-60)*
Sexually Abused (N=120)	47 (39.17)	73 (60.83)
Non-sexually Abused (N=120)	81 (67.50)	39 (32.50)

Base: All Respondents

A comparative picture of data with regard to level of emotional adjustment among sexually abused and non-abused girl children have been drawn in Fig. 4.6 in order to facilitate visual presentation of the same data.

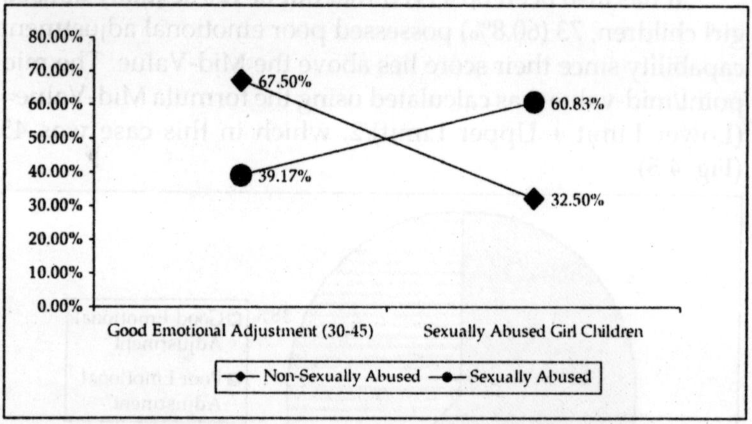

Fig. 4.6: Comparative Picture of Level of Emotional Adjustment among Sexually Abused and Non-Sexually Abused Girl Children

Qualitative analysis of data of the Social Adjustment Inventory indicated that sexually abused girl children were more affected while dealing with the following emotional statements:

'I am often baffled while facing either a minute or a tough problem'
'I feel jealous when anybody supercedes me'
'I get angry whenever things are not according to my wish'
'Often it occurs in my mind that nobody loves me'
'Often it occurs in my mind that it is better to die rather than remain alive'
'When anybody gets annoyed with me, I feel dejected'

The data were then processed properly for the verification of the seventh hypothesis, i.e.,

'Emotional adjustment of sexually abused and non-abused girl children differs significantly, irrespective of age group'.

To prove the above hypothesis, 't'-test was applied with a view to compare the means and standard deviations of sexually abused and non-sexually abused girl children with regard to 'emotional adjustment' variable as displayed in Table 4.17.

Data in Table 4.17 shows that 'p'-value is less than 0.05 in case of the 'emotional adjustment' variable. Therefore, it may be stated that at given 0.05 level of significance, the seventh hypothesis, i.e., *'emotional adjustment of sexually abused and non-abused girl children differs significantly, irrespective of age group'*, is retained.

Table 4.17: Comparison of Emotional Adjustment of Sexually Abused and Non-Sexually Abused Girl Children

Sample Group	*Sample Size*	*Mean*	*S.D.*	*t* (Test Statistic)*	*'p' Value*	*Level of Significance 'α'*
Sexually Abused	120	47.10	5.50	6.23	0.00	0 .05
Non-Sexually Abused	120	43.00	4.80			

Base: All Respondents.

For verification of eighth hypothesis as given below, the processed data have been presented in Table 4.18.

> *'Emotional adjustment of sexually abused girl children aged between 13-15 years and 16-18 years differs significantly, irrespective of effectiveness of counselling as perceived by the subjects '.*

To verify the above hypothesis, 't'-test was applied for comparing the means and standard deviations of the 13-15 years old and 16-18 years old sexually abused children with regard to 'emotional adjustment' as exhibited in Table 4.18.

Data in Table 4.18 reveals that sexually abused girl children whose age groups were varied did not differ significantly with respect to 'emotional adjustment' ($p > .05$). Hence, hypothesis number eight i.e., *'emotional adjustment of sexually abused girl children aged between 13-15 years and 16-18 years differs significantly, irrespective of effectiveness of counselling as perceived by the subjects'*, has been disapproved.

Since the mean score of 13-15 years old sexually abused girl children was marginally higher as compared to 16-18 years old sexually abused children, it may be inferred that the younger age group had poor emotional adjustment capability than that of their slightly older counterparts (Table 4.18).

Table 4.18: Comparison of Emotional Adjustment of Different Age Groups of Sexually Abused Girl Children

Sample Group	*Sample Size*	*Mean*	*S.D.*	*t* (Test Statistic)*	*'p' Value*	*Level of Significance 'α'*
13-15 Years	45	47.80	5.72	1.09	0.280	0 .05
16-18 Years	75	46.68	5.32			

Base: All Respondents who were Sexually Abused.

For verification of ninth hypothesis, data were presented in Table 4.19.

'Emotional adjustment of sexually abused girl children who received counselling and perceived it to be beneficial and those who did not receive counselling and/or did not perceive it to be beneficial differs significantly, irrespective of age group'.

To confirm the above hypothesis, 't'-test was applied for comparing the means and standard deviations of the sexually abused girl children who acknowledged counselling to be beneficial and those who did not, as displayed in Table 4.19.

It has been observed that 'p' value is less than 0.05 in case of the 'emotional adjustment' variable. Therefore, it may be stated that the ninth hypothesis is retained.

The sexually abused girl children who perceived counselling to be beneficial were emotionally more stable as compared to their counterparts.

Table 4.19: Comparison of Emotional Adjustment of Sexually Abused Girl Children who Benefited and/or Not Benefited from Counselling

Sample Group	*Sample Size*	*Mean*	*S.D.*	*t* (Test Statistic)*	*'p' Value*	*Level of Significance 'α'*
Benefited from counselling	70	45.24	4.66	–4.78	0.00	0 .05
Not benefited from counselling	50	49.70	5.52			

Base: All Respondents who were Sexually Abused.

Social Adjustment

Data pertaining to 'social adjustment' of the sexually abused girl children and for comparison of the same with the non-sexually abused girl children were collected by 'Social Adjustment Inventory'—a standardized psychological test. The distributions of measures of central tendency and deviations have been provided in Table 4.20.

Table 4.20: Central Tendency Measures and Deviations of Social Adjustment Scores

Sample Group	*Central Tendency Measures*			*Deviations*	
	Mean	*Median*	*Mode*	*SD*	*SK*
Sexually Abused (N=120)	49.90	51.00	54.00	5.90	–1.079
Non-Sexually Abused (N=120)	52.70	53.00	53.00	3.60	–3.7

Base: All Respondents.

The mean value of the sexually exploited children with regard to social adjustment was found to be 49.90, which was less than the mean value of non-sexually abused girl children with respect to the same attribute, i.e., 52.70.The standard deviations of the scores of the above mentioned dimension of the abused children was 5.90 while in the case of their counterparts it was 3.60.

On further analysis of the data, it was found that out of 120 sexually abused girl children, 25 (20.83%) did not possess good social adjustment capacity and their score lies below the Mid Value (Fig. 4.7).

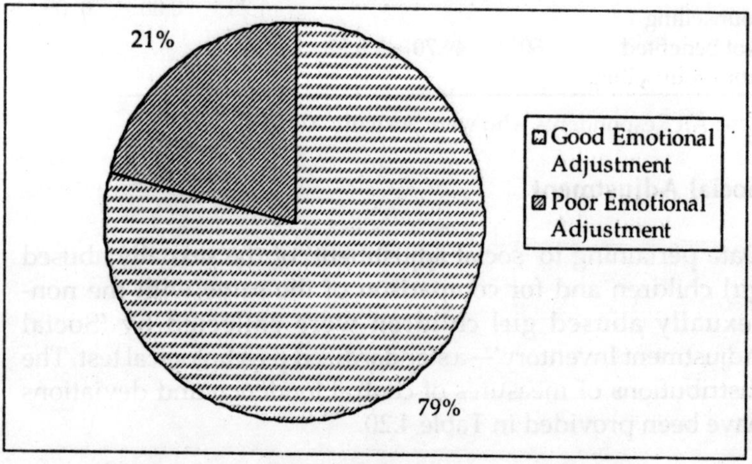

Fig. 4.7: Level of Social Adjustment among Sexually Abused Girl Children

Data with regard to level of social adjustment among sexually abused and non-abused girl children have been provided in Table 4.20a.

Table 4.20a: Comparison of Social Adjustment of Sexually Abused and Non-abused Girl Children

Sample Group	*Level of Emotional Adjustment (Score Range)*	
	Good Social Adjustment(46-60)	*Poor Social Adjustment (30-45)*
Sexually Abused (N=120)	95 (79.17)	25 (20.83)
Non-Sexually Abused (N=120)	115 (95.83)	5 (4.17)

Base: All Respondents.

A comparative picture of data with regard to social adjustment of sexually abused and non-abused girl children have been drawn in Fig. 4.8 in order to facilitate visual presentation of the same data.

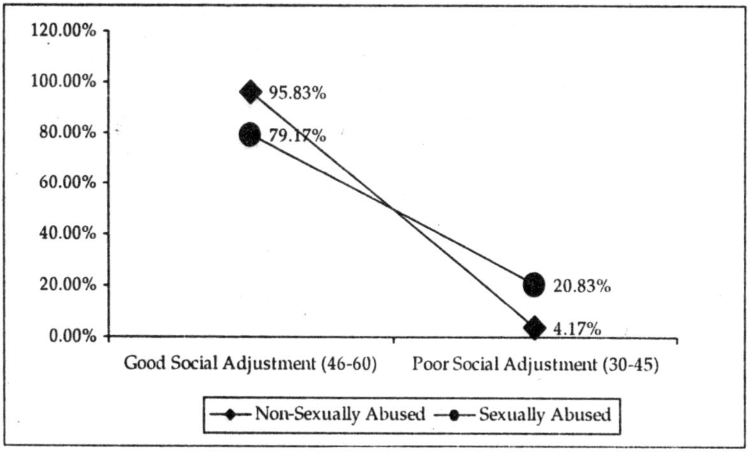

Fig. 4.8: Comparative Picture of Level of Social Adjustment among Sexually Abused and Non Abused Girl Children

The following statements produced a negative response with regard to social adjustment in case of the sexually abused girl children:

'It is better to make good friends than earn money'
I feel pleasure on seeing other's happiness or progress'
'I do not feel hesitation or fear even among unknown people'
'In my view, it is better to work in a group rather than individually'
'I don't have any problem mixing up with people'
'Before taking decisions, I certainly take other's suggestion'

The data were then processed for the verification of the tenth hypothesis i.e.,

'Social adjustment of sexually abused and non-abused girl children differs significantly, irrespective of age group'.

In order to substantiate the above hypothesis, 't'-test was applied for comparison of the means and standard deviations of sexually abused girl children and non-sexually abused girl children with regard to 'social adjustment' variable as displayed in Table 4.21.

Table 4.21 shows that the 'p' value is less than 0.05 and therefore, the tenth hypothesis, i.e., *'social adjustment of sexually abused and non-abused girl children differs significantly, irrespective of age group'*, has been retained, which indicates that sexually abused girl children possessed lesser capability of good social adjustment when compared with the non-sexually abused.

Table 4.21: Comparison of Social Adjustment of Sexually Abused and Non-Sexually Abused Girl Children

Sample Group	*Sample Size*	*Mean*	*S.D.*	*t* (Test Statistic)*	*'p' Value*	*Level of Significance 'α'*
Sexually Abused	120	49.90	5.90	4.44	0.00	0 .05
Non-Sexually Abused	120	52.70	3.60			

Base: All Respondents.

For verification of eleventh hypothesis, data have been presented in Table 4.22.

'Social adjustment of sexually abused girl children aged between 13-15 years and 16-18 years differs significantly, irrespective of effectiveness of counselling as perceived by the subjects'.

From Table 4.22, it has been observed that there was no significant difference in social adjustment between sexually abused children of different age groups (p>.05), though from the mean scores it can be derived that older sexually abused children are better socially adjusted *vis-à-vis* the younger ones. Therefore, the eleventh hypothesis, i.e., *'social adjustment of sexually abused girl children aged between 13-15 years and 16-18 years differs significantly, irrespective of effectiveness of counselling as perceived by the subjects'*, cannot be retained.

Table 4.22: Comparison of Social Adjustment of Different Age Groups of Sexually Abused Girl Children

Sample Group	*Sample Size*	*Mean*	*S.D.*	*t* (Test Statistic)*	*'p' Value*	*Level of Significance 'α'*
13-15 Years	45	49.27	5.30	-0.93	0.354	0 .05
16-18 Years	75	50.29	6.15			

Base: All Respondents who were Sexually Abused.

For verification of twelfth hypothesis as given below, the data have been presented in Table 4.23.

> *'Social adjustment of sexually abused girl children who received counselling and perceived to be beneficial and those who did not receive counselling and/or did not perceive it to be beneficial differs significantly, irrespective of age group'.*

To verify the above hypothesis, 't'-test was applied for comparing the means and standard deviations of the sexually abused children who perceived themselves to have been benefited from counselling and who did think differently as displayed in Table 4.23.

Table 4.23: Comparison of Social Adjustment of Sexually Abused Girl Children who Benefited and/or Not Benefited from Counselling

Sample Group	*Sample Size*	*Mean*	*S.D.*	*t* (Test Statistic)*	*'p' Value*	*Level of Significance 'α'*
Benefited from counselling	70	51.94	4.50	4.93	0.00	0 .05
Not benefited from counselling	50	47.06	6.35			

Base: All Respondents who were Sexually Abused.

It has been observed that the sexually abused children who sensed that counselling was beneficial for them possessed better social adjustment than those who did not ($p< .05$). Hence, the twelfth hypothesis, i.e., '*social adjustment of sexually abused girl children who received counselling and perceived it to be beneficial and those who did not receive counselling and/or did not perceive it to be beneficial differs significantly, irrespective of age group*', has been accepted.

Personality Dispositions

To understand the personality dispositions of the sexually abused girl children and for comparison of the same with the non-sexually abused girl children, Multi-dimensional Personality Inventory was used, which is a standardized psychological test which was further locally adapted. The distributions measures of central tendency and deviations have been provided in Table 4.24.

Table 4.24: Central Tendency Measures and Deviations of Data Collected Through Personality Dispositions Inventory (Sexually Abused 120 and Non-abused 120)

Sub-Scales	*Sample Group*	*Central Tendency Measures*			*Deviations*	
		Mean	*Median*	*Mode*	*SD*	*SK*
Introversion/ Extroversion	Sexually Abused	42.71	42.50	43.00	5.30	0.159
	Non-Sexually Abused	41.30	42.00	44.00	4.10	–2.3
Self-concept	Sexually Abused	40.83	40.50	41.00	4.51	0.612
	Non-Sexually Abused	42.23	43.00	43.00	6.07	–1.2
Dependence/ Independence	Sexually Abused	48.06	47.00	47.00	3.69	0.588
	Non-Sexually Abused	48.19	48.00	48.00	4.35	–7.3
Temperament	Sexually Abused	40.70	40.00	39.00	5.91	0.275
	Non-Sexually Abused	38.35	38.00	36.00	4.38	0.166
Anxiety	Sexually Abused	45.78	46.00	47.00	4.72	–1.00
	Non-Sexually Abused	42.27	42.00	42.00	4.71	–3.6

Base: All Respondents.

The mean value of the sexually exploited children with regard to personality variables like self-concept and independence/dependence was found to be 40.83 and 48.06 respectively which were less than the mean value of non-sexually abused children with respect to the same personality variables, i.e., 42.23 and 48.19 respectively. However, with regard to extroversion/introversion, it has been observed that the mean value of the sexually abused children was more (42.71) than that of their counterparts (41.30). In case of the fourth variable, i.e., temperament, the mean of the victim children was again found to be more (40.70) *vis-à-vis* the non-victim children (38.35). Therefore, it can be deduced that the former group possessed better temperament than the latter one. Similarly, for the last variable, the mean value of the sexually abused children was 45.78 whereas for the non-abused children it was 42.27, which indicates that the former group is more anxiety prone. The standard deviations of the scores of the said personality variables of the sexually abused children were 5.30, 4.51, 3.69, 5.91 and 4.72 while in case of non-abused children it was 4.10, 6.07, 4.35, 4.38 and 4.71 respectively.

The data also revealed that about 20 (17.0%) of the victim girls were introvert and only 2 (1.7%) were extrovert in nature. Majority of the victim girls (74.2%) possessed low self-concept. In case of the dimension of 'dependence-independence', about 107 (89.2%) of the respondents were perceived to be highly independent. Good temperament was a quality that the overwhelming number (83.3%) of victim girls was said to have possessed. Eleven (9.2%) of the victims reported high anxiety while only 3 (2.5%) of them were seen to suffer from low anxiety.

Qualitative analysis of data revealed that sexually abused girl children tended to be more introverted, possessed low self-concept and were more anxiety prone. The way the victim girls dealt with the following qualitative statements with regard to different personality variables were indicative of their personality:

Introversion-Extroversion

'I wish to work alone so that I may be able to do it according to myself'
'A work done in co-operation gets spoilt'
'I have a few friends because I have a suspicious nature'

Low score responses to the following statements were instrumental in sexually abused girl children having low self-concept.

Self-Concept

'I wish my friends should honour me'
'I give priority to the present and do not think about the future'
'I easily influence anyone with my personal appearance'
'I am an expert in finding solutions to problems'

Scoring more in the below mentioned items also demonstrate the respondents anxious nature.

Anxiety

'Everybody believes that I am not capable of doing anything'
'My friends are jealous of me'
'I worry that everyone gets angry with me'

The data were then processed properly for the verification of the thirteenth hypothesis i.e.,

'Personality disposition of sexually abused and non-abused girl children differs significantly, irrespective of age group'.

To verify the above hypothesis 't'-test was applied for comparing the means and standard deviations as displayed in Table 4.25. It has been observed that 'p' value is less than 0.05 in case of all (extroversion/introversion, self-concept, temperament and anxiety) but one of the personality variables, viz., independence/dependence.

Hence, it may be stated that thirteenth hypothesis, i.e., *'personality dispositions of sexually abused and non-abused girl children differs significantly, irrespective of age group'*, cannot be retained.

Conclusively, it may be stated that sexually abused girl children were more introvert, possess low self-concept and more anxious than their normal counterparts with respect to the said personality variables (Table 4.25). On the other hand, it can be said that the desire to stand up on their own feet and gain financial independence, after silently suffering so much, is equally realized by them as with their non-victim counterparts.

Table 4.25: Comparison of Sub-scales of Personality Dispositions of Sexually Abused and Non-Sexually Abused Girl Children

Sub-scales	*Sample Group*	*Sample Size*	*Mean*	*S.D.*	*t* (Test Statistic)*	*'p' Value*	*Level of Significance 'α'*
Introversion/ Extroversion	Sexually Abused	120	42.71	5.30	2.3	0.022	0.05
	Non-Sexually Abused	120	41.30	4.10			
Self-concept	Sexually Abused	120	40.83	4.51	-2.03	0.044	0.05
	Non-Sexually Abused	120	42.23	6.07			
Dependence/ Independence	Sexually Abused	120	48.06	3.69	-0.26	0.798	0.05
	Non-Sexually Abused	120	48.19	4.35			
Temperament	Sexually Abused	120	40.70	5.91	3.5	0.001	0.05
	Non-Sexually Abused	120	38.35	4.38			
Anxiety	Sexually Abused	120	45.78	4.72	5.77	0.000	0.05
	Non-Sexually Abused	120	42.27	4.71			

Base: All Respondents.

The data were then processed again for the verification of the fourteenth hypothesis, i.e.,

'Personality disposition of sexually abused girl children aged between 13-15 years and 16-18 years differs significantly, irrespective of effectiveness of counselling as perceived by the subjects'.

From the Table 4.26, it has been observed that 'p' value is more than 0.05 in case of all the personality variables, viz., extroversion/introversion, self-concept, independence/dependence, temperament and anxiety of sexually abused girl children of dissimilar age group.

Hence, it may be stated that fourteenth hypothesis, i.e., *'personality disposition of sexually abused girl children aged between 13-15 years and 16-18 years differs significantly, irrespective of effectiveness of counselling as perceived by the subjects'*, has been rejected.

However, it has been observed that the mean scores for older sexually abused girl children were greater in case of all the personality variables as compared with the younger ones.

Sexually abused girl children of 16-18 years old seemed to be more independent as well as more anxious about their future and better tempered than their younger similitude. Both the population possessed quite low self-concepts.

Table 4.26: Comparison of Sub-scales of Personality Dispositions of Different Age Group of Sexually Abused Girl Children

Sub-scales	*Sample Group*	*Sample Size*	*Mean*	*S.D.*	*t* (Test Statistic)*	*'p' Value*	*Level of Significance 'α'*
Introversion/ Extroversion	13-15	45	42.51	4.97	-0.31	0.754	0.05
	16-18	75	42.83	5.52			
Self-concept	13-15	45	40.73	4.51	-0.19	0.852	0.05
	16-18	75	40.89	4.54			
Dependence/ Independence	13-15	45	47.22	3.44	-1.94	0.054	0.05
	16-18	75	48.56	3.77			
Temperament	13-15	45	39.51	5.15	-1.72	0.088	0.05
	16-18	75	41.41	6.25			
Anxiety	13-15	45	45.51	5.35	-0.49	0.627	0.05
	16-18	75	45.95	4.33			

Base: All Respondents who were Sexually Abused.

For verification of the fifteenth and final hypothesis as stated below, data were processed accordingly and have been provided in Table 4.27.

Table 4.27: Comparison of Sub-scales of Personality Dispositions of Sexually Abused Girl Children who Benefited and/or Not Benefited from Counselling

Sub-scales	*Sample Group*	*Sample Size*	*Mean*	*S.D.*	*t* (Test Statistic)*	*'p' Value*	*Level of Significance 'α'*
Introversion/ Extroversion	Benefited from counselling	70	42.63	4.42	-0.19	0.846	0.05
	Not benefited from counselling	50	42.82	6.39			
Self-concept	Benefited from counseling	70	41.97	4.61	3.41	0.001	0.05
	Not benefited from counselling	50	39.24	3.88			
Dependence/ Independence	Benefited from counselling	70	48.34	3.12	1.00	0.320	0.05
	Not benefited from counselling	50	47.66	4.37			
Temperament	Benefited from counselling	70	40.73	5.23	0.06	0.950	0.05
	Not benefited from counselling	50	40.66	6.80			
Anxiety	Benefited from counselling	70	45.40	4.68	-1.05	0.295	0.05
	Not benefited from counselling	50	46.32	4.78			

Base: All Respondents who were Sexually Abused.

'Personality disposition of sexually abused girl children who received counselling and perceived it to be beneficial and those who did not receive counselling and/or did not perceive it to be beneficial differs significantly, irrespective of age group'.

It has been observed that 'p' value of two categories of sexually abused girl children, i.e., those who profited from counselling and those who did not, were more than 0.05 in case of all (viz. extroversion/introversion, independence/dependence, temperament and anxiety) but one the personality variable, i.e., self-concept (Table 4.27).

Hence, it may be stated that the last hypothesis i.e., *'personality disposition of sexually abused girl children who received counselling and perceive it to be beneficial and those who did not receive counselling and/or did not perceive it to be beneficial differs significantly, irrespective of age group'*, has been rejected.

The mean score was greater with regard to self-concept in case of sexually abused girl children who seemed to benefit from counselling as likened to sexually abused girl children who did not perceive counselling to be helpful in their overall development. It means that the group, which benefited from counselling possessed higher self-concept in comparison to those who did not profit from counselling. It can also be deduced from the above mentioned data that the first category of sexually abused children, as seen by their mean scores, were marginally more independent, possessed better temperament and were less anxious than those of their counterparts.

SECTION III: FUTURE ASPIRATION, SKILL BUILDING AND PERCEPTION ABOUT THE HOME

From the below mentioned Table 4.28, it may be stated that about 46.7% of the sexually abused children had other ideas of gaining financial independence, like being a farmer, domestic assistant, teacher or an ayah. About 24.2% of the sexually abused children wanted to receive some kind of vocational training like sewing, block printing, batik, stained glass, candle making in the shelters they are put up in to stand on their own feet. About 26.7% had absolutely no idea as to what they want for themselves in the future while 2.5% wanted to emulate the counsellors and other home employees and become a social worker.

Table 4.28: Future Aspiration of the Sexually Abused Girl Children (N=120)

What is your future aspiration	*Mode of Response*	
	Frequency	*Percentage*
• Want to be a social worker	3	2.5
• Want to receive meaningful vocational training and do something	29	24.2
• No idea	32	26.7
• Others (farmer, maid, engaging in ayah and so on)	56	46.7

Base: All Respondents who were Sexually Abused

Table 4.29 clearly indicates that a whopping majority of 75.8% of the inmates of these shelters had some experience in various vocational training programmes or had been undergoing them while 24.2% did not acquire any vocational skill.

Table 4.29: Vocational Training Knowledge of the Sexually Abused Girl Children (N=120)

Whether attended any vocational training or currently undergoing any vocational training	*Mode of Response*	
	Frequency	*Percentage*
• Yes	91	75.8
• No	29	24.2

Base: All Respondents who were Sexually Abused.

As per Table 4.30, most of the sexually abused children had attended and acquired knowledge about more than one vocational training which included block printing, sewing, batik, stained glass, mushroom harvesting, candle making, jute work etc.

Table 4.30: Vocational Training Received by the Sexually Abused Girl Children (Multiple Response) {N=91}

What training have you attended or are attending	*Mode of Response*	
	Frequency	*Percentage*
• Printing	20	16.7
• Sewing	33	27.5
• Others	48	40.0

Base: Respondents who attended/are attending vocational training.

About 65.0% of the victim girls were seen to be delighted to be at a secure shelter and away from the traumatic environment while 35.0% did not seem to be enjoying their apparently transient halt, according to Table 4.31.

Table 4.31: Perception of the Sexually Abused Children about Home (N=120)

Are you enjoying your stay in this home	*Mode of Response*	
	Frequency	*Percentage*
• Yes	78	65.0
• No	42	35.0

Base: All Respondents who were Sexually Abused

SECTION IV: PERCEPTION OF COUNSELLORS IN DEALING WITH SEXUALLY ABUSED CHILDREN

As stated earlier, the term 'Counselling' refers to a relationship between a counsellor and a person looking for help with a problem. It also means work with individuals and with relationships, which may be developmental, crisis support, psychotherapeutic, guiding or problem solving.

The counselor helps one to understand one's self and her problems better. Subsequently, this understanding can be utilized to make better choices in life. One should perceive, requiring the help of a counselor not as a weakness, but as an intelligent way to solve a problem.

A counsellor can help a victim of child sexual abuse in various ways, some of them being:

(1) Help take the parent and the child through the painful details of the abuse one small step at a time, so the whole experience is easier to handle and less frightening.
(2) She can also aid the child and her family in understanding the complex and confusing emotions while the sexual abuse took place and after it had ended.
(3) Help the child and her parents to understand why the abuse happened and how neither of the parties should be blamed for it.
(4) Assist the child to become free from the effects of the past so she can enjoy happier lives in the future.

To address the concerns and be aware of the suggestions of the mental health professionals regarding child sexual abuse, seven available counsellors from different homes were asked to respond to a semi-structured questionnaire. Most of them held a post-graduate degree in psychology and had about two to five years of work experience in this field. All of them mentioned to having received some training in counselling. Most of the counsellors stated that the periodicity of counselling of inmates was roughly once a week and that individual file for each case are maintained for them to record their feedbacks. Majority of them also averred that they found positive changes in the sexually abused girl children after counselling. Mental health professionals are also aware that the lack of psychological test tools for the victims are an impediment in further improvement of their overall personality.

Some problems that the professionals in various shelters confronted while counselling were lack of confidential space, authority not being so keen on counselling, no system for rendering feedbacks, no action is taken after giving feedback, no psychological tests available for the inmates and the fact that the skeletal counselling staff have to multitask most of the time which affords them less time for counselling.

All the shelters visited had an arrangement for vocational training programmes ranging from block printing, knitting, embroidery, batik, mushroom harvesting to stained glass painting, tailoring, book binding, jute work, candle making, soft toys etc.

The counsellors have implemented group activities in most of the homes, to facilitate more social interaction among the children, like, HIV support groups, advocacy groups, issue addressal groups, prefect groups, music therapy groups and conflict resolution groups.

The psychological problems, which affect the children, as perceived by the professionals were lack of self-confidence, low self-esteem, depression, suicidal tendencies, self-image distortion, poor adjustment capability, non-trusting nature, attention disorder, identity crisis, withdrawal, mood fluctuation and high aggression levels.

Medical services were available in most of the shelters. Weekly check-up by a general practitioner along with psychiatric check up and the services of a dermatologist were also available.

Most of the counsellors felt that achievement of financial independence was the future aspiration of the majority of the sexually abused children.

The suggestions offered by seven counsellors to render better psychological, social and other services to the sexually abused children were as follows—

(1) Awareness generation programme in the communities about sexual abuse and its impact,
(2) Construction of support groups at different levels,
(3) Involvement of local youth groups in sensitizing the issue,
(4) Lobbying with the Government to provide more job opportunities to the victim girls,
(5) Training for law enforcement authorities on the issue, and
(6) Family counselling even after the child has been rehabilitated.

5

Discussion, Conclusion and Recommendation

There seems to be a dramatic rise world-wide in the incidence of child sexual abuse/exploitation due to various factors including globalization and free trade. Child pornography, juvenile prostitution and trafficking in children for sexual purposes have emerged as significant problems on the national, regional, and international stages (Barr, 1996; Botti, 2000; Caldwell et al., 1997; Ennew, 1986; Hughes and Roche, 1999; Ireland, 1993; Jaffe and Rosen, 1996; Lederer, 2001; Munir and Yasin, 1997). So, too, has sex tourism (Hughes and Roche, 1999; Pettman, 1997), including child sex tourism (Gray, 2000; Klain, 1999; Seabrook, 1997).

Statistics show that child sexual abuse occurs at an alarming rate.At least one in five girls and one in ten to twenty boys will be sexually abused at some point in their childhood, according to most reliable studies of child sexual abuse in the United States (Finkelhor, D. 1994). The enormity of the child sexual abuse problem has been described as 'one of the most discouraging discoveries of our era' (Finkelhor 1990:394).

In India, child trafficking for commercial sexual exploitation has become a serious social problem. In the present study, out of a total 120 sexually abused girl children, more than half were trafficked children who were subjected to sexual, physical and emotional abuse through false promises and pretensions (Deb, 2002; Deb 2005; Deb et al., 2005; Chatterjee et al., 2006).

Although, its incidence, nature and magnitude is more and/or grave in some of the developing countries, in India, too, child sexual abuse has been an age-old social and health problem. Though, there exists no population based data on the nature and magnitude of the problem of child sexual abuse in India, micro study indicates that both male and female children remain the victims of child sexual abuse for a number of reasons like poverty, demand for children as sexual commodities, myths and misconception attached with sexually transmitted diseases and lack of adequate supervision by parents. In India, till the begining of 21st century, there existed a strong social stigma attached to this issue, which inhibited the parents in reporting the abused cases to the police or other equally powerful and competent authorities. The psychological, medical and rehabilitation support services for the sexually abused children still continue to be inadequate and pitiable. Hence, majority of the sexually abused children live with the psychological trauma of the abuse lifelong, which affects their interpersonal relationship, personality and career development (Deb et al., 2005). Though, lots of studies (Collin-Vezina and Cyr, 2003; Fergusson et al., 1996; Mullen et al., 1993) have been conducted on different dimensions of the same problem in the industrial countries, very few studies attempted to address the issue in India specially the impact of sexual abuse on mental health.

Given the above background, necessity was felt to investigate the issue with a view to understanding the impact of sexual abuse on mental disposition of girl children. There were altogether nine specific objectives of the study as stated in Chapter 2.

In order to achieve the objectives of the present study, a group of 120 sexually abused children between 13-18 years were covered from four rehabilitation homes, which included one Government home and three non-governmental shelters located in and around Kolkata, India and they were selected following purposive sampling method. For comparison of the data of sexually abused children with non-sexually abused girl children an equal number of sample were covered in the study from four schools located in and around the homes and the population was matched in terms of age and gender. Three basic screening questions were asked to the normal population to select the non-sexually abused children for comparison. In addition, to the screening tool, six questionnaires were used for achieving the nine specific objectives. Out of six, two were semi-structured questionnaires and rest four was standardized psychological tests. The psychological tests were used after local adaptation.

Majority (62.5%) of the sample covered in the study belonged to 16-18 years age group and were either illiterate and/or studied up to primary level. An overwhelming number of them were single (80.0%) and had more than two siblings (67.5%), which suggests that parents tend to be less concerned about family planning and in turn are generally unable to provide the basic amenities to their children and consequently jeopardize their proper development by placing them in vulnerable situations. It is relevant to mention here that especially in the rural areas in our country, opting for a large family is a common practice among poor people since they believe that the children will look after and financially support them in their old age. Unfortunately, they tend to overlook the educational aspect along with the welfare of the children by following this path.

Nuclear families, with no stand in support, are found to be more vulnerable especially in case of girl children with regard to sexual abuse as indicated in the earlier chapter. An overwhelming (93.3%) number of the sexually abused children came from nuclear families. Parental educational and occupational background and income of the family are found to be directly related to the problem. It is also seen that the children of families residing in the rural areas are more prone to sexual abuse.

It is evident from the present study that the girl child becomes more vulnerable to sexual abuse after attaining the stage of puberty. Although, in more than half of the cases strangers maltreated the child, a large number of children were sexually abused by relatives (29.2%).

So far as situation of abuse is concerned, findings reveal that about one-fifth (24.2%) were abused when nobody was at home while the vast majority (73.3%) of them were abused outside their secure surroundings primarily after they were lured with better future prospects and consequently sold to the brothels.

More than half of the sample were abused thrice and above and eventually were forced to work as child sex workers/ prostitutes or bar girls/dancers. At the same time, a large number of children (30.8%) were abused once by people who they were acquainted with, either while dwelling with immediate family or while working as a domestic help.

Although data shows that 98.3% were examined by the doctor and received medical treatment, it should be noted here, that this did not happen immediately after the sexual abuse. The medical care and supervision was rendered to them only after they were rescued from their life of ignominy and disgrace and sent to rehabilitation homes.

As stated earlier, the number of sexual abuse cases that gets reported, ultimately, to either the law enforcement authorities such as the police or non-governmental organizations is pathetic in Kolkata as indicated by the data. Perceived harassment, threat by the perpetrators and strong social stigma and thereby fear of losing social relationships, dignity and/or getting ostracized by the society, are the factors, which deter the victim and their families to report the crime to the respective authority.

Coming to the issue of reaction of family members to the incident of abuse, attitude of 64/120 family members could be ascertained after they became cognizant of the event. Findings reveal a positive picture, i.e., non-discriminatory attitude of family members towards victim girls.

The reactions of the family members, who were intimated about the condition of the girls and were made aware of their current geographical location, were mostly non-discriminatory, as stated above. Only a minority (7.5%) of them possessed discriminatory attitude towards their own children. Out of the 120 girls interviewed for the study, the families of about 56 of them could still not be traced and consequently the attitude of their family members regarding the heinous incident could not be gauged. The reason for lack of this data were mostly incomplete and wrong address provided by the girls to the home authorities, inability to furnish their address at all and also the geographical distance which complicated matters a bit more, since some of the girls were procured for this kind of business and/or job from neighbouring countries like Bangladesh, Nepal etc.

More than half (55.0%) of the respondents did not have any communication with their families while about 54 of the 120 girl children selected for the study has had some involvement with their parents and siblings. It is of importance to mention here that one of the girls, interviewed, did not want to have any correspondence with her family though her parents did not possess a negative attitude towards her because she felt that the shelter she was residing has afforded her much more security and equipped with better facilities to improve herself.

Majority of the family members, when they came to know the whereabouts of their children (latest status), wanted to take them back but the child did not want to return to the poor environment because of earlier awful experiences (e.g., lack of minimum basic facilities). The parents, who maintain contact or visit their children, try to do so at least once a month. There is a system of parents meeting with the authorities of rehabilitation homes for positive facilitation of the rehabilitation process.

Most of the sexually abused children, who were covered in the study, from different rehabilitation homes, had had the opportunity to undergo counselling to overcome psychological stress and trauma. It's relevant to state here that there exists a lack of trained counselors in Kolkata and that is specifically the reason that only three rehabilitation homes had minimal in-house counselling staff while one had an arrangement of referral counselling, of the 4 shelters that were covered. More than half (58.3%) reported counselling to be of value in overcoming psychological crisis and/or trauma.

Mental Disposition

Depression

The worst after effects of sexual abuse is psychological trauma and/or depression (Brayden et al., 1995; Dinwiddie et al., 2000; Finkelhor and Browne, 1985; Beitchman et al., 1992; Deb et al.,

2005). Findings of the present study on the Kolkata sample corroborate the previous study findings as mentioned above. It has been observed that almost half of the sexually abused children were above the median value in depression scale, which indicates that they are highly depressed. Further analysis highlighted the specific areas of depression in case of the present study sample (e.g., pessimism, guilty feelings, self-dislike, worthlessness, concentration difficulty and loss of interest in sex).

An attempt was also made to understand the impact of sexual abuse on children of two different age groups (viz. 13-15 years and 16-18 years) with respect to depression. As revealed, children of these two age groups are equally affected by the problem ($p > .05$).

Psychological intervention (namely counselling) has a significant role in improving the status of mental health as has been demonstrated by many researches worldwide. It should be noted, however, that the quality of counselling is of utmost importance in minimizing the effects of sexual abuse on mental health. In order to verify this issue, data were further segregated and an attempt was made to understand the benefits of counselling. Findings disclose that the children who perceived counselling to be beneficial are less depressed as compared to their counterparts (i.e. those who did not perceive counselling to be beneficial) and both the groups differed significantly at 0.05 level.

Aggression

So far as the second prime psychological factor considered in the study, i.e., aggression, findings show that sexually abused girl children are more aggressive than that of normal children ($p < .05$). Further analysis of qualitative data indicates that the main areas of aggression, which were by and large positively responded to, are as follows:

> *'How much do I agree in tit for tat'*
>
> *'How much anger do I experience when people do not work according to me'*

'How much anger do I experience in arguments with other people'
'How much anger do I experience when people do not consider my opinion'
'How much anger do I experience when someone is late in returning my things'

No significant difference (p>.05) was observed in age-wise comparison of abused children with respect to aggression, which indicates that, the incidence of sexual abuse and/or unpleasant experiences in life equally affect the children of the two stated age groups (namely 13-15 years and 16-18 years).

Effective counselling is found to be beneficial for appeasing and pacifying the aggressive propensity of sexually abused children (p<. 05).

Emotional and Social Adjustment

Previous study findings (Burnam et al., 1988; Ernst et al., 1993; Fromuth, 1983; Mullen et al., 1996; Roesler and McKenzie, 1994; Finkelhor et al., 1990; Conte and Schuerman, 1987) indicate that adjustment pattern of sexually abused children is also equally affected by abuse. The present study also affirms and validates the same fact about the Kolkata sample, i.e., both emotional and social adjustment of sexually abused children was impacted, in case of majority of the sample. In this regard, they differed from non-sexually abused girl children (p<. 05) but no significant difference was obtained in the age-wise sample selection (p>.05). Counselling in the rehabilitation homes helped the children to become more adjustable especially in case of children who perceived it to be beneficial. It is relevant to mention here that all the counselors are not equally competent in dealing with sensitive issues. Moreover, there is a want of opportunity for professional training for counsellors. It could be mentioned here that children of homes with requisite educational background benefited more from interactive sessions with adequately trained councillors than those who were not fortunate enough to have expert guidance (p<.05).

Personality Disposition

Multi-dimensional Personality Inventory, which was locally adapted, explored five personality dimensions/dispositions of the sexually abused children and the data were then compared with the normal sample. It has been observed that out of the five dimensions (viz. introversion-extroversion, self-concept, dependence-independence, temperament and anxiety), they differed significantly ($p < .05$) in four of them, namely introversion-extroversion, self-concept (Brayden et al., 1995; Roosa et al., 1999), temperament and anxiety (McLeer et al., 1998; Mullen et al., 1993) while there was an insignificant difference among sexually abused and non-sexually abused girl children with respect to dependence-independence. It indicates that crude reality teaches them to live independently in the face of crisis and uncertainty. In other words, it can be said, that they recognize the importance of financial independence in their life ($p > .05$). Similarly, with regard to another dimension, i.e., temperament, it can be pointed out that perhaps overtly, they seek to sustain a healthy and smooth relationship with the authorities and their peers and cope up with the perceived unfavourable situations taciturnly since there are is no stand in support.

On the contrary, in the case of aggression as revealed by the Aggression Scale, sexually abused girl children differed significantly from non-sexually abused girl children, i.e., the sexually abused girl children seemed to have more covert aggression which might get exposed in case of adverse and untoward situations as revealed by Table 4.13. Interestingly, no significant difference was observed between the stated two age groups (13-15 years and 16-18 years) of the experimental sample with respect to the five personality dimensions likewise the other psychological parameters as measured by Beck Depression Inventory, Aggression Scale and Social Adjustment Inventory.

Respondents who perceived counselling to be beneficial differed with those who did not recognize this particular kind of intervention to be of help in only one of the five personality dimensions, viz., self-concept. The other dimensions, namely introversion-extroversion, dependence-independence, temperament and anxiety did not yield any significant difference between the two above-mentioned samples. This issue requires further investigation.

Future Aspiration

Each and every study should have some pragmatic application. In the present study an attempt was also made to understand the future aspiration of the children and their skill for designing effective rehabilitation programme. The basic understânding was to unearth the interest of the subject and design future interest and skill oriented vocational programmes accordingly that provides them with maximum benefit. Regarding this issue, a good number of them (24.2%) expressed their interest in receiving vocational training, which will enable them to become economically independent. On the other hand, a large number of them expressed their interest for some basic, immediate mode of earning for survival (46.7%) while some of them had no such vision about their future (26.7%).

It was also revealed that a large number of them (75.8%) received some sort of arranged vocational training in the regular programme, which was not perceived by them as being immediately beneficial in terms of earning but would ultimately aid them in the coming future to obtain jobs.

Finally, the overall perceptions of more than two-thirds of the sample about rehabilitation homes were positive which is a good indication of activities of rehabilitation homes although some of them may lack specialized training programmes.

Conclusion

In fine, it may be stated that a large number of sexually abused children in Kolkata have been suffering from depression and high aggression. They also possess poor emotional and social adjustment capability and experience problems in four personality dimensions out of the five that were measured and they differed significantly from the non-sexually abused children on the above-mentioned variables. It is clear from the present study that mental health, (specifically the variables considered in the present study) of sexually abused girl children of different age groups is equally affected because of incidence of abuse. Psychological intervention, more specifically counselling, was found to be beneficial in majority of the cases in improving the mental health condition of the sexually abused girls. The findings of the present study revealed another interesting characteristic of the victims, i.e., although the mistreated children differed significantly from non-sexually abused girl children with respect to aggression, their temperament was found to be better than their normal counterparts.

It is relevant to mention here that significant progress has been achieved in the field of child sexual abuse in the last 10 years, mostly in the developed countries. However, in developing countries like India, little progress has been made in identification, investigation, intervention, and treatment of sexually abused children. Sexual abuse cases, perhaps even more than other types of maltreatment, require multi-disciplinary, multiagency collaboration in order to address the issue professionally for the interest of the victim and victim's family. However, there still exists a problem in reporting of incidences of sexual abuse to respective authorities because of social stigma and harassment.

Despite the 'marginal' progress, many cases still go undetected in our country. Further, the investigative techniques do not guarantee all victimized children will disclose, and many cases are still inadequately investigated. Moreover, in too many instances children's disclosures are met with skepticism, and the conscientious work of professionals acting on their behalf is challenged. In a country like ours, even when an incident of such magnitude eventually gets reported to the law enforcement authorities, the deterrents for proper justice are many. Most of the police stations do not have confidential space to carry interviews with the child. Moreover, for want of female police officials are a huge impediment in investigating and recording of the incidence. Sometimes, the children are coerced to delineate the traumatic incident over and again while facing the prospect of lack of guarantee of confidentiality of the information they render. This subsequently, makes them more vulnerable in the hands of the perpetrators who had abused them in the first place. Most importantly, the greatest hindrance to the child's disclosure comes from her immediate family. Sexual abuse being perceived as it is, family members find it difficult to acknowledge the incident and accept the child, extending unconditional affection and cooperation, henceforth.

Although in part professional shortcomings relate to the fact that one's ability to address sexual abuse is still developing, they are largely the outcome of lack of adequate resources. Caseloads for staff in the shelters are too large; their training is sometimes inadequate and stresses of the job are too high. Also, the lack of privacy, inaction after giving feedback and multitasking are the handicaps that the professionals confront. There is a deficiency of mental health professionals who can provide treatment to families and individuals involved in sexual abuse, and also lack of fund is a constraint in producing skilled professionals. Finally, the funding for research to help us better understand sexual abuse and how to address it is in very short supply.

Nevertheless, professionals in the field of child sexual abuse strive to educate the public and other professionals about this problem and its pervasive effects as was observed while interacting with the mental health professionals in different shelters.

It is relevant to mention here that since the inception, MIDSW, an NGO based in Kolkata, organized a number of multi-disciplinary training programmes funded by the International Society for Prevention of Child Abuse and Neglect (ISPCAN) and Oak Foundation through ISPCAN for the professionals like police, doctors and NGO personnel in Kolkata with a view to sensitizing them about the nature and magnitude of child abuse and neglect in India, especially child sexual abuse and to improve their skills for diagnosis and effective intervention. Training programmes helped to develop a good number of trained resource persons for conducting similar training for other professionals for combating child abuse and neglect in Koikata. In one such training programme for the doctors with different specializations, they developed a Child Protection Protocol for the Medical Colleges and Hospitals, which they propose to introduce in two or three Medical Colleges in Kolkata. Although it is not so easy to introduce a new system in Indian society, the authority of Calcutta Medical College had shown keen interest to implement the same as an experiment. Similar multi-disciplinary training programmes for the professionals in other selected cities in India are going to start soon with the support from ISPCAN and other international agencies. Meanwhile, the Government of India also created an independent Ministry for Women and Child Development for addressing the issue of child protection more effectively. A new stringent law is also going to be introduced in the Indian Parliament for prevention of child abuse and neglect and this would be a good legal step towards child protection in the Indian Society.

Recommendations for Future Study

- Effectiveness of vocational training for sexually abused children.
- Efficacy of psychological intervention for post-traumatic stress disorder and results of follow up with the family members for reunion of the children with the family.
- Developing culturally sensitive risk assessment instruments that contemplate the local characteristics and scope of the problem.
- Comparison studies on the effect of childhood sexual abuse among boys and girls and also of high-risk families of different religions could be beneficial in recognizing and identifying the vulnerable families.
- Relation between child sexual abuse and depression among various Indian ethnic groups.
- Developmental studies which take intervening variables into consideration are needed.
- Studies exemplifying why some children become symptomatic and others do not, why some have no immediate reaction and may develop symptoms only

years later, and why some develop one set of symptoms and others develop different symptoms.

Recommendations for Intervention and Prevention

Child sexual abuse is a widespread problem that has been associated with a variety of negative physical and mental health outcomes. There has been a call for prevention of first occurrences of child sexual abuse. The need for systematic public and professional education on child sexual abuse along with prevention and harm reduction are priorities for sensitizing this issue. Earlier identification and more intensive supervision of sexually offending adults and juveniles also are priorities as is the need for more in-depth research into other societal factors that contribute to child sexual abuse and the identification of those sub-groups of children who are at the greatest risk of exploitation. Realization of these priorities would require a higher level of public policy focus, commitment and coherence than currently exists. Their realization also requires new human, fiscal and other resources to support the activities of state and local governments, service providers, planners, child advocacy organizations, researchers and others that are seeking to protect children from sexual abuse. Only a comprehensive approach to the elimination of child sexual abuse can succeed.

Intervention

(1) Understanding of the extent of psychological trauma along with suicidal ideations by professional psychologists.
(2) Arrangement of individual and periodic group counselling by professionally trained clinical psychologists.
(3) Arrangement of potential vocational training for immediate economic independence.
(4) Establishing network/relationship with the family.
(5) Periodic evaluation/assessment of existing rehabilitation/intervention programme.

(6) Sharing of outcome of rehabilitation programmes in different platforms so that people can be more aware and sensitized about issues.

(7) Providing children with behavioural rehearsal of prevention strategies and offering feedback on their performance to facilitate children's depiction of their involvement in abusive as well as unpleasant interactions.

(8) Repeatedly stressing the need for children to tell every time someone continues to touch them in a way that makes them uneasy.

(9) Encouraging children to come forward to report and teaching professionals to screen for sexual abuse.

(10) Developing extended after-school programmes and more in-depth discussion opportunities for certain high-risk groups (e.g., former victims, teen parents).

(11) Public education efforts to improve the public's understanding of the underlying cause and forms of child sexual abuse.

(12) Support groups for children experiencing specific trauma that may leave them feeling isolated and, therefore, more vulnerable to advances by perpetrators.

(13) Support groups for vulnerable adults going through difficult transitions that limit their ability or interest in protecting their children.

(14) Directed education to those who are offending children in an effort to encourage perpetrators to seek out services and to alter their behaviours.

(15) Parenting education programmes that strengthen a parent's protective instincts and provide parents information on how to discuss the issue with their children and how to secure help if their children are being victimized. Specific guidelines that help parents distinguish among appropriate, potentially troublesome and inappropriate sexual interests or behaviours also can offer parents a means of monitoring their child's behaviours.

(16) Life skills training for young adolescents that help them establish positive relationships and avoid abusive behaviours with their peers. These attributes include communication skills; problem-solving and planning skills; assertiveness skills; negotiated conflict resolution; friendship skills; peer resistance skills; low-risk choice-making skills; stress reduction skills; self-improvement skills; consumer awareness skills; self-awareness skills; critical thinking skills; and basic academic skills.

(17) Teaching generic concepts such as assertive behaviour, decision-making skills, and communication skills that children can use in not just to fend off abuse but also in everyday situations.

(18) Focusing on increasing the national pool of legal, correctional and human service professionals with specialized expertise in the nature, extent, dynamics and impact of sexual exploitation/abuse on children and their families.

Prevention

(1) Identification of families living below poverty line and having an adolescent girl child and bringing them under intervention programme of NGOs.

(2) Helping rural population living below poverty line for formation of self-help groups and taking up NGO's income generated programmes.

(3) Local administration should ensure sincere implementation of primary education programme for each every child, which in terms of South Asia is still not a reality.

(4) Formation of Mahila Mandal for sharing and exchanging different positive and/or negative experiences in a group.

(5) Sensitization of Panchayat members as well as local administration including police about child sexual abuse and child trafficking.

(6) Allocation of responsibility and accountability to Panchayats and other local self-government units regarding missing and trafficked children.
(7) Arranging training programmes for Anganwadi and health workers for prevention of sexual abuse, identification of high-risk families.
(8) Stringent enforcement of laws such as ITPA and the Juvenile Justice Act to target the perpetrators, brothel keepers and prostitute users, whether local or foreign.
(9) Community awareness programmes targeting both adults and children. The media can play a role in terms of warning children about child sexual abusers.
(10) Political commitment by state authorities to combat child sexual abuse.
(11) Supporting aggressive prosecution of offenders who victimize children within local communities and have an action plan and protocol in place to alert the community and assuage their fears when a high-profile arrest is made.

The road ahead to protecting India's children and youth from child sexual abuse is long, and success is uncertain. It is clear that there is the need for collateral first generation policy development and strategic planning in dealing with child sexual abuse at the local, state, national, and, because of the great human mobility involved, international levels. These developments must engage the talents and resources of all those persons and organizations working to protect children from child sexual abuse and these efforts must be adequately financed. Nothing short of a comprehensive and well-coordinated approach to enhancing the nation's capacity for preventing and protecting children from the horrors of child sexual abuse will succeed.

APPENDICES

APPENDIX I

Date of Interview: .... Qre. Serial No........

Sexual Abuse Screening Questionnaire

Developed by
Dr. Sibnath Deb and Aparna Mukherjee
Department of Applied Psychology,
University of Calcutta
(2004)

Introduction: Child sexual abuse is a serious problem in India. There is no reliable data on the same issue since there is no system of mandatory reporting of the same. Hence, the present made an attempt to understand the magnitude of the problem and its impact on mental disposition. The broad objective of this screening questionnaire is to find out whether the children were either sexually molested and/or raped.

Please note that the information to be shared by you will be exclusively used for research purpose and in no way it will be shared with any outsiders. Therefore you can be ensured about the confidentiality of the information. After hearing the questions if you feel uncomfortable to answer, you can withdraw yourself from the study. Participation in the study is completely voluntary.

---

(1) Are you willing to participate in the study voluntarily?
Yes 1
No...................................2

(If the answer in Question 1 is 'yes', then only ask the following three questions)

(2) Were you ever asked by a grown-up to touch their private parts or did they touch yours in an inappropriate manner, when you did not like?
Yes 1
No.................................2

(3) Were you ever forced to have sex or do sexual things with another grown-up?
Yes 1
No.................................2

(4) Were you ever forced to have sexual intercourse, even if it did not take place?
Yes 1
No.................................2

Thanks for Your Kind Cooperation

APPENDIX II

Date of Interview: .... Qre. Serial No.........

Background Information Schedule

Developed by

Dr. Sibnath Deb and Aparna Mukherjee
Department of Applied Psychology
University of Calcutta

(2004)

Introduction: The objective of this questionnaire is to understand the socio-economic and demographic background of the respondents, history of abuse, contact with the family members, skill and perception about counselling. The information to be collected from the respondents will be utilized for research purpose only.

Section I: Socio-economic and Demographic Information

1.1 Name: ____________________
1.2 Age: 13-15 years ________1, 16-18 years __________2
1.3 Education: Illiterate ______1, Up to Primary ________2, Up to Secondary ________3
1.4 Marital Status: Single ________ 1, Married ________2
1.5 No. of Siblings: Single child ________________1, One ________________2, Two____________3, More than two ________________4
1.6 Family Type: Joint __________1, Nuclear __________2
1.7 Family Size: Below 4 ___________1, 4-6 _________2, 7 and above __________3
1.8 Parent's Education:

Education	*Father*	*Mother*
Illiterate		
Up to Primary		
Up to Secondary		
Passed Secondary Exam		
Passed H.S.		

1.9 Parent's Occupation:

Occupation	*Father*	*Mother*
Service		
Business		
Housewife		
Casual Worker, please specify		
Unemployed		
Others, please specify		

1.10 Total monthly income of the family from all sources

Less than Rs.1000	
Rs.1001-Rs.2000	
Rs.2001-Rs.3000	
Rs.3001 and above	

1.11 Place of Living: Rural __________1, Urban __________2, Semi-Urban ________3

Section II: History of Abuse

2.1 Perpetrator of abuse: Father __________1, Relative __________2, Stranger __________3, Others, please specify __________4

2.2 Situation when abused:
Nobody was at home __________1
While going to somebody's place/coming from school __________2
While working in the field __________3
Others, please specify __________4

2.3 Whether examined by a doctor and received treatment after being rehabilitated?
Yes __________1, No __________2

2.4 Frequency of sexual abuse: Once __________1, Twice __________2, Thrice and above __________3

2.5 Have you ever been pregnant as a result? Yes __________1, No __________2

Section III: Reporting

3.1 Whether the incident was reported to the police? Yes __________1, No __________2

3.2 If No, why?
Because of perceived harassment __________1
Police refused to file an FIR __________2
Threatened by the perpetrator __________3
Social stigma __________4
Others, please specify __________5

3.3 Whether the incident was reported to the local NGO?
Yes __________1, No __________2

3.4 If No, why?

Because of perceived harassment __________1
There is no NGO in the locality __________2
There is an NGO but they do not work in this field __________3
Threatened by the perpetrator __________4

Social stigma ______ 5
Others, please specify ______ 6

3.5 If Yes to Question 3.1 or Question 3.3, what was the result?

______

Section IV: Reaction of Family Members and Future Aspiration

4.1 What was the reaction of the family members about the incident?
Discriminated ______ 1
Did not discriminate ______ 2
Others, please specify ______ 3

4.2 Is there any contact with the family members? Yes ______ 1, No ______ 2

4.3 If Yes, periodicity of contact with the family members:
Once a week ______ 1
Once a month ______ 2
Once or twice a year ______ 3
No fixed time ______ 4

4.4 If No, why?

______

______

4.5 What is your future aspiration?
Want to be a social worker ______ 1
Want to receive meaningful vocational training and do Something ______ 2
No idea ______ 3
Others, please specify ______ 4

Section V: Skill Building and Perception about the Home

5.1 Have you attended any vocational training or currently undergoing any vocational training?
Yes ______ 1, No ______ 2

5.2 If Yes, what training are/have you attending/ attended?
Weaving ________________________1
Printing ________________________2
Sewing ________________________3
Others, please specify ________________4

5.3 Are you enjoying your stay in this home? Yes ________1, No________2

5.4 Why do you feel so?
____
____

5.5 Perception about behaviour of the staff of the home:
____

Section VI: Perception regarding Counseling Benefits

6.1 Have you attended any counselling session or currently undergoing any counselling session?
Yes ________1, No ________2

6.2 Do you think counselling is/was beneficial Yes ________1, No ________2

Thanks for Your Kind Cooperation

APPENDIX III

Semi-structured Questionnaire for Counsellors

Developed by
Dr. Sibnath Deb and Aparna Mukherjee
Department of Applied Psychology
University of Calcutta
(2004)

Introduction: Child sexual abuse is a serious problem in India. There is no reliable data on the same issue since there is no system of mandatory reporting of the same. At the same time, intervention facilities are limited like lack of safe shelters and trained psychologists for psychological intervention of sexually abused children. The broad objective of this semi-structured questionnaire is to understand the experience of the counsellors in dealing with abused children, nature of intervention services available and problems encountered by them.

Please note that there no right or wrong answer. We are interested to learn from your experience only. Information to be shared by you will be exclusively used for research purpose. Therefore you can be ensured about the confidentiality of the information. After hearing the questions if you feel uncomfortable to answer any question, you can withdraw yourself from the study or ignore that particular question. Participation in the study is completely voluntary.

Section I: Background Information

Name: ____________________ Age: ____________________
Education: ________________ Designation: ______________

Years of work experience especially in dealing with sexually abused children: ______________________________

Have you received any training on counselling: Yes/No

Number of counselors working in your organization: ______________________

Total number of inmates/disadvantaged children in the Home: ______________

Section II: Counselling of Children

1. Number of sexually abused children in the shelter (approx): ________________
2. Periodicity of counselling of inmates:
   ____
   ____
   ____
3. Do you apply any psychological tests for understanding the mental disposition of the sexually abused children? Yes/No
4. If Yes, what are the tests applied and why?
   ____
   ____
   ____
   ____
   ____
5. Do you maintain individual file for each case? Yes/No
6. If Yes, will you show me some of them?
   ____
   ____
   ____
   ____
   ____

7. According to you what type of psychological problems do sexually abused children suffer from?

____

____

____

____

____

8. How do you deal with sexually abused children to help them become more emotionally stable? What type of psychological intervention programmes do you have for the sexually abused children?

____

____

____

____

____

9. Do you find any positive changes in sexually abused children owing to your intervention programme? Yes/No

10. If Yes, can you tell how many of them are benefited, if possible in terms of percentage?

____

____

11. In case of sexually abused children where you did not perceive any success, what could be the probable causes for the same?

____

____

____

____

____

Section III: Counselling of Parents

12. Do you try to contact the family member(s)? Yes/No

13. If Yes, please specify the success rate, i.e., how many parents come to see their children?

    ____
    ____
    ____

14. Periodicity of visit of family member(s):

    ____
    ____
    ____

15. Do you counsel the parents, if so; specify the result (any positive changes in the outlook of parents):

    ____
    ____
    ____
    ____
    ____

Section IV: Problems in Counselling

16. Do you face any problem while counselling the children? __________

    Problems in rendering effective counselling

    __________lack of confidential space

    __________too many counsellors

    __________no system of recording information

    __________no psychological tests available

    __________did not receive any training on counselling

    __________authority is not keen on counselling

    __________no system for giving feedback

    __________even if feedback is given, no action is taken

    __________I am given/asked to perform various jobs, hence unable to give more time to counselling

17. Do you have any arrangement of vocational training for the sexually abused girl children? Yes/No

18. If Yes, what are they?

____

____

____

____

____

19. Nature of medical services available:

____

____

____

____

20. Do you have any group activities in the Home? Yes/No

21. If Yes, what are those?

____

____

____

____

____

22. Do all the sexually abused children participate in these group activities? Yes/No

____

____

____

____

____

23. If No, why?

24. In general, what is the perceived future aspiration of the sexually abused children?

____

____

____

____

____

Section V: Recommendations

25. According to you, what needs to be done to render better psychological, social and other services to sexually abused children?

____

____

____

____

____

26. How do you think the participation of family member(s) in the programme can be ensured?

____

____

____

____

____

27. How do you think sexually abused children can be returned to their families?

____

____

____

____

____

Thanks for Your Kind Cooperation

APPENDIX IV

Beck Depression Inventory (BDI-II)

Developed by

Aaron T. Beck (1994) and locally adapted by

Aparna Mukherjee and Dr. Sibnath Deb (2004)

Name: ________________ Marital Status: ______________
Age: ______ Sex: __________ Occupation: ________________
Education: _________________________

Instructions: This questionnaire consists of 21 groups of statements. Please read each group of statements carefully and then pick out the **one statement** in each group that best describes the way you have been feeling during the **past two weeks, including today**. Circle the number beside the statement you have picked. If several statements in the group seem to apply equally well, circle the highest number for that group. Be sure that you do not choose more than one statement for any group, including Item 16 (Changes in Sleeping Pattern) or Item 18 (Changes in Appetite).

1. Sadness

0 I do not feel sad.
1 I feel sad much of the time.
2 I am sad all the time.
3 I am so sad or unhappy that I can't stand it.

2. Pessimism

0 I am not discouraged about my future.
1 I feel more discouraged about my future than I used to be.
2 I do not expect things to work out for me.
3 I feel my future is hopeless and will only get worse.

3. Past Failure
0 I do not feel like a failure.
1 I have failed more than I should have.
2 As I look back, I see a lot of failures.
3 I feel I am a total failure as a person.

4. Loss of Pleasure
0 I get as much pleasure as I ever did from the things I enjoy.
1 I don't enjoy things as much as I used to.
2 I get very little pleasure from the things I used to enjoy.
3 I can't get any pleasure from the things I used to enjoy.

5. Guilty Feelings
0 I don't feel particularly guilty.
1 I feel guilty over many things I have done or should have done.
2 I feel guilty most of the time.
3 I feel guilty all of the time.

6. Punishment Feelings
0 I don't feel I am being punished.
1 I feel I may be punished.
2 I expect to be punished.
3 I feel I am being punished.

7. Self-Dislike
0 I feel the same about myself as ever.
1 I have lost confidence in myself.
2 I am disappointed in myself.
3 I dislike myself.

8. Self-Criticalness
0 I don't criticize or blame myself more than usual.
1 I am more critical of myself than I used to be.
2 I criticize myself for all my faults.
3 I blame myself for everything bad that happens.

9. Suicidal Thoughts or Wishes
0 I don't have any thoughts of killing myself.
1 I have thoughts of killing myself, but I would not carry them out.
2 I would like to kill myself.
3 I would kill myself if I had the chance.

10. Crying
0 I don't cry anymore than I used to.
1 I cry more than I used to.
2 I cry over every little thing.
3 I feel like crying but I can't.

________________**Sub-total Page 1**

11. Agitation
0 I am no more restless or wound up than usual.
1 I feel more restless or wound up than usual.
2 I am so restless or agitated that it's hard to stay still.
3 I am so restless or agitated that I have to keep moving or doing something.

12. Loss of Interest
0 I have not lost interest in other people or activities.
1 I am less interested in other people or things than before.
2 I have lost most of my interest in other people or things.
3 It's hard to get interested in anything.

13. Indecisiveness
0 I make decisions about as well as ever.
1 I find it more difficult to make decisions than usual.
2 I have much greater difficulty in making decisions than I used to.
3 I have trouble making any decisions.

14. Worthlessness
0 I do not feel I am worthless.
1 I don't consider myself as worthwhile and useful as I used to.
2 I feel more worthless as compared to other people.
3 I feel utterly worthless.

15. Loss of Energy

0 I have as much energy as ever.
1 I have less energy than I used to have.
2 I don't have enough energy to do very much.
3 I don't have enough energy to do anything.

16. Changes in Sleeping Pattern

0 I have not experienced any change in my sleeping pattern.
1a I sleep somewhat more than usual.
1b I sleep somewhat less than usual.
2a I sleep a lot more than usual.
2b I sleep a lot less than usual.
3a I sleep most of the day.
3b I wake up 1-2 hours early and can't get back to sleep.

17. Irritability

0 I am no more irritable than usual.
1 I am more irritable than usual.
2 I am much more irritable than usual.
3 I am irritable all the time.

18. Changes in Appetite

0 I have not experienced any change in my appetite.
1a My appetite is somewhat less than usual.
1b My appetite is somewhat greater than usual.
2a My appetite is much less than before.
2b My appetite is much greater than usual.
3a I have no appetite at all.
3b I crave food all the time.

19. Concentration Difficulty

0 I can concentrate as well as ever.
1 I can't concentrate as well as usual.
2 It's hard to keep my mind on anything for very long.
3 I find I can't concentrate on anything.

20. Tiredness or Fatigue

0 I am no more tired or fatigued than usual.
1 I get more tired or fatigued more easily than usual.
2 I am too tired or fatigued to do a lot of the things I used to do.
3 I am too tired or fatigued to do most of the things I used to do.

21. Loss of Interest in Sex

0 I have not noticed any recent change in my interest in sex.
1 I am less interested in sex than I used to be.
2 I am much less interested in sex now.
3 I have lost interest in sex completely.

____________________**Sub-total Page 2**

Thanks for Your Kind Cooperation

APPENDIX V

Aggression Scale

(A-SCALE)

Constructed and Standardized by
Km. Roma Pal and Dr. (Smt.) Tasneem Naqvi
and locally adapted by
Aparna Mukherjee and Dr. Sibnath Deb
(2004)

Name ________________________________ Age ________
Education ____________________ Rural/Urban ______________
Occupation _________________________ Caste ______________
Father/Guardian's Name ______________________________
Monthly Income ____
Address ____

Instruction

Some statements are given in this booklet, related to your personality. Please go through them carefully. There are six answers for every statement. Please tick (√) mark only to that answer to which you strongly agree. You are required to tick (√) mark only one answer for each statement. Please try to attempt answers to all the statements. There is no time limit but still try your best to complete it at the earliest.

Item No.	*Mode of Response*					
	Very much	*Much*	*Ordinary*	*Less*	*Very less*	*Not at all*
1. How much liking do I have in breaking the rules of the family, if needed....						
2. How much anger do I experience when people do not accept even reasonable things						
3. How far do I feel it proper to break the social traditions when they obstruct in my way....						
4. How much do I like to do daring things....						
5. How much do I like dreadful warriors in a pitched battle....						
6. How much do I think of beating one who abuses me....						
7. How much do I like to see movies that are full of fighting scenes....						

Item No.	*Mode of Response*					
	Very much	*Much*	*Ordinary*	*Less*	*Very less*	*Not at all*
8. How much anger do I experience even in small events....						
9. How much do I agree in 'tit for tat'....						
10. How much do I like to hang the pictures related to war in all the rooms of my house....						
11. How much anger do I experience when people do not work according to me....						
12. How much do I like pictures of warriors with sword in comparison to others....						
13. How much anger do I experience in arguments with people....						
14. How much do I like to think over before arguing....						
15. How much do I like to tear off my clothes when elders do not agree with me....						

Item No.	Mode of Response					
	Very much	*Much*	*Ordinary*	*Less*	*Very less*	*Not at all*
16. How much do I agree in hitting the colleagues if they joke about me....						
17. How much do I like the loud voice of the candidate in the election campaign....						
18. How much do I like to make friends who revolt against society....						
19. How much do I like to read the stories of warriors....						
20. How much anger do I experience when people do not consider my opinion....						
21. How much feeling of hitting do I experience when a child intentionally incorrectly answers examination questions....						
22. How much feeling of discarding an irregular teacher do I feel....						

Item No.	Mode of Response					
	Very much	Much	Ordinary	Less	Very less	Not at all
23. How much do I agree to the views that books, which are not appropriate for our culture, should be torn off and burnt....						
24. How much do I agree to the views that a thief caught red-handed should be killed....						
25. How much interest do I have in war news in comparison to others....						
26. How much does the thought of hitting the players of my team occur when they are defeated....						
27. How much anger do I experience when someone is late in returning my thing....						
28. How much do I agree to the thought of hitting my						

Item No.	Mode of Response					
	Very much	*Much*	*Ordinary*	*Less*	*Very less*	*Not at all*
youngsters when they insult me....						
29. 'I like to organize an exhibition in which pictures of only the brave are included'. With this statement I agree...	______					
30. How much do I agree with the thought of rusticating an indisciplined student from the school....	______					

Sub-total Page 2

Thanks for Your Kind Cooperation

APPENDIX VI

Social Adjustment Inventory (S.A.I.)

Constructed and Standardized by Dr. Roma Pal (1985) and locally adapted by Aparna Mukherjee and Dr. Sibnath Deb (2004)

Name ____________________________

Education __________ Age ______________ Sex __________

Address ____________________________

Instruction: There are sixty statements followed by 'Yes' and 'No' responses. Kindly go through them carefully. If you agree with the statement then tick (√) mark on 'Yes' and if you do not agree, then tick (√) mark on 'No'. Respond to all the statements without leaving any one behind. There is no time limit but still try to complete it, at the earliest.

Statements	*Mode of Response*	
	Yes	*No*
1. Minute things trouble me so much that I often feel sad.	________	
2. I agree with the fact that one should take active part in social customs and rituals.	________	
3. I often get afraid while talking with others.	________	
4. I am often baffled while facing either a minute or a tough problem.	________	
5. I get pleasure in respecting the aged people of the society.	________	
6. Apart from my family members, the neighbours, also, often like my views.	________	
7. My eyes get wet on seeing anybody in trouble or distress.	________	
8. I feel jealous when anybody supercedes me.	________	
9. I fear going out alone at night.		
10. It has become my habit to take active part in social functions.	________	

Statements	*Mode of Response* Yes	No
11. I agree that one should lead a joyful life.	______	
12. I get angry whenever things do not happen according to my wish.	______	
13. My friends and colleagues certainly take my suggestion in whatever they plan.	______	
14. It is better to make good friends than earn more money.	______	
15. When my younger brother/sister does not accept my advice, I get angry.	______	
16. I get frightened even at the mere name of examination.	______	
17. I do not harass others for my pleasure.	______	
18. Often I get nervous at the feeling that I may be a burden on my family.	______	
19. While travelling, people become my friends due to my behaviour.	______	
20. I never want to joke/make fun about/of others.	______	
21. If anybody insults me, I become very excited.	______	
22. I feel that most of my ideals and theories match with others.	______	
23. Even at the simple jokes people make, I get angry and feel like beating them.	______	
24. I don't hesitate in mixing up even with low caste people.	______	
25. Often it occurs in my mind to run away from home.	______	
26. In my views, for the progress of society, it is essential that boys and girls get married in different castes.	______	
27. When my friends criticize me without any cause, I feel sad.	______	
28. Even when I come to know that my friends criticized me, I do not say anything to them but stay upset for several days.	______	
29. In elections, I vote for such a party or candidate which/who works for the upliftment of the society.	______	
30. If anybody gets dejected because of familial dispute, I try my best to help him.	______	
31. I like to leave some of my habits but can't do so.	______	
32. I feel pleasure on seeing other's happiness or progress.	______	

Statements	Mode of Response Yes	No
33. Often I get tired and feel monotony even at the slightest work.	________	
34. However disturbed I may be, I don't stay back from helping the needy people.	________	
35. I can't work for a long time even if the job interests me.	________	
36. I altogether agree with the fact that it is better to break a promise rather than keep it.	________	
37. While helping, I don't consider my loss, even.	________	
38. I do not feel hesitation or fear even among unknown people.	________	
39. Even the simplest of events upset me so much that I can't sleep.	________	
40. I satisfy even the unknown people with my behaviour.	________	
41. Even after hard labour, I can't complete my work in time.	________	
42. Often it occurs in my mind that nobody loves me.	________	
43. It is my interest to take active part in cultural programmes.	________	
44. In my view, it is better to work in a group rather than individually.	________	
45. I like to cry loudly when even after being innocent, I am being considered as a culprit.	________	
46. In my view, competition and co-operation are essential for the upliftment of the society.	________	
47. Often I feel sleepy while reading.	________	
48. I don't have any problem in mixing up with people.	________	
49. Often it occurs in my mind that it is better to die rather than remain alive.	________	
50. I can't speak frankly in front of unknown people.	________	
51. I have affectionate terms with my neighbours.	________	
52. I enjoy playing jokes with people in the parties.	________	
53. Even the simplest events upset me so much, that I can't take it out of my mind for several days.	________	
54. In spite of being busy it is my habit to help anyone who is in trouble.	________	
55. I get upset on seeing other's progress.	________	
56. Before taking decisions, I certainly take other's suggestion.	________	

Statements	*Mode of Response*	
	Yes	*No*
57. When I don't get the desired thing, I become so angry, that I even lose self control.	———	
58. After much thinking, I place my views before my friends and they accept it without any hesitation.	———	
59. Before accepting social customs and rituals, I judge their utility and take decision.	———	
60. When anybody gets annoyed with me, I feel dejected.	———	

Thanks for Your Kind Cooperation

APPENDIX VII

Multi-dimensional Personality Inventory

Developed by

Km. Manju Agarwal (1988) and locally adapted by Anjana Bhattacharjee and Dr. Sibnath Deb (2002)

Instruction: Some statements are given here. Please go through these statements carefully. There are three possible answers, i.e., 'Yes', 'Sometimes' and 'No' beside each statement. If you totally agree to the statement then put a tick (√) mark to the category of 'Yes' and if you do not agree then put a tick (√) mark to 'No'. Similarly, if you feel that the statement is sometimes applicable to you, please put a tick mark (√) to 'Sometimes.'

There is no right or wrong answer in this inventory. Please respond to all the items without any hesitation. There is no time limit but still try your best to complete these statements as early as you can. If you feel any difficulty, please tell me. Your responses will be kept confidential.

Name:..

Age:..................................Date:.......................................

Education:.............................Occupation:...............................

Address: ....

....

STATEMENTS

Sl. No.	*Statements*	*Mode of Response*		
		Yes	*Sometimes*	*No*

(A)

1. I wish to work alone so that I can work according to myself.
2. A work done in cooperation gets spoiled.
3. Without any reason I do not meet people.
4. I go with my friends in social occasions.
5. I feel uneasy if my friends do not sit beside me in the office or in the cinema hall.
6. I use to stand beside of my neighbours in both pleasures –sad full situation.
7. I do not hesitate to highlight others faults.
8. I work according to myself even after knowing faults and weaknesses of others.
9. I have a habit to make friendship even with the strangers at a new place.
10 Often on seeing me my friends use to tell me that I do not take their opinions in my work.
11. Often I share I belongings to others.
12. Often I sit alone and do my study.
13. I prefer to study alone in a closed room while listening to music rather than studying jointly with my friends.
14. As I am suspicious minded, I do not have many friends.
15. I can easily make my work done from my strangers.
16. I cannot keep my secretes with in myself.
17. I feel very happy in taking active participation in social activities.
18. I do not take part in pleasure sorrow activities of the society thinking that such events happen very often in this world.
19. I become upset whenever any past event comes to my mind.
20. Whenever I travel, many travellers become my friend.

(B)

1. I think that I am an efficient person.
2. I wish to get respect from my friends.
3. I am capable of doing everything.

Sl. No.	*Statements*	*Mode of Response*		
		Yes	*Sometimes*	*No*
4.	I think that I am very powerful.			
5.	I have faith on ability and hard work.			
6.	I have many qualities so I can solve my problems by my own.			
7.	I work according to my own wish.			
8.	I use to think very deeply about my own problems.			
9.	People know it very well that I do have all qualities.			
10.	I can do any kind of work.			
11.	I give priority to my present rather than thinking of my future.			
12.	I do not care of others anger.			
13.	Every body praises my work and me.			
14.	I am of stubborn in nature.			
15.	My friends think that I am very proudy.			
16.	I can easily impress others by my personality.			
17.	I become very upset when I see others sorrow.			
18.	I am efficient to solve problem.			
19.	I am very much concern about my responsibilities rather than giving priority to my rights.			
20.	I have a strong desire to become a rich person.			
	(C)			
1.	I want to do such work, which will make me self-dependent.			
2.	I use to solve my problem in such a way that I may lead a happy life.			
3.	I like such kind of syllabus that may help me to get a job in future.			
4.	I am mature enough now so I wish to work seriously.			
5.	I don't want to be a burden on my family and society.			
6.	Everybody likes me for my work procedure.			
7.	I become very much angry if my parents interfere too much in my activities.			
8.	I do not worry of getting job because I have enough quality to get a job.			
9.	I feel that I am mentally mature.			
10.	I like to work without any help.			
11.	I like to work rather than living in fantasy.			

Sl. No.	Statements	Mode of Response		
		Yes	Sometimes	No
12.	I believe in the theory that outcome will certainly be the result of one's own work.			
13.	I do not do any such work, which can make me frightened.			
14.	Seeing my self-dependency, people think that I will become a very rich person.			
15.	I do not like any interference in my thoughts and works.			
16.	I am not a burden on my parents.			
17.	I don't like anyone to object me while roaming with my friends.			
18.	I like to stay alone because I make most of my planning by my own.			
19.	I feel irritated, as people do not consider me as self-dependent.			
20.	My friends and my family members have faith on me.			
	(D)			
1.	My friends think that my nature faulty.			
2.	I wish my friends didn't oppose me.			
3.	Often I face lots of problems due to my nature.			
4.	My teachers get irritated on account of my nature and my behaviour.			
5.	I get angry even for silly matters.			
6	I least bother about whether my friends talk to me or not.			
7.	Due to my blunt and critical talk my friends do not behave properly with me.			
8.	People are jealous of me due to my nature.			
9.	When I see that people want me to flatter, I hate them.			
10.	I know that due to my nature I can't make many friends.			
11.	I became mentally disturbed when my family members tell me to do such work, which I don't want to do.			
12.	Often my friend takes advantage of my simplicity.			
13.	Whatever people say, I don't mind.			
14.	When I am unsuccessful, I become upset for several days.			

Sl. No.	Statements	Mode of Response: Yes	Sometimes	No
15.	I feel like biting my younger if they disobey me.			
16.	My behaviour changes when I find things are in disorder.			
17.	I became upset if any work is not done according to my wish.			
18.	Generally my personality is balanced.			
19.	When I get angry, I never say anything to others but I stop taking food.			
20.	I use to keep my patience in any work even if that work is against my nature.			
	(E)			
1.	I like this world.			
2.	My friends like me very much.			
3.	Being intelligent in class, my teachers consider me a good student.			
4.	I wish to have many friends and have friendly terms with them.			
5.	My friends and family members like me very much.			
6.	I think that there are many means available in this world to live a luxurious life.			
7.	When I will be grown up I would like to work in such a way so that everybody could lead a happy and prosperous life.			
8.	My younger and elder brothers and sisters like me very much.			
9.	I am more eager to know that for which job or business I will be eligible rather than concentrating on studies.			
10.	After being educated only I will do job.			
11.	I do not bother whether friendship remains or not.			
12.	I can't control my emotions.			
13.	There is no value for a good person in this world.			
14.	My father considers my opinion in every family matters.			
15.	Everybody is eager to make friendship with me.			
16.	I never oppose my parents.			
17.	I try to keep everybody happy.			
18.	My neighbours like me very much.			
19.	In social activities I energetically take part.			

Sl. No.	Statements	Mode of Response		
		Yes	Sometimes	No
20.	Whenever I get time, I use to help my family members in the household work.			
	(F)			
1.	Sometimes I feel to change the society.			
2.	Everybody thinks I am worthless.			
3.	I don't bother over that each individual in this world suffers from misery on account of one or the other cause.			
4.	I am free from all anxiety.			
5.	I like more sad songs.			
6.	The cause of my anxiety is the inability in studies.			
7.	I fear of failure in the examination.			
8.	My friends are jealous of me.			
9.	The world is so selfish that no one can live here with truth and honesty.			
10.	There is risk in every work.			
11.	Everyone in this world feels jealous of me and hates me.			
12.	I am anxious of getting a good job.			
13.	Nothing to worry about a job, only that will happen what is written in fate.			
14.	I worry over that everybody gets angry with me.			
15.	I am anxious of becoming self-dependent.			
16.	I am anxious of making my life prosperous.			
17.	Often I feel anxious about my general physical health.			
18.	I try to keep proper adjustment with the society.			
19.	I worry about how to make good friends.			
20.	I try to behave nicely with the family members yet they assault me even for the very minor things.			

Thanks for Your Kind Cooperation

References

Abel et al., (1994). Screening tests for paedophilia. *Criminal Justice and Behaviour*, 21, 115-131.

Abel, G. G., and Rouleau, J. L. (1990). The nature and extent of sexual assault. In W. L. Marshall, D. R. Laws and H. E. Barbaree (Eds.), *Handbook of Sexual Assault: Issues, Theories, and Treatment of the Offender* (pp. 9-12). New York: Plenum. (Req. #88)

Angus, G., and Woodward, S. (1995). Child abuse and neglect, Australia, 1993-94. *Child Welfare Series*, No.13, Australian Institute of Health and Welfare, AGPS.

Arata, C.M. (1998). To tell or not to tell: Current functioning of child sexual abuse survivors who disclosed their victimization. *Child Maltreatment*, 3. 63-71.

Aytes et al., (2001). Cognitive/behavioural treatment for sexual offenders: An examination of recidivism; *Sexual Abuse: A Journal of Research and Treatment*, 13, 4.

Azaola, Elena (2001). Stolen childhood. Girl and boy victims of sexual exploitation in Mexico. (Mexico DF: UNICEF).

Azaola, Elena (2001). The commercial sexual exploitation of children in Mexico, in Richard J. Estes and Neil A. Weiner (Editors). *The Silent Emergency: The Sexual Exploitation of Children in the U.S., Canada and Mexico* (Westport CT: Greenwood Publishing Group).

Bagley, C., and King, K. (1990). Child sexual abuse: The search for healing. London: Tavistock-Routledge.

Bagley, C. (1991). The prevalence and mental health sequels of child sexual abuse in a community sample of women aged 18-27. *Canadian Journal of Community Mental Health*, 10, 103-116.

Bagley, C., Wood, M., and Young, L. (1994). Victim to abuser: mental health and behavioural sequels of child sexual abuse in a community survey of young adult males. *Child Abuse and Neglect*, 18, 683-697.

Baker, H.J. and Stroller, R.J. (1968). Sexual psychopathology in the hypogondal male. *Archives of General Psychiatry*, 18, 631-634.

Baker, A.W. and Duncan, S.P. (1985). Child sexual abuse: A study of prevalence in Great Britain. *Child Abuse and Neglect*, 9, 457-467.

Bancroft, J. (1978). The relationship between hormones and sexual behaviour in humans, in J. Hutchison (Ed.). *The Biological Determinants of Sexual Behaviour*. Chichester: Wilcy.

Banyard, V. L., and Williams, L. M. (1997). Characteristics of child sexual abuse as correlates of women's adjustment: A prospective study. *Journal of Marriage and the Family*, 58, 853-865.

Barbaree et al., (2001) Evaluating the predictive accuracy of six risk assessment instruments for adult sex offenders. *Criminal Justice and Behaviour, 28*, 490-521.

Barbaree, H.E., and Marshall, W.L. (1991). The role of male sexual arousal in rape: Six models. *Journal of Consulting and Clinical Psychology, 59*, 621-630.

Barr, C.W. (1996). *Child sex trade: Battling a scourge.* (Boston MA: Christian Science Publishing).

Baxter et al., (1984). Deviant sexual behaviour: Differentiating sex offenders by criminal and personal history, psychometric measures, and sexual response. *Criminal Justice and Behaviour*, 11, 477-501.

Beck, A.T., Ward, C.H., Mendelson, M., Mock, J., and Erbaugh, J. (1961). An inventory for measuring depression. *Archives of General Psychiatry*, 4, 561-571.

Becker, Judith. (1994). Offenders: Characteristics and treatment. *The Future of Children*, 4(2): 179, 186.

Beitchman, J. H., Zucker, K. J., Hood, J. E., DaCosta, G. A., Akman, D., and Cassavia, E. (1992). A review of the long-term effects of child sexual abuse. *Child Abuse and Neglect*, 16, 101-118.

Belkin, D.S., Greense, A. F., Rodrigue, J. R., and Boggs, S. R. (1994). Psychopathology and history of sexual abuse. *Journal of Interpersonal Violence*, 9 (4), 535-547.

Berlin, F.S. (1983). Sex offenders: A biomedical perspective and a status report on biomedical treatment, in J.G. Greer (Ed.) The Sexual Aggressor: Current Perspectives on Treatment (pp. 83-123). New York: Van Nostrand Reinhold.

Berliner, L., and Conte, J. (1995). The effects of disclosure and intervention on sexually abused children. *Child Abuse and Neglect*, 19, 371-384.

Bhattacharjee, A., (2006). A study on personality dispositions, self-esteem, emotional control and suicidal tendencies of depressive patients. An Unpublished Doctoral Dissertation. University of Calcutta.

Bickley, J.A., and Beech, A.R. (2001). Classifying child abusers: Its relevance to theory and clinical practice. *International Journal of Offender Therapy and Comparative Criminology*, 45: 51-69.

Bickley, J.A., and Beech, A.R. (2002). An investigation of the Ward and Hudson Pathways Model of the sexual offense process with child abusers. *Journal of Interpersonal Violence*, 17, 372-393.

Billy, J., et al., (1993). The sexual behaviour of men in the United States. *Family Perspectives*, 25: (2) 52-60.

Botti, Anita (2000). Remarks at the opening of the ARIAT meeting (in Manila, Philippines). (Washington: U.S. State Department, International Information Programmes).

Bradford, J.M.W. (1990). The anti-androgen and hormonal treatment of sex offenders cited in W.L. Marshall (Ed.). *Handbook of Sexual Assault: Issues, Theories, and Treatment of the Offender* (pp. 297-310). New York: Plenum Press.

Bradley, A.R., and Wood, J.M. (1996). How do children tell? The disclosure process in child sexual abuse. *Child Abuse and Neglect*, 20, 881-891.

Brayden et al., (1995).In Nereo, N.A. (2002) Willingness to self—disclose among late adolescent female survivors of child sexual abuse. *Journal of Youth and Adolescence.*

Briere, J., and Zaidi, L. Y. (1989). Sexual abuse histories and sequelae in female psychiatric emergency room patients. *American Journal of Psychiatry*, 146, 1602-1606.

Briere, J. N., and Elliot, D.M. (1994). Immediate and long-term impacts of child sexual abuse. *The Future of Children*, 4, 54-69.

Briggs, L., and Joyce, P.R. (1997). What determines post-traumatic stress disorder symptomatology for survivors of childhood sexual abuse? *Child Abuse and Neglect, 21,* 575-582.

Browne et al., (1998). Predicting treatment drop-out in sex offenders. *Child Abuse Review*, 7, 402-419.

Brown, L. K., Lourie, K. J., Zlotnick, C., and Cohn, J. (2000). Impact of sexual abuse on the HIV-risk-related behaviour of adolescents in intensive psychiatric treatment. *American Journal of Psychiatry*, 157(9), 1413-1415.

Budapest Group (1999). The relationship between organized crime and trafficking in aliens (Austria: International Centre for Migration Policy Development).

Bucky, S. J., and Dallenberg, C. (1992). The relationship between training of mental health professionals and the reporting of ritual abuse and multiple personality disorder symptomatology. *Journal of Psychology and Theology*, Vol. 20, pp. 233-238.

Burnam, M. A., Stein, J. A., Golding, J. M., Siegel, J. M., Sorenson, S. B., Forsythe, A. B., and Telles, C. A. (1988). Sexual assault and mental disorders in a community population. *Journal of Consulting and Clinical Psychology*, 56, 843-850.

Caldwell, G., Galster, S., and Steinsor, N, (1997). Crime and servitude: An expose of the traffic in women for prostitution from the newly independent states. (Moscow: Global Survival Network).

Campis et al., (1993). Developmental differences in detection and disclosure of sexual abuse. *Journal of the American Academy of Child and Adolescent Psychiatry*, 32, 920–924.

Centers for Disease Control and Prevention. (2000). Youth risk behaviour surveillance—United States, 1999. Morbidity and mortality weekly report, 49(SS05), 1-96.

Chatterjee, P., Chakraborty, T., Srivastava, N., and Deb, Sibnath (2006). Short and long-term problems faced by the trafficked children: A qualitative study. *Social Science International*, 22, 1, 167-182.

Chauhan, N.S., and Tiwari, G.P. (1972). *Guide to using Nairashya Maapa*. Agra Psychological Research Cell, Agra.

Chauhan, N.S., Tiwari, G.P., and Khatter, I. (1972). Anxiety as a function of intelligence and adjustment. *Indian Journal of Experimental Psychology*, 10(2), 250-263.

Choquet et al., (1997). Self-reported health and behavioural problems among adolescent victims of rape in France: Results of a cross-sectional study. *Child Abuse and Neglect*, 21:823-832.

Clark, R. (1995). Child protection services in Victoria. Family Matters, No.40, Australian Institute of Family Studies, Melbourne.

Cohen M., Deamant C., Barkan S., Richardson J., Young M., Holman S., Anastos K., Cohen J., and Melnick S. (2000). Domestic violence and childhood sexual abuse in HIV-infected women and women at risk for HIV.

CORE Center, Cook County Hospital, Chicago, IL 60612, USA. *American Journal of Public Health*, Vol. 90, Issue 4 560-565.

Collin-Vezina, D., and Cyr, M. (2003). Current understanding about inter-generational transmission of child sexual abuse. *Child Abuse and Neglect*, 27(5):489-507.

Collings, S. (1995). The long-term effects of contact and non-contact forms of child sexual abuse in a sample of university men. *Child Abuse and Neglect, 19*, 1-6.

Conte et al., (1991). Evaluating children's reports of sexual abuse: Results from a survey of professionals. *American Journal of Orthopsychiatry, 61*, 428–437.

Conte, J., and Shore, D. (1982). Social work and sexual abuse. *Journal of Social Work and Human Sexuality*, Vol.1, No.1-2, Haworth Press, New York.

Conte, J. R., and Schuerman, J. R. (1987). Factors associated with an increased impact of child sexual abuse. *Child Abuse and Neglect*, 11, 201-211.

Conway, M., Mendelson, M., Giannopoulos, C., Csank, A.R., Patricia, L., and Holm, Susan (2004). Childhood and adult sexual abuse, rumination on sadness and dysphoria. *Child Abuse and Neglect*, 28(4), 393-410.

Cook, J.A. (1997). National Conference on Women and HIV. Abstract 122.4.

Craig, L.A., Browne, K.D., and Stringer, I. (2003). Treatment and sexual offence recidivism. *Trauma, Violence and Abuse*, 4(1): 70-89.

Csorba, R., Lampe, L., Borsos, A., Balla, L., Poka, R., and Olah, E. (2006). Female child sexual abuse within the family in a Hungarian county. *Gynecol Obstet Invest.* 2; 61(4), 188-193.

Dalenberg, C. J., and Palesh, O. G. (2004). Relationship between child abuse history, trauma and dissociation in Russian college students. *Child Abuse and Neglect*, 28(4), 461-474.

Dancu, C. V., Riggs, D. S., Hearst-Ikeda, D., Shoyer, B. G., and Foa, E. B. (1996). Dissociative experiences and post-traumatic stress disorder among female victims of criminal assault and rape. *Journal of Traumatic Stress, 9*, 253-267.

Danni et al., (2002). An analysis of predictors of child sex offender types using Presentence Investigation Reports. *International Journal of Offender Therapy and Comparative Criminology*, 44, 490-504.

Daro, D. (1994). "Prevention of childhood sexual abuse." *The Future of Children*, 4:2 (Summer/Fall), pp. 198-223.

Deb, Sibnath, and Mitra, Kathakali (2002). Nature and types of abuse and neglect among migrant child labour: A qualitative study. *The 14th International on Child Abuse and Neglect* held in Denver in July 2002.

Deb, Sibnath, (2002). Child sexual abuse: An overview with special reference to role of Police. *Social Defense*, 53, 154, 44-58.

Deb, Sibnath (2005). A study on socio-economic profile of young trafficked women, their substance abuse and HIV status. Presented in *'the European Conference on Child Abuse and Neglect'* held in Germany during Sept 11-13, 2005.

Deb, Sibnath (2005). Child Abuse and Neglect: The Indian Scenario, *Social Science International*, 21, 1, 3-19.

Deb, Sibnath (2005). Child abuse and neglect in a metropolitan city: A qualitative study of migrant child labour in South Kolkata. *Social Change*, 35, 3, 56-67.

Deb, Sibnath and Sen, Purba (2005a). A study on psychological trauma of young trafficked women. Presented in the 6th Asian Conference on Child Abuse and Neglect held in Singapore during November 16-18, 2005.

Deb, Sibnath, Srivastava, N., Chatterjee, P., and Chakraborty, T. (2005). Processes of child trafficking in West Bengal: A qualitative study. *Social Change*, 35, 2, 112-123.

DeJong, A.R., Emmett, G.A., and Hervada, A.A. (1982). Epidemiologic factors in sexual abuse of boys. *American Journal of Diseases of Children*, 136, 990-993.

Denenberg, Risa (1997). Childhood sexual abuse as an HIV risk factor in women. Gay Men's Health Crisis.

Department of Labour (1996). Forced labour: The prostitution of children: Symposium proceedings (Washington: U.S. D.o.L., Bureau of International Affairs).

DeVoe, E.R., and Coulborn-Faller, K. (1999). The characteristics of disclosure among children who may have been sexually abused. Child Maltreatment: *Journal of the American Professional Society on the Abuse of Children*, 4, 217-227.

DeYoung, M. (1982). The sexual victimization of children, McFarland, Jefferson, NC.

DiBlasio, F. (1992) Forgiveness in psychotherapy: Comparison of older and younger therapists. *Journal of Psychology and Christianity*, 11(2), 181-187.

Dinwiddie, S. et al., (2000) Early sexual abuse and life-time psychopathology: a co-twin control study. *Psychology and Medicine* 30:41-52.

Dionne, P. (2001). The commercial sexual exploitation of children in Canada, Richard J. Estes and Neil A. Weiner (Editors). *The Silent Emergency: The Sexual Exploitation of Children in the U.S., Canada and Mexico* (Westport CT: Greenwood Publishing Group).

DiPietro et al., (1997). Predictors of disclosure during medical evaluation for suspected sexual abuse. *Journal of Child Sexual Abuse*, 6 (1), 133–142.

Dodge, K.A., Bates, J. E., and Pettit, G.S. (1990). Mechanisms in the cycle of violence. *Science*, 250, 1678-1683.

Draijer, N., and Langeland, W. (1999) Childhood trauma and perceived parental dysfunction in the etiology of dissociative symptoms in psychiatric inpatients. *Am. J. Psychiatry*, 156; 379-385.

Drossman, D.A. (1992). The link between early abuse and GI disorders in women. *Emerg. Med.*, 2:171-175.

Dunne, M., and Legosz, M. (2000). The consequences of childhood sexual abuse. *An AXIS Project*, Queensland.

EASCAP-HRD, United Nations, NY (2002). Training manual on psychosocial and medical services for sexually abused and sexually exploited children and youth.

Eccles, A., and Marshall, W.L. (1999). Relapse prevention. In W.L. Marshall, D. Anderson and Y.M. Fernandez, *Cognitive behavioural treatment of sexual offenders* (pp. 127-146). London: John Wiley and Sons.

Eccles, A., and Walker, W. (1998). Community-based treatment with sexual offenders. In W. L. Marshall, Y. M. Fernandez, S. M. Hudson, and T. Ward (Eds.) *Sourcebook of treatment programmes for sexual offenders* (pp. 93-103): New York: Plenum.

Ellerstein, N. S., and Canavan, J. W. (1980). Sexual abuse of boys. *American Journal of Diseases of Children, 134,* 255-257.

End Child Prostitution, Child Pornography, and the Trafficking of Children for Sexual Exploitation (ECPAT). (1996). Europe and North America Regional Profile (issued by the World Congress Against Commercial Sexual Exploitation of Children held in Stockholm, Sweden, August 1996, p.70.)

Ennew, Judith (1986). The sexual exploitation of children New York: St. Martin's Press.

Epstein, J.N., Saunders, B.E., Kilpatrick, D.G., and Resnick, H.S. (1998). PTSD as a mediator between childhood rape and alcohol use in adult women. *Child Abuse and Neglect*, 22, 223-234.

Ernst, C., Angst, J., and Foldenyi, M. (1993). The Zurich study: XVII. Sexual abuse in childhood: Frequency and relevance for adult morbidity data of a longitudinal epidemiological study. *European Archives of Psychiatry and Clinical Neuroscience*, 242, 293-300.

Estes, Richard J. (1996). Social development trends in Latin America, 1970-1994: In the shadows of the 21st century, *Social Development Issues*, 18(1): 25-52.

Estes, Richard J. (1996). Social development trends in Asia, 1970-1994: The challenges of a new century," *Social Indicators Research*, 37(2): 119-148.

Estes, Richard J., and Weiner, Neil A. (2001). *The silent emergency: The sexual exploitation of children in the U.S., Canada and Mexico* (Westport CT: Greenwood Publishing Group).

Fairburn et al., (1997). Risk factors for Bulimia Nervosa: a community based case-control study. *Archives of General Psychiatry*, 54, 509-517.

Feltham, C., and Dryden, W. (1993). *Dictionary of counselling*. Whurr.

Fergusson, D.M., Lynskey, M.T., and Horwood, J. (1996). Childhood sexual abuse and psychiatric disorders in young adulthood: I. Prevalence of sexual abuse and factors associated with sexual abuse. *Journal of the American Academy of Child Psychiatry*, 34, 1355-1364.

Fergusson, D., Horwood, L., and Lynsky, M. (1996). Child sexual abuse and psychiatric disorder in young adulthood II. *Journal of Child and Adolescent Psychiatry*, 34, 1365-1374.

Fields, P.J. (1981). Parent-child Relationships, childhood sexual abuse, and adult interpersonal behaviour in female prostitutes. *Dissertation Abstracts International*, 42, 5, 20536-20546.

Finkelhor, D. (1979). *Sexually victimized children*. New York: Free Press.

Finkelhor, D., and Russell, D.E.H. (1984). The gender gap among perpetrators of sexual abuse cited in D.E.H. Russell (Ed.) Sexual Exploitation: Rape, Child Sexual Abuse, Sexual Harassment (pp. 215-228). Beverly Hills, CA: Sage.

Finkelhor, D. (1984). Child sexual abuse: New theory and Research. New York: The Free Press.

Finkelhor, D., and Browne, A. (1985). The traumatic impact of child sexual abuse: A conceptualization. *American Journal of Orthopsychiatry*, 55, 530-541.

Finkelhor, D., and Browne, A., (1986). Initial and long-term effects: A conceptual framework. In D. Finkelhor and Associates (Eds.). *A Sourcebook on Child Sexual Abuse* (pp.180-198). Beverly Hills, CA: Sage Publications.

Finkelhor, D. (1990). "New ideas for child sexual abuse prevention." In Oates, R.K. (Ed.). *Understanding and Managing Child Sexual Abuse.* Australia: Harcourt Brace Jovanovich Group Pty. Limited, pp. 385-396.

Finkelhor, D., Hotaling, G., Lewis, I.A., and Smith, C. (1990). Sexual abuse in a national survey of adult men and women: Prevalence, characteristics and risk factors. *Child Abuse and Neglect*, 14, 19-28.

Finkelhor D. (1994). The international epidemiology of child sexual abuse. *Child Abuse and Neglect*, 18:409-417.

Fleming et al., (1999). The long-term impact of childhood sexual abuse in Australian women. *Child Abuse and Neglect*, 23, 145-159.

Freeman-Longo, R.E. (1996). Nation-wide survey of juvenile and adult sex offender treatment programmes and models (Orwell VT: The Safer Society).

Freund et al., (1972). "The female child as a surrogate object." *Archives of Sexual Behaviour*, 2 (2), 119-133.

Fritz, C.C., Stoll, K., and Wagner, N.N. (1981). A comparison of males and females who were sexually molested as children. *Journal of Sex and Marital Therapy*, 1, 54-60.

Fromuth, M.E. (1983) The long-term psychological impact of childhood sexual abuse. Unpublished Doctoral Dissertation, Auburn University, Auburn, AL.

Fromuth, M. E., and Burkhart. B. R. (1987). Sexual victimization among college men: Definitional and methodological issues. *Violence Victims* 2: 241.253.

Gebhard P.H. and Gagnon, J.H. (1965). Male sex offenders against very young children. *American Journal of Psychiatry*, 121, 576-579.

Goddard, C.R., and Carew, R. (1993). Responding to children: Child welfare practice, Longman Chesire, Melbourne.

Golding, J. M., and Hauselt, J. (1994). When instructions to forget become instructions to remember. *Personality and Social Psychology Bulletin*, 20, 178-183.

Goldman, R., and Wheeler, V., (1986). Silent shame: The sexual abuse of children and youth (Danville IL: The Interstate).

Goodman-Brown, Edelstein, and Goodman (2003). Why children tell: A model of children's disclosure of sexual abuse. *Child Abuse and Neglect, 27*, 525–540.

Goodwin, J. (1985). Post-traumatic symptoms in incest victims. In S. Eth and R. S. Pynoos (Eds.), *Post-Traumatic Stress Disorder in Children* (pp. 155-168). Washington D.C.: American Psychiatric Press, Inc.

Gray, W. D. (2000). The nature and processing of errors in interactive behaviour. *Cognitive Science*, 24(2), 205-248.

Green, A.H. (1993). Child sexual abuse: Immediate and long-term effects and intervention. *Journal of the American Academy of Child and Adolescent Psychiatry*, 32 (5), 890-902.

Greene et al., (1999). Prevalence and correlates of survival sex among runaway and homeless youth. *American Journal of Public Health*, 89(9): 1406-1409.

Gries, L.T., Goh, D.S., and Cavanaugh, J. (1996). Factors associated with disclosure during child sexual abuse assessment. *Journal of Child Sexual Abuse*, 5, 1-20.

Groth, A.N. (1978). Men who rape. New York: Plenum Press.

Groth, A.N., and Birnbaum, H.J. (1978). Adult sexual orientation and attraction to underage persons. *Archives of Sexual Behaviour*, 7 (3), 175-181.

Groth, A.N., and Burgess, A.W. (1979). Sexual trauma in the life histories of rapists and child molesters. *Victimology—An International Journal*, 4, 10-16.

Groth A.N., Hobson, W.F., and Gary, T.S. (1982). The child molester: Clinical observations. In J. Conte and D.A. Shore (Eds.). *Social Work and Child Sexual Abuse*. New York; Haworth.

Grubin, D. (1997). Inferring predictors of risk: Sex offenders. *International Review of Psychiatry*, 9, 225-231.

Grubin, D. (2000). Complementing relapse prevention with medical intervention. In D.R. Laws (Ed.). *Remaking Relapse Prevention with Sex Offenders* (pp. 201-212). California: Sage Publications.

Gutman L.T., St. Claire K.K., Weedy C., Herman-Giddens M.E., Lane B.A., Niemeyer J.G., and McKinney R.E. Jr. (1991). Human immunodeficiency virus transmission by child sexual abuse. *Am. J. Dis. Child,* 145(8): 847-8.

Hall, G.C. (1995). Sexual offender recidivism revisited: A meta-analysis of recent treatment studies. *Journal of Consulting and Clinical Psychology,* 63:802-809.

Hanson, K., and T. Bussiere, M. (1998). Predicting relapse: A meta-analysis of sexual offender recidivism studies, *Journal of Consulting and Clinical Psychology,* 66(2): 348-362.

Hanson, R.K., and Harris, A. (2000). Where should we intervene? Dynamic predictors of sexual offense recidivism. *Criminal Justice and Behaviour,* 27 (1) 6-35.

Hanson, R.K., and Thornton, D. (2000). Improving risk assessments for sexual offenders: A comparison of three actuarial scales. *Law and Human Behaviour,* 24, 119-136.

Harris, M. (1998). *Trauma Recovery and Empowerment: A clinician's guide for working with women in groups.* New York: The Free Press.

Hastings, T., and Kern, J.M. (1994). Relationship between bulimia, childhood sexual abuse, and family environment. *International Journal of Eating Disorders,* 15, 103-111.

Haywood, T.W., and Grossman, L.S. (1994). Denial of deviant sexual arousal and psychopathology in child molesters. *Behaviour Therapy, 25,* 327-340.

Hecht, M. (1997). Canada's Bill C-27, how does it compare to extraterritorial legislation in other countries? *Human Rights Tribune,* 4(1): 10ff.

Hiebert-Murphy, D. (2001) Partner abuse among women whose children have been sexually abused: an exploratory study. *Journal of Child Sexual Abuse,* 10(1): 109-118.

Holmes, R.M., and Holmes, S.T. (1997). *Profiling violent crimes: An investigative tool.* Thousand Oaks, CA; Sage Publications.

Holmes S.T., and Holmes, R.M. (2002). *Sex crimes: Pattern and Behaviour.* California: Sage Publications, Inc.

Hucker S.J., and Bain, J. (1990). Androgenic hormones and sexual assault cited in W.L. Marshall (Ed.). *Handbook of Sexual Assault: Issues, Theories, and Treatment of the Offender* (pp. 93-102). New York: Plenum Press.

Hughes, D., and Roche, C. (Editors) (1999). Making the harm visible: Global sexual exploitation of women and girls (Kingston RI: Coalition Against Trafficking in Women).

Hughes, Donna M. (2000). The "Natasha" trade—The transnational shadow market of trafficking in women, *Journal of International Affairs* (Spring).

Ireland, T., and Widom, C. S. (1993). Childhood victimization and risk for alcohol and drug arrests. *The International Journal of the Addictions*, 2(2): 235–274.

Jaffe, M., and Rosen, S. (Editors). (1996). *Forced labor: The prostitution of children* (Upland: Diane Publishing Company).

Jenny et al., (1994). Are children at risk for sexual abuse by homosexuals? 94 *Pediatrics* 41.

Keary, K., and Fitzpatrick, C. (1994). Children's disclosure of sexual abuse during formal investigation. *Child Abuse and Neglect*, 18, 543–548.

Kempe, C. H., Silverman, F., Steele, B., Droegemueller, W., and Silver, H. (1962). The battered child syndrome. *Journal of the American Medical Association*, 181, 17-24.

Kendler, K.S., et al., (2000). Childhood sexual abuse and adult psychiatric and substance use disorders in women: An epidemiological and co-twin control analysis. *Archives of General Psychiatry* 57(10): 953-959.

Kerchner, G., and McShane, M. (1984). The prevalence of child sexual abuse victimization in an adult sample of Texas residents. *Child Abuse and Neglect, 8*, 495-501.

Kilpatrick et al., (1992). Rape in America: A Report to the Nation (Arlington VA: National Victim Center).

Kim, H.S., and Kim, H.S. (2005) Incestuous experience among Korean adolescents: prevalence, family problems, perceived family dynamics, and psychological characteristics. *Public Health Nursing*, 22(6): 472-82.

Klain, Eva J. (1999). Prostitution of children and child-sex tourism: An analysis of domestic and international responses (Arlington VA: National Center for Missing and Exploited Children).

Knight, R.A., and Prentky, R.A. (1990). Classifying sexual offenders: The development and corroboration of taxonomic models cited in W. L. Marshall (Ed.). *Handbook of Sexual Assault: Issues, Theories, and Treatment of the Offender* (pp. 23-52). New York: Plenum Press.

Korbin, J.E. (1990), 'Child sexual abuse: a cross-cultural view', In R.K. Oates (Ed.) *Understanding and Managing Child Sexual Abuse,* Harcourt Brace Jovanovich, Sydney.

Koss, M.P., Woodruff, W.J., and Koss, P.G. (1990). Relation of criminal victimization to health perceptions among women medical patients. *Journal of Consulting and Clinical Psychology*, 58, pp. 147-152.

Kral, Alex H. et al., (1997). Prevalence of sexual risk behaviour and substance use among runaway and homeless adolescents in San Francisco, Denver and New York City, *International Journal of STD and AIDS*, 109 ff.

Lalor, K. (2004). Child sexual abuse in sub-Saharan Africa: a literature review. *Child Abuse and Neglect*, 28(4), 439-460.

Lamb S., and Edgar-Smith, S. (1994). Aspects of disclosure: Mediators of outcome of childhood sexual abuse. *Journal of Interpersonal Violence*, 9, 307-326.

Lamb et al., (2003). Differences between accounts provided by witnesses and alleged victims of child sexual abuse. *Child Abuse and Neglect*, 27(9): 1019-31.

Launay, G. (2001). Relapse prevention with sex offenders: practice, theory and research. *Criminal Behaviour and Mental Health*, 11, 38-54.

Laws, D.R. (1999). Relapse prevention: The state of the art. *Journal of Interpersonal Violence*, 14, 285-302.

Laws D.R., Hudson, S.M., and Ward (2000). The original model of relapse prevention with sex offenders: Promises unfulfilled. In D.R. Laws (Ed.). *Remaking Relapse Prevention with Sex Offenders* (pp. 3-24). California: Sage Publications.

Lawson, L., and Chaffin, M. (1992). False negatives in sexual abuse disclosure interviews: Incidence and influence of caretaker's belief in abuse in cases of accidental abuse discovery by diagnosis of STD. *Journal of Interpersonal Violence*, 7, 532-542.

Lawson, C. (1993). Mother/son sexual abuse: Rare or underreported? A Critique of the Research, *Child Abuse and Neglect* 17, 26169.

Laws, D.R., and Marshall, W.L. (1990). A conditioning theory of the etiology and maintenance of deviant sexual preference and behaviour. In W.L. Marshall (Ed.). *Handbook of Sexual Assault: Issues, Theories, and Treatment of the Offender* (pp. 209-229). New York: Plenum Press.

Laws, D.R., and Marshall, W.L. (2003). A brief history of behavioural and cognitive behavioural approaches to sex offenders: Part 1. Early developments. *Sexual Abuse: A Journal of Research and Treatment*, 15, 75-92.

Lederer, L. (2001). *Human rights report on trafficking of women and children* (Baltimore MD: Johns Hopkins University, The Paul H. Nitze School of Advanced International Studies).

Leserman et al., (1997). Severe stress, depressive symptoms, and changes in lymphocyte subsets in Human Immunodeficiency Virus-Infected men: a two year follow up study, *Archive of General Psychiatry*, 54 (3): 279-285.

Leventhal, J.M. (1990). Epidemiology of child sexual abuse, In R.K. Oates (Ed.), *Understanding and Managing Child Sexual Abuse*, Harcourt Brace Jovanovich, Sydney.

Lindegren, M. L., Hanson, I. C., Hammett T. A, Beil, J., Fleming, P. L., Ward, J. W. (1998). *Sexual abuse of children: Intersection with the HIV epidemic.*

Lisak, D., and Luster, L. (1994). Educational, occupational, and relationship histories of men who were sexually and/or physically abused as children. *Journal of Traumatic Stress*, 7, 507-523.

Lisak, D., Hopper, J., and Song, P. (1996). Factors in the cycle of violence: Gender rigidity and emotional constriction. *Journal of Traumatic Stress*, 9, 721-743.

Looman et al., (2000). Recidivism among treated sexual offenders and matched controls: Data from the Regional Treatment Centre. *Journal of Interpersonal Violence*, 15 (3), 279-290.

Looman et al., (2001). Replication of the Massachusetts treatment center child molester typology in a Canadian sample. *Journal of Interpersonal Violence*, 16 (8), 753-767.

Lysaker, P.H., Beattie, N.L., Strasburger, A.M., and Davis, L.W. (2005) Reported history of child sexual abuse in schizophrenia: associations with heightened symptom levels and poorer participation over four months in vocational rehabilitation. *J. Nerv. Ment. Dis.*, 193(12): 790-5.

Lysaker, P.H., Davis, L.W., Gatton, M.J., and Herman, S.M. (2005). Associations of anxiety-related symptoms with reported history of childhood sexual abuse in schizophrenia spectrum disorders. *Journal of Clinical Psychiatry*, 66(10): 1279-84.

Marques et al., (2002). In responsivity issues in the treatment of sexual offenders, In Looman et al., *Trauma Violence Abuse*, 6: 330-353.

Marques, J. K., Nelson, C., West, M. A. and Day, D. M. (1994). The relationship between treatment goals and recidivism among child molesters. *Behaviour Research and Therapy*, 32, 577-588.

Marques, J. K., D. M. Day, et al., (1994). "Effects of cognitive-behavioural treatment on sex offender recidivism." *Criminal Justice and Behaviour*, 211(1): 28-54.

Marshall and Barbaree (1978). Marshall, W. and Barbaree, H. (1978). The reduction of deviant arousal: Satiation treatment for sexual aggressors, *Criminal Justice and Behaviour*, 5(4), 294-303.

Marshall, W.L. (1989). Intimacy, loneliness and sexual offenders. *Behaviour Research Therapy*, 27, 491-503.

Marshall et al., (Eds.) (1990). *Handbook of sexual assault: Issues, theories and treatment of the offender*. New York: Plenum Press.

Marshall, W.L., and Anderson, D. (2000). Do relapse prevention components enhance treatment effectiveness? In D.R. Laws,

S.M. Hudson and T. Ward (Eds.), *Remaking relapse prevention with sex offenders: A sourcebook* (pp. 39-55). Newbury Park, CA: Sage Publications.

Marshall, W.L., and Barbaree, H.E. (1990). An integrated theory of the etiology of sexual offending, in W.L. Marshall (Ed.). *Handbook of Sexual Assault: Issues, Theories, and Treatment of the Offender* (pp. 257-275). New York: Plenum Press.

Marshall, W., Anderson, D., and Fernandez, Y. (1999). *Cognitive behavioural treatment of sex offenders.* West Sussex, England: Wiley.

Marshall, L.E., and Marshall, W.L. (2002). The role of attachment in sexual offending: An examination of preoccupied-attachment-style offending behaviour cited in B. Schwartz (Ed.). *The Sex Offender: Current Treatment Modalities and Systems Issues* (pp. 1-7).

Martin, G., Bergen, H.A., Richardson, A.S., Roeger, L., and Allison, S. (2004). Sexual abuse and suicidality: gender differences in a large community of adolescents. *Child Abuse and Neglect*, 28(5), 491-503.

Mathoma, A.M., Maripe-Perera, D.B., Khumalo, L.P., Mbayi, B.L., and Seloilwe, E.S. (2006). Knowledge and perceptions of parents regarding child sexual abuse in Botswana and Swaziland. *Journal of Pediatric Nursing*, 21(1), 67-72.

McFadden, E. J. (1989). Counseling abused children. Ann Arbor, MI: ERIC Counseling and Personnel Services Clearinghouse, The University of Michigan.

McFall, R. (1990). The enhancement of social skills cited in W. L. Marshall (Ed.), *Handbook of Sexual Assault: Issues, Theories, and Treatment of the Offender* (pp. 311-327). New York: Plenum Press.

McGrath, R.J., Hoke, S.E., and Vojtisek, J.E. (1998). Cognitive-behavioural treatment of sex offenders: A treatment comparison and long-term follow-up study. *Criminal Justice and Behaviour*, 25, 203-225.

McGrath, R.J., Cumming, G., Livingston, J. A., and Hoke, S. E. (2003). Outcome of a treatment programme for adult sex offenders: From prison to community. *Journal of Interpersonal Violence*, 18, 3-17.

McLeer et al., (1998). Psychopathology in non-clinical referred sexually abused children. *Journal of the American Academy of Child and Adolescent Psychiatry*, 37 (12), 1326-1333.

Metcalfe et al., (1990). Childhood sexual experiences reported by male psychiatric patients. *Psychological Medicine*, 20:925-929

Miller et al., (1995). Adolescent female offenders: Unique considerations. *Adolescence*, 30(118), 429-435.

Mohr et al., (1964).*Pedophilia and exhibitionism*. Toronto: University of Toronto Press.

Money, J. (1970). Use of an androgen-depleting hormone in the treatment of male sex offenders. *Journal of Sex Research*, 6, 165-172.

Moran, P.B., Vuchinich, S., and Hall, N.K. (2004). Association between types of maltreatment and substance use during adolescence. *Child Abuse and Neglect*, 28(5), 565-574.

Mullen et al., (1993). Childhood sexual abuse and mental health in adult life, *British Journal of Psychiatry*, Vol. 163, pp. 721-732.

Mullen, P. E., Martin, J.L., Anderson, J.C., Romans, S.E., and Herbison, G.P. (1996). The long-term impact of the physical, emotional, and sexual abuse of children: A community study *Child Abuse and Neglect*, 20(1): 7-20.

Mulloy, R, and Marshall, W.L. (1999). Social functioning , In W.L. Marshall, D. Anderson, and Y. Fernandez (Eds.). *Cognitive Behavioural Treatment of Sexual Offenders* (pp. 93-110). England: John Wiley and Sons, Ltd.

Munir, AB., and Yasin, S. (1997). Commercial sexual exploitation (of children), *Child Abuse Review*, 6(2): 147-153.

Muntarbhorn, V. (1996). Report of the Rapporteur-General on the World Congress against commercial sexual exploitation of children.

Nayak (1996) Report presented in the World Congress against Commercial Sexual Exploitation of Children, Stockholm, Sweden, 7-31.

Nicholaichuk, T., Gordon, A., Gu, D., and Wong, S. (2002). Outcome of an institutional sexual offender treatment programme: A comparison between treated and matched untreated offenders. Sexual Abuse: *A Journal of Research and Treatment*, 12, 139-153.

Nunes et al., (2002). A comparison of modified versions of the Static-99 and the Sex Offender Risk Appraisal Guide. *Sexual Abuse: A Journal of Research and Treatment*, 14, 253-269.

Oates, R.K. (1990). Understanding the problem , In R.K. Oats (Ed.) *Understanding and Managing Child Sexual Abuse*, Harcourt Brace Jovanovich, Sydney.

Oates, R. K. (1996). The spectrum of child abuse. *See Also* Sagatun and Edwards, *Supra* Note 10.

Okami, P.(1990). Socio-political biases in the contenporary scientific literature on adult human sexual behaviour with children and adolescents. In J.R. Feierman (Ed.), *Pedophilia: Bio-social dimensions* (pp. 91-121). New York: Springer-Verlag.

Oppong, B.A., Nickels, M.W., and Sax, H.C. (2006). The impact of a history of sexual abuse on weight loss in gastric bypass patients. *Psychosomatics*, 47(2): 108-11.

Pagare, D. (2003). A study of physical and sexual abuse and behavioural problems amongst boys from an observation home in Delhi. *Unpublished Doctoral Dissertation in Community Medicine*, University of Delhi.

Paine, M. L., and Hansen, D. J. (2002). Children's self-disclosure of sexual abuse: effects of victim, perpetrator, and abuse characteristics. *Current Opinion in Psychiatry*, 15(4 441-466.

Paone, D., and Chavkin, W. (1991) SIECUS Report: 1.

Pecukonis, E.V. (1996) Childhood sex abuse in women with chronic intractable back pain. *Social Work in Health Care*. 23, 3.

Pettman, J.J. (1997). Body politics: International sex tourism, *Third World Quarterly*, 18(1): 93-108.

Pirke, K.M., Kockott, G., and Dittmar, F. (1974). Psychosexual stimulation and plasma testosterone in ma *Archives of Sexual Behaviour*, 3, 577-584.

Pithers, W.D., Marques, J.K., Gibat, C.C., and Marlatt, G.A. (1983). Relapse prevention with sexual aggressives: A self-control model of treatment and maintenanchange cited in J.G. Greer (Eds.). *The Sexual Aggressor: Curt Perspectives on Treatment* (pp. 214-239). New York: Van Nostrand Reinhold.

Pithers, W.D. (1990). 'Relapse prevention with sexual aggressors' in *Handbook of Sexual Assault*, Eds W.L. Marshall, D.R. Laws and H.E. Barbaree, Plenum Press, New York.

Prentky, R., Knight, R., and Lee, A. (1997). *Child sexual molestation: Research issues.* Washington: National Institute of Justice.

Quinsey, V.L. and Earls, C.M. (1990). The modification of sexual preferences , In W.L. Marshall, D.R. Laws and H.E. Barbaree (Eds.), *Handbook of Sexual Assault: Issues, theories and treatment of the offender* (pp. 343-361). New York, NY: Plenum Press.

Quinsey, V.L., Steinman, C.M., Bergerson, S.G., and Holmes, T.F. (1975) Penile circumference, skin conductance and ranking responses of child molesters and "normals" to sexual and non-sexual visual stimuli. *Behaviour Therapy, 6,* 213-219.

Rada, R., Laws, D., and Kellner, R. (1976). Plasma testosterone levels in the rapist. *Psychosomatic Medicine*, 38:257-268.

Raj, A., Silverman, J.G., Wingood G., and DiClemente, R. (1999). Prevalence and correlates of relationship abuse among a community-based sample of young African-American women. *Violence against Women*, 5, 272-291.

Reid, S.A. (2001). Fact sheet on sexual orientation and child abuse. *An Internet Report.*

Reinhart, M. (1987). Sexually abused boys. *Child Abuse and Neglect*, 11, 229--235.

Rellini, A.H., and Meston, C.M. (2006) Psychophysiological sexual arousal in women with a history of child sexual abuse. *J. Sex Marital Ther.*, 32(1): 5-22.

Reppucci, N.D., and Haugaard, J.J. (1993), Problems with child sexual abuse prevention programmes, In R.J. Gelles and D. R. Loseke (Eds) *Current Controversies on Family Violence*, Sage Publications, Newbury Park, California.

Richard, Amy O'Neil (1999). *International trafficking in women to the U.S.: A contemporary manifestation of slavery and organized crime.* (Washington: U.S. State Department Bureau of Intelligence and Research).

Rind, B., Tromovitch, P., and Bauserman, R. (1998). 'An examination of assumed properties of child sexual abuse based on non-clinical samples.' Paper presented to the symposium sponsored by the Paulus Kerk, Rotterdam, The Netherlands.

Risin, L.I., and Koss, M.P. (1987). 'The sexual abuse of boys: Frequency and descriptive characteristics of childhood victimizations' reported by a national sample of male post-secondary students. Kent, OH: Kent State University.

Roberts, R., O'Connor, T., Dunn, J., and Golding, J. (2004). The effects of child sexual abuse in later family life; mental health, parenting and adjustment of offspring. *Child Abuse and Neglect*, 28(5), 525-545.

Rodgers, C.S., Lang, A. J., Laffaye, C., Satz, L.E., Dresselhaus, T.R., and Stein, M. B. (2004). The impact of individual forms of childhood maltreatment on health behaviour. *Child Abuse and Neglect*, 28(5), 575-586.

Roesler, T.A., and McKenzie, N. (1994). Effects of childhood trauma on psychological functioning in adults sexually abused as children. *Journal of Nervous and Mental Disease*, 182:145-150.

Roesler, T.A., and Weissmann-Wind, T. (1994). Telling the secret: adult women describe their disclosures of incest. *Journal of Interpersonal Violence*, 9, 327-338.

Romans, S.E., Gendall, K.A., Martin, J.L., and Mullen, P.E. (2001). Child sexual abuse and later disordered eating: New Zealand epidemiological study. Department of Psychological Medicine, University of Otago Medical School, Dunedin, New Zealand.

Roosa, M.W., Reinholtz, C., and Angelini, P.J. (1999). The relation of child sexual abuse and depression in young women: comparison across four ethnic groups. *Journal of Abnormal Child Psychology*, Vol. 27.

Rorty M., Yager J., and Rossotto, M.A. (1994). Childhood sexual, physical and psychological abuse in Bulimia Nervosa *American Journal of Psychiatry*, 151, 8: 1122-1126.

Rosenfeld, S., and Lewis, D. (1993). *AIDS and Public Policy Journal*, 8(4): 108-13.

Rösler, A., and Witztum, E. (2000). Pharmacotherapy of paraphilias in the next millennium. *Behavioural Sciences and the Law*, 18, 43-56.

Roth et al., (1997). Complex PTSD in victims exposed to sexual and physical abuse: Results from the DSM-IV Field Trial for Posttraumatic Stress Disorder. *Journal of Traumatic Stress, 10(4)*, 539–555.

Runtz, M. G., and Schallow, J. R. (1997). Social support and coping strategies as mediators of adult adjustment following childhood maltreatment. *Child Abuse and Neglect*, 21(2), 211-226.

Report of Sahil—An NGO (2003). *Drug abuse and its relationship to sexual abuse of street children.*

Sakshi Violence Intervention Centre Report (1997).

Sandnabba et al., (2003). Age and gender specific sexual behaviours in children. *Child Abuse and Neglect*, 27(6): 579-605.

Schei, B., and Bakketeig, L. S. (1989). Gynaecological impact of sexual and physical abuse by spouse: A study of random sample Norwegian women. *British Journal of Obstetrics and Gynaecology*, 96, 1379-1383.

Schecter, M.D., and Roberge, L. (1976). Sexual exploitation, In Hefer, R.E., and Kempe, C.H. (Eds).

Schultz, T., Passmore, J.L., and Yoder, C.Y. (2003) Emotional closeness with perpetrators and amnesia for child sexual abuse. *Journal of Child Sexual Abuse*, 12(1):67-88.

Schwartz, B.K. (1995). Characteristics and typologies of sex offenders, In B. Schwartz (Ed.). *The Sex Offender: Corrections, Treatment and Legal Practice* (Vol. 2). New Jersey: Civic Research Institute, Inc.

Scott, M.B., and Lyman, S.M. (1968). Paranoia, homosexuality, and game theory. *Journal of Health and Social Behaviour*, 9, 179-187.

Scully, D. and Marolla, J. (1990). Convicted rapists' vocabulary of motive: Excuses and justifications cited in D. Brissett, and C. Edgley (Eds.). *Life as Theater: A Dramaturgical*

Sourcebook (pp. 261-280, second edition). Hawthorne, NY: Aldine de Gruyter.

Seabrook, J. (1997). North-South relations: The sex industry. (Third World Network Features).

Seidman, B.T., Marshall, W.L., Hudson, S.M., and Robertson, P.J. (1994). An examination of intimacy and loneliness in sex offenders. *Journal of Interpersonal Violence*, 9, 518-534.

Silbert, M. H., and Pines, A.M. (1983). Early sexual exploitation as an influence in prostitution. *Social Work*, July-August, 285-289.

Simkins, L. (1993). Characteristics of sexually repressed child molesters. *Journal of Interpersonal Violence*, 8, 3-17.

Simkins, L., Ward, W. W., Bowman, S., and Rinck, C. M. (1989). The Multiphasic Sex Inventory as a predictor of treatment response in child sexual abusers. *Annals of Sex Research*, 2, 205-226.

Simon, L.M.J., Sales, B., Kaskniak, A., and Kahn, M. (1992). Characteristics of child molesters: Implications for the fixated-regressed dichotomy. *Journal of Interpersonal Violence*, 7, 211-225.

Smith, D.W., Letourneau, E.J., and Saunders, B.E. (2000). Delay in disclosure of childhood rape: Results from a national survey. *Child Abuse and Neglect*, 24, 273-287.

Smolak, L., and Murnen, S.K. (2002). *A meta-analytic examination of the relationship between child sexual abuse and eating disorders*, Department of Psychology, Kenyon College, Gambier, Ohio 43022, USA.

Sorenson, T., and Snow, B. (1991). How children tell: the process of disclosure in child sexual abuse. *Child Welfare*, 70, 3-15.

Spak, L., Spak, F., and Allebeck, P. (1998). Sexual abuse and alcoholism in a female population, *Addiction*, 93(9), 1365-1373.

Spangenberg, M. (2001) *Prostituted youth in New York city: An Overview*.

Steele, B.E., and Alexander, H. (1981). Long-term effects of sexual abuse on childhood. In P.B.Mrazek And C.H. Kempe (Eds.), *Sexually Abused Children And Their Families* (pp. 223-233). New York: Pergamon Press.

Stovall, B. (1981). *Child sexual abuse.* Ypsilanti, MI: Eastern Michigan University

Sullivan, P.F., Bulik, C.M., Carter, F.A., and Joyce, P. R. (1995). The significance of a history of childhood sexual abuse in Bulimia Nervosa. *Br. J. Psychiatry,* 167(5): 679-682

Summit, R.C. (1983). The child sexual abuse accommodation syndrome. *Child Abuse and Neglect,* 7, 177-193.

Swanston, H.Y., Plunkett, A.M., O'Toole, B.I., Shrimpton, S., Parkinson, P.N., and Oates, R.K. (2003). Nine years after child sexual abuse. *Child Abuse and Neglect,* 27(8):967-84.

Sykes, G., and Matza, D. (1957). Techniques of neutralization: a theory of delinquency. *American Sociological Review,* 22(6), 664-670.

Terry, K. J., and Tallon, J. (2001). Child sexual abuse: A Review of Literature

Tower, C.C. (1989), Understanding child abuse and neglect, Allyn and Bacon, Boston.

Urquiza, A., and Keating, L.M. (1990). The prevalence of sexual victimization in males, In M. Hunter (Ed.), *The sexually abused male* (Vol. 1, pp. 89-104). Lexington, MA: Lexington Books.

Vlahov, D. et al., (1996). Self-reported Antiretroviral Therapy in injecting drug users. XI International Conference on AIDS. Abstract Tu.D.135.

Vittachi, A. (1989). *Stolen childhood: In search of the rights of the child* (New York: Polity Press).

Vogelman, L. (1990). *The sexual face of violence.* Johannesburg: Raven Press.

Walrath, C., Ybarra, M., Holden, E.W., Liao, Q., Santiago, R., and Leaf, P. (2003). Children with reported histories of sexual abuse: Utilizing multiple perspectives to understand clinical and psychosocial profiles. *Child Abuse and Neglect,* 27(5): 509-24.

Ward, T., and Keenan, T. (1999). Child molesters' implicit theories. *Journal of Interpersonal Violence,* 14, 8, 821-838.

Ward, T., and Hudson, S.M. (2000). A self-regulation model of relapse prevention. In D. R. Laws and S. M. Hudson and T. Ward (Eds.), *Remaking Relapse Prevention with sex offenders: A sourcebook* (pp. 79-101). Newbury Park: CA: Sage.

Warren, H.C. (Ed.) (1934). *Dictionary of Psychology*. Houghton, Miffin and Co.

Whealin, J.M. (2002) Women's report of unwanted sexual attention during childhood. *Journal of Child Sexual Abuse*, 11(1): 75-93.

Wolfe, D.A. (1999). *Child abuse: Implications for child development and psychopathology*, 2nd ed. Thousand Oaks, CA, Sage.

Wonderlich, S.A., Donaldson, M.A., Carson, D.K., Staton, D., Gertz, L., Leach, L., and Johnson, M. (1996). Eating disturbance and incest. *Journal of Interpersonal Violence*, 11, 195-207.

Wood, J. M., and Garven, S. (2000). How sexual abuse interviews go astray: Implications for prosecutors, police, and child protection services. *Child Maltreatment: Journal of the American Professional Society on the Abuse of Children, 5*, 109–118.

Wooley, S. (1994). Feminist perspective on eating disorders, Guilford Press, London.

Wurtele, S., and Miller-Perrin, C. (1992). Preventing child sexual abuse: Sharing the responsibility. Lincoln, NB: University of Nebraska Press.

Wyatt, G.E., and Newcomb, M.D. (1990). Internal and external mediators of women's sexual abuse in childhood. *Journal of Consulting and Clinical Psychology*, 58 , 758-767.

Wyatt, G.E., Carmona, J.V., Loeb, T.B., and Williams, J.K. (2005) HIV-positive black women with histories of childhood sexual abuse: patterns of substance use and barriers to health care. *J Health Care Poor Underserved* 16(4 Suppl B): 9-23.

Zierler, S. (1995). *American Journal of Public Health*, 81(5): 572-575.

Zuravin, S., McMillen, C., DePanfilis, D., and Risley-Curtiss, C. (1996). The intergenerational cycle of child maltreatment. *Journal of Interpersonal Violence*, 11(3): 315-334.

Index